Legal English through the Ages

Vanessa Leonardi • Patrizia Giampieri

Legal English through the Ages

A Corpus-Based Investigation of Change and Continuity

palgrave
macmillan

Vanessa Leonardi
Humanities and Modern Cultures
Sapienza University of Rome
Rome, Italy

Patrizia Giampieri
Human and Social Sciences
Mercatorum University
Rome, Italy

ISBN 978-3-032-02171-7 ISBN 978-3-032-02172-4 (eBook)
https://doi.org/10.1007/978-3-032-02172-4

This Palgrave Macmillan imprint is published by the registered company Springer Nature Switzerland AG.
The registered company address is: Gewerbestrasse 11, 6330 Cham, Switzerland

Foreword

In their volume Legal English Through the Ages: A Corpus-based Investigation of Change and Continuity, Vanessa Leonardi and Patrizia Giampieri provide a balanced and engaging assessment of how legal English has evolved over time.

Indeed, it is precisely this sense of balance that constitutes one of the leitmotifs of this book. Over the five chapters constituting the volume, the authors guide the reader through the intricacies of legal English, showing in detail how it came to have the distinctive features that characterise legal English today. The authors also highlight the importance of plain language initiatives in recent decades which have attempted to eliminate some of the worst excesses of legalese in order to make legal English more comprehensible to non-experts. However, their analysis is always carefully thought out and objective. For example, while they clearly show their approval of those plain language initiatives that facilitate our understanding of legal English, they also illustrate on various occasions why certain long-established words and expressions may occasionally still be preferable in particular contexts, even when more modern alternatives may be available.

The authors examine in depth the various features of legalese, not merely from a theoretical viewpoint, but with the help of selected corpora they give us a precise idea of how each feature has evolved over time. They also highlight an area that has received increasing attention over the years, namely, the phenomenon of sexist language and gender bias that was an inherent part of legal English for centuries, but which is now being addressed through the introduction of gender-neutral language: further proof that legal language, despite its inherently conservative nature, does in fact adapt—albeit slowly—with the times and with the needs of a changing society.

In their final chapter, the authors offer a fascinating glimpse into an area that is bound to affect the future of legal English (as well as countless aspects of our daily lives) in the coming decades: the development of Artificial Intelligence in the legal field. Here the authors meticulously outline the potential advantages and pitfalls that AI offers in shaping the future of legal English, once again applying corpus analysis in order to give a solid scientific basis to their observations. The volume will undoubtedly be of interest to linguists and members of the legal profession, but also to laypersons wanting to learn more about the fascinating and ever-evolving phenomenon of legal English.

The authors are to be congratulated for adding to our knowledge of legal English by investigating both its complex past as well as how it may evolve in the future.

Foggia, Italy Christopher Williams

Acknowledgements

We would like to express our deepest thanks to all the members of the Research Unit for *Variation, Linguistic Change and Grammaticalization* from the Department of English and German at the University of Santiago de Compostela for their generous permission to use the CHELAR corpus in this monograph. This work would not have been possible without their invaluable support and resources and we are deeply appreciative of the opportunity to incorporate this vital corpus into our research. The CHELAR corpus has provided a rich foundation for our exploration!

We would also like to express our heartfelt gratitude to Professor *Christopher Williams* for his unwavering support and guidance throughout our research journey. His expertise, insightful feedback and patience have been invaluable, significantly enhancing the quality of our work. We are particularly appreciative of his dedication to reviewing our manuscript, which has greatly contributed to its development. Thank you, Professor Williams, for your commitment and encouragement; it has been a privilege to work under your mentorship.

With sincere thanks,

Vanessa Leonardi and Patrizia Giampieri

Although this monograph is a collaborative work, the authors wish to clarify their respective contributions. Vanessa Leonardi was responsible for writing Chaps. 2 and 5, as well as Sects. 6.4, 6.5 and 6.6 of Chap. 6. Patrizia Giampieri authored Chaps. 3 and 4 and contributed Sects. 6.1, 6.2 and 6.3 of Chap. 6. Chaps. 1 and 7 were a joint effort by both authors.

Contents

Abbreviations

AI	Artificial Intelligence
BLaRC	British Law Report Corpus
BoLC	Bonomia Legal Corpus
CHELAR	Corpus of Historical English Law Reports
CUE	Corpus Universal Examiner
JCUE	Java Corpus Universal Examiner
NLP	Natural Language Processing
pmT	Per Million Tokens
SGML	Standard Generalized Markup Language

List of Tables

1

Introduction

In *Bleak House*, Charles Dickens criticises the British legal system, especially the Court of Chancery, by describing London covered in thick, murky fog. This fog represented the confusion and lack of clarity that often surrounded legal proceedings, thus implying that people can get trapped in a complicated web of legal language and processes that make it hard to find justice. This critique remains relevant today, as legal English, the specialised language of law, continues to be known for its dense and formulaic style. Unlike many other specialised fields of discourse which have experienced rapid linguistic change in response to societal, technological and cultural shifts, legal English has been characterised by a markedly slow and conservative evolution. This resistance to change is largely due to its fundamental reliance on precision, consistency and the preservation of tradition. Legal language demands a certain degree of accuracy that leaves little room for ambiguity, as even the slightest misinterpretation can have profound legal consequences, thus potentially altering the outcomes of cases, the interpretation of statutes or the execution of contracts, among others. As such, the legal profession has historically prioritised stability and continuity in its linguistic practices, often at the expense of intelligibility and accessibility.

V. Leonardi, P. Giampieri, *Legal English through the Ages*,
https://doi.org/10.1007/978-3-032-02172-4_1

This prioritisation of precision and tradition in legal English, while serving the function of maintaining the integrity of the legal system, has led to widespread perceptions of legal language as being unnecessarily complex, opaque and impenetrable to those outside the profession. Unlike technical jargon found in other professional fields, the features of legal English go beyond mere specialised vocabulary. They encompass a complex web of archaic terminology and syntactic structures that are markedly more complex than those found in modern standard English. Legal texts, indeed, are often constructed with multiple layers of meaning, thus requiring readers to deal with long, multi-clausal sentences that seek to cover every conceivable legal nuance. The result is a form of communication that, while ensuring precision, is often inaccessible to laypeople, thus raising significant concerns in an era increasingly focused on transparency, inclusivity and access to justice.

The historical roots of legal English play a key role in explaining its complexity. Much of the terminology used in legal texts has remained unchanged for centuries, thus reflecting the conservative nature of the legal profession and its attachment to historical precedent. Many legal terms and phrases are derived from Latin or Norman French, legacies of England's legal history and its medieval connections to the Roman and French legal traditions. These linguistic remnants, though vital to the historical continuity of legal language, have created a linguistic distance between legal English and the forms of English used in everyday communication. The reliance on archaic terminology reinforces the perception of legal English as a distinct and "isolated" language, separated from the rest of the linguistic community.

The syntactic complexity of legal English further compounds the difficulties associated with its comprehension. Legal texts are replete with lengthy sentences, often stretching over multiple lines, punctuated by subordinate clauses, conditional phrases and legal formulae. These sentences are designed to be exhaustive, thus leaving no room for ambiguity or misinterpretation, but they often come across as awkward and complicated. The desire for comprehensiveness, while necessary in legal drafting, results in a writing style that can be daunting even for trained legal professionals, let alone for laypeople or those learning English as a second language. For instance, contracts and statutes frequently employ *legalese*, which is a dense, formalised language that seeks to codify legal principles with extreme precision but often alienates those who are unfamiliar with its structure.

For many individuals, particularly foreign students of legal English and those who are unfamiliar with or outside the legal profession, understanding even basic legal documents can be a significant challenge. The highly formal and often archaic vocabulary, coupled with the complex sentence structures, creates a steep learning curve that requires years of education and practice to master. This situation is particularly problematic in today's increasingly globalised world where non-native English speakers frequently engage with legal systems based on English common law, whether for academic, professional or personal reasons. Legal systems vary significantly across jurisdictions, and understanding how legal language functions in one context may not necessarily translate into another. As such, foreign students face the dual challenge of learning both the language and the underlying legal principles that govern its use in a specific jurisdiction.

In addition to the linguistic and syntactic complexities of legal English, another issue that warrants further investigation is the persistence of gender-biased language in legal texts. Despite broader societal movements towards gender equality and inclusivity, legal language has been slow to adapt. Many legal documents continue to use language that reflects outdated notions of gender roles, thereby excluding women and non-binary individuals from full linguistic representation. This use of gender-biased language is not only a linguistic issue but also a matter of social justice, as it perpetuates the marginalisation of individuals who do not conform to traditional gender norms. This persistence of gender-biased language in legal texts is particularly concerning given that the law is supposed to embody fairness, justice and equality. When legal language fails to reflect these values, it undermines the credibility of the legal system and contributes to the exclusion of certain groups from full participation in legal processes. Addressing gender bias in legal language is, therefore, not only a linguistic task but also an ethical imperative. It requires a critical examination of the ways in which language shapes and reflects social power dynamics as well as a commitment to reforming legal texts to ensure that they are truly inclusive and representative of all members of society.

Given the challenges posed by legal English, plain language has gained considerable momentum in recent decades as a tool for creating clearer, more accessible legal documents, communications and proceedings. Advocates of plain language aim to make legal documents understandable to laypeople, thus reducing the barriers created by complex legal jargon. As a result, many jurisdictions and countries have adopted plain language initiatives to enhance transparency, fairness and inclusivity in legal texts, such as laws, contracts and court records.

In parallel with these efforts to simplify legal language, the use of corpora, which are systematically organised collections of texts, has emerged as an essential resource to gain a deeper understanding of the intricacies of legal terminology. Through the analysis of word frequencies and phrases, corpora enable researchers to identify jargon, formulaic expressions and recurring terminology within legal language. This analysis not only highlights specific linguistic patterns but also provides insights into how legal language operates within its specific contexts. Legal corpora, often focused on particular areas of law or specific types of documents, mirror the language used in different legal genres. The examination of corpora, therefore, allows researchers to track the evolution of legal language historically and across various legal systems, potentially uncovering variations in terminology and interpretation that may impact legal outcomes.

In light of these developments in legal communication and accessibility, the increasing reliance on artificial intelligence (AI) within the legal domain cannot be overlooked. AI has proven to significantly reduce costs associated with contract life-cycle management, including drafting, review, negotiation and enforcement. Moreover, AI algorithms manage repetitive tasks more efficiently than human professionals, thus leading to substantial cost savings for both law firms and individuals. This technological innovation offers the potential to enhance efficiency while also democratising access to legal services, thereby ensuring that justice is more effective and fairly distributed among individuals.

Nevertheless, alongside these benefits come important considerations regarding the drawbacks and potential biases inherent in AI-driven tools.

The effectiveness of AI applications in contracts or the delivery of justice is significantly dependent on the quality and representativeness of the data used for their training. If these training data are biased, the outputs generated by AI will inevitably reflect those prejudices. Consequently, many law firms and professionals may rely almost indiscriminately on AI-generated outputs without fully considering the risks involved. As AI technology continues to advance, it becomes increasingly crucial to ensure that its application is both responsible and ethical, thus enhancing the legal system while safeguarding the rights of all parties involved.

This work seeks to explore the evolution of legal English by focusing on the challenges posed by both *legalese* and gender-biased language. In addition, it is aimed at investigating the extent to which AI-driven solutions can significantly enhance clarity in legal documents and in the understanding of legal discourse. Through a corpus-based analysis, this study aims to address three central research questions:

1. How can diachronic analyses of legal language be conducted through corpus-based studies?
2. What observable trends exist in the evolution of legal language, particularly regarding the simplification of legal discourse?
3. How can AI-driven tools assist in analysing *legalese* and gendered language within legal texts?

This book is organised in five distinct chapters. Chapter 2 explores the civil law and common law systems as a foundation for tracing the origins and features of legal language. It provides a chronological account of the evolution of legal English, highlighting how its modern features stem from sociolinguistic interactions across different historical periods. The chapter examines the enduring influence of historical elements, which contribute to the stability of legal terminology. It also discusses the plain language movement, which emerged in response to the complexity of traditional legal language, and how legal language continues to evolve in response to societal demands for clarity. Chapter 3 provides an in-depth exploration of corpora, tracing their historical development and their crucial role in linguistic research. It examines the evolution of corpora and their significance in studying language, with particular emphasis on legal discourse. The chapter outlines different types of corpora and key features such as representativeness and methodological considerations, highlighting their relevance to legal linguistic studies. It also introduces three diachronic legal corpora, CHELAR, BLaRC and BoLC, which will be used for a detailed analysis of the evolution of legal English, focusing on *legalese* and gendered language. Chapter 4 outlines the methodological and analytical framework necessary for corpus-based analyses of specific aspects of legal language, particularly legalese and sexist terminology in the evolution of legal English. It focuses on complex prepositional and adverbial phrases, deictic elements, vague expressions, archaic verbs and nouns, Law Latin, Law French and formulaic expressions. Furthermore, this chapter examines prevalent gender biases in legal language, offering a structured approach for their systematic analysis. Chapter 5 presents a corpus-based analysis of legal language, focusing on *legalese* and instances of sexism and gender bias within three diachronic legal corpora, namely the *Corpus of Historical English Law Reports* (CHELAR), the *British Law Reports Corpus* (BLaRC) and the *Bononia Legal Corpus* (BoLC). This chapter systematically displays the *legalese* features and gender-biased language identified in the previous chapter, categorising these elements by their linguistic and thematic characteristics to facilitate comparison and interpretation across the corpora. Chapter 6 deals with artificial intelligence and its applications in the legal field. It firstly traces the historical background of AI in the legal field. It then discusses state-of-the-art AI interfaces that are used by legal professionals and scholars. It describes the potentialities and drawbacks of AI-driven solutions. To this aim, the chapter provides two hands-on AI applications. The first one concerns a chatbot-based analysis of an extract of a law report sourced from CHELAR. The chatbot system is prompted to find *legalese* elements and replace them with plain expressions. The second application revolves around automated translations and back-translations performed by both MT and AI-based systems. This part of the chapter is aimed at bringing to the fore both advantages and shortcomings of automated (back-)translations. It also discusses gender bias in AI, showing how it can reinforce existing biases and how AI can support gender-neutral language.

This study adopts a dual methodological framework to examine legal language through the lenses of both historical evolution and contemporary technological transformation. It integrates diachronic corpus linguistics with discourse analysis of AI applications in legal contexts, thereby offering a comprehensive perspective on how legal English has adapted across temporal and technological paradigms. The historical strand of the research is grounded in the analysis of the three specialised British legal corpora mentioned above. CHELAR contains genuinely historical material that spans several centuries of legal tradition, while BLARC and BoLC reflect more recent developments in legal discourse, including transitional periods that bridge past and present legal practices. Together, these corpora provide extensive and representative samples of authentic legal texts, enabling a systematic empirical investigation into lexical, syntactic, and semantic changes in legal English. Employing both quantitative and qualitative corpus-based methods, this component of the study traces linguistic patterns of change and continuity within their wider socio-legal contexts. The contemporary strand explores the linguistic implications of AI technologies in legal practice. It examines AI-generated legal texts, investigates the challenges posed by machine interpretation of legal language and considers the legal and ethical dimensions of algorithmic decision-making. In light of the rapid pace of AI development, this component adopts a primarily qualitative, interdisciplinary approach, informed by discourse analysis and perspectives from the digital humanities.

The integration of these methodological approaches reflects the dual character of contemporary legal English, that is, it remains rooted in historical precedent while simultaneously responding to technological innovation. By combining the empirical rigour of corpus linguistics with the interpretative depth of discourse analysis, this framework captures both the enduring features and dynamic transformations of legal language across temporal and technological contexts. Ultimately, this methodological synthesis allows for a nuanced inquiry into whether AI technologies signify a fundamental rupture in legal linguistic tradition or a continuation of established patterns of adaptation and change.

2

Historical Development of Legal English

2.1 Introduction

Language plays a fundamental role in shaping and clarifying legal principles across various genres within the legal system, with the objective of constructing and perpetuating an idealised societal model. Once formulated, this regulatory system undergoes interpretation and application within society to govern human conduct and fortify desired norms. Bhatia (2006) highlights the complexity of this task, noting that legislators must grapple with the entirety of unpredictable human behaviour, incorporating a wide spectrum of scenarios and contingencies into the textual framework.

The primary objective of written legal language is the meticulous specification of legislative intentions, characterised by clarity, precision, unambiguity and inclusivity. This legislative genre serves as the foundation and essence of all other legal practices within any societal group. Legal formulation, codification, interpretation and application across societies are entrusted to institutions and legal professionals employing a shared linguistic code.

V. Leonardi, P. Giampieri, *Legal English through the Ages*,
https://doi.org/10.1007/978-3-032-02172-4_2

Language stands as the primary medium through which the law is conceptualised, codified, interpreted, and enforced. It encompasses a phonological, lexical, and morphosyntactic structure governed by particular operational principles. However, its essence predominantly emerges as a reflection of a linguistic community, embodying the overt and surface-level aspects of the history, customs, socio-cultural practices, and identity of its speakers. From this perspective, the development of legal English, as a variant of the English language used in legal contexts, can be attributed to the mutual influence and contamination resulting from interactions among different linguistic communities. This ongoing process has led to changes in the structure and fundamental characteristics of legal English, ultimately shaping it into its current form. In parallel, legal systems exhibit distinctive linguistic features that set them apart from everyday language. These features may vary, with some legal systems closely aligning with ordinary language, especially in oral or emerging legal traditions. Conversely, in more established systems, legal professionals, including lawyers and judges, often employ language that deviates considerably from everyday speech. Modern legal regimes typically fall between these extremes, characterised by the incorporation of technical vocabulary and, at times, archaic linguistic elements. Consequently, comprehending the speech and written documents produced within these legal systems may prove challenging for the general public, even when they are presented in ordinary language.

Embedded within legal systems, language bears the traces of historical influences, serving as a reflection of the individuals who employed it. English legal language, for instance, has been shaped by the presence of Anglo-Saxons, Danes and Normans, all of whom settled in England during various periods. Nevertheless, legal systems have distinct origins that may not necessarily align with the histories of the countries in which they are practised. The legal language used in Continental Europe, which has been greatly influenced by Roman law, has had an impact even on nations that were never under Roman occupation. In contrast, despite the historical association of England as a Roman colony, the impact of Roman law on its legal language has been minimal. The investigation, therefore, focuses on the two prevailing legal traditions adopted worldwide: the civil law system originating in continental Europe and the common law system that emerged in England.

2.2 Legal Language and the Civil Law Tradition

The enduring influence of Roman law is evident in the development of the civil law tradition in western Europe. Roman law has demonstrated an exceptional level of resilience compared to the legal systems of other ancient civilisations, which have mostly been forgotten over time. Its enduring influence goes beyond the actual content of the law, encompassing its effective use in writing, procedural rules and the systematic categorisation of legal concepts (Tiersma 2012). A key element contributing to the preservation and dissemination of Roman legal principles was the class of individuals known as *jurists* or *jurisconsults*. Operating not as modern lawyers but as affluent individuals committed to studying and offering legal opinions, these jurists played a pivotal role in shaping Roman legal thought. A significant portion of the understanding of Roman law stems from the written commentaries produced by these jurists, particularly during the first three centuries A.D. (ibid.).

The fourth century witnessed the fall of the Western Roman Empire, leading to the rise of smaller states that operated under customary law. Despite this transition, remnants of Roman law continued to exist in specific regions. In stark contrast, the Byzantine Empire thrived for a thousand years, with rulers such as Justinian viewing themselves as the rightful heirs to the original Roman emperors (Merryman 1985). Justinian, aiming to revive and consolidate Roman law, commissioned scholars to compile the *Corpus Juris Civilis*, a comprehensive body of civil law. This corpus, consisting of the *Digest*, *Code*, *Novels*, and *Institutes*, written mostly in Latin, became the law of the Byzantines. During the eleventh century, a significant turning point took place when a manuscript was discovered in Pisa, marking a resurgence in the influence of Roman law across the Western world. This discovery sparked the intellectual fervour of legal scholars, known as glossators, based in Bologna, who devoted themselves to the meticulous study and interpretation of Justinian's legal corpus. Their scholarly pursuits encompassed not only dissecting and analysing the intricacies of Roman law but also creating comprehensive commentaries to elucidate its principles. Bologna, as a scholarly centre, became a magnet for students from various parts of Europe who were attracted by the opportunity to immerse themselves in the study of Roman law under the guidance of these esteemed glossators. The influx of students contributed to the vibrant intellectual atmosphere of Bologna, fostering lively debates and exchanges of legal ideas. As a result, the influence of Roman law spread outwards from Bologna, permeating various European regions as returning students disseminated the knowledge and insights they had acquired. This revival of Roman legal scholarship not only revitalised the study of law but also played a crucial role in shaping the legal landscape of Europe, laying the foundation for the development of legal systems that would endure for centuries to come (Merryman 1985; Robinson et al. 2000).

The legal systems of civil law countries today have a shared historical background that can be traced back to the legal traditions of ancient Rome. This legal heritage underwent a process of organisation and structure during the Byzantine Empire, and later experienced a notable resurgence in northern Italy, specifically in cities such as Bologna. From there, it gradually spread throughout Europe. The fundamental legal concepts and terminology, which were heavily influenced by the Latin language of the Corpus Juris, have played a crucial role in establishing a common "conceptual language" among European lawyers. As a result, the legacy of Roman law continues to have a lasting impact on contemporary legal systems (Mattila 2006). The common conceptual language shared among European civil law practitioners finds its roots in the profound historical role of Latin within their professional sphere. During the medieval era, while English legal scholars were immersed in the intricacies of Law French, their counterparts in civil law, grounded in the traditions of Roman jurisprudence, studied through the medium of Latin within university settings. Latin, esteemed as the language of scholarship and erudition across Europe, asserted its supremacy within legal contexts, shaping the landscape of statutes, treaties, judicial decisions and legal literature (ibid.). Although Latin has experienced a decrease in usage over the past few centuries, it continues to play a significant role in designating fundamental concepts, particularly those deriving from Roman law, within the civil law tradition. Noteworthy examples encompass terms like *causa*, *ex aequo et bono*, *culpa in contrahendo*, *jus soli* and *jus sanguinis*. Latin expressions have also become integrated into various languages or translated, thereby exemplifying its enduring influence. Despite a decline in everyday use, Latin still maintains a presence in contemporary legal language. Moreover, in Eastern Europe, there has been a resurgence in the utilisation of Latin as nations transition from socialist law to revive the civil law tradition. It is worth mentioning that Latin legal maxims, such as *pacta sunt servanda*, *nulla poene sine lege* and *in dubio pro reo*, have withstood the test of time and pose challenges when it comes to accurate translation, thereby retaining their erudite and authoritative essence in their original form (ibid.).

Despite its significant influence in contracts and torts, the *Corpus Juris* did not encompass rules for all aspects of life, even in regions where it was recognised as binding law. In matters of marriage and family, the Catholic church's Canon law held authority, while property and succession were governed by customary and feudal law. The regulation of commerce fell under the jurisdiction of the *lex mercatoria*, collectively forming the *jus commune* (common law) in many parts of Europe (Merryman 1985; Robinson et al. 2000). Although sharing a similar name, the common law of England has a distinct historical background. Initially, the *jus commune* aimed to create a unified legal culture across Europe, but it eventually gave way to the rise of nationalism. Indigenous or customary law gained prominence, leading to the application of local laws in courts and the documentation of oral customs in vernacular languages. Legal professionals, educated in universities, possessed extensive knowledge of Roman law, primarily in Latin. The *Sachsenspiegel*, also known as the Saxon mirror, played a pivotal role in shaping German jurisprudence. Its impact reverberated across German territories for over three centuries, until the adoption of Roman law in the sixteenth century. It is worth noting that in certain regions, such as Prussia, the *Sachsenspiegel* retained its legal validity until the establishment of the Prussian *Landrecht* (land law) promulgated in 1794. France witnessed a division between the *pays de coutumes* (the land of customary law) in the north and the *pays de droit écrit* (the land of written law, mostly Roman law) in the south. During the sixteenth century, northern French customs were codified, resulting in diverse legal systems (Robinson et al. 2000). While Roman law influenced civil law countries worldwide, many retained their customary law, as seen in Indonesia inheriting the Dutch civil law system. Colonial officials respected customary or *adat* law, which, to some extent, persisted even after independence. Additionally, Arabic legal terms, including the Indonesian word for "law" (*hukum*), are commonly used (Hooker 1978; Mattila 2006).

During the eighteenth century, Europe experienced significant political and industrial changes that led to the Enlightenment era. This period not only sparked political revolutions but also prompted a re-evaluation of existing legal systems. Jeremy Bentham, an English lawyer, played a crucial role in proposing comprehensive legal reform during this time. Despite the prevalence of customary law in continental Europe and the English common law, Bentham advocated a radical shift towards legislation. His vision involved transforming customary practices into statutory law through codification. This ground-breaking idea did not find widespread acceptance in England but gained favour in the continent, particularly in France, where Bentham was honoured with citizenship (Merryman 1985). The implementation of legal codification in the eighteenth and nineteenth centuries marked a revolutionary period in Europe. For instance, the Prussian *Landrecht*, promulgated in 1794 under Frederick the Great, aimed to articulate the law clearly and exhaustively. The objective was to enable citizens to understand the law without the need for legal professionals, envisioning judges simply applying rather than interpreting the law. The codification was carried out in German in order to make the law more accessible and understandable to the general population. Similarly, the French Civil Code, often referred to as the Code Napoléon, emerged from the French Revolution but was enacted chiefly through Napoleon's efforts in an attempt to unify and reform French law by repealing all prior legislation. Drawing inspiration from the Institutes of Justinian, the French Civil Code aimed to be accessible to ordinary citizens by stating legal principles rather than detailed rules, resulting in approximately 2000 articles compared to over 17,000 of the

Prussian *Landrecht* (Merryman 1985; Robinson et al. 2000). The influence of these legal codes extended far beyond their countries of origin. Napoleon's conquests introduced the French Civil Code to Belgium, the Netherlands, Portugal, Spain, and parts of Italy and Germany. The influence exerted by the Code Napoléon extended far beyond the borders of Europe, resonating notably across former colonial territories. Its reach encompassed substantial areas of Africa and Latin America, where it stood as a cornerstone for the establishment and development of legal frameworks. As highlighted by Robinson et al. (2000), the Code Napoléon served as a paradigm for legal systems in these regions, shaping the trajectory of jurisprudence and governance in diverse cultural and geographical contexts.

In Germany, the process of legal codification took a distinctive path. While the Prussian *Landrecht* encountered difficulties and ultimately proved unsuccessful, Roman law, the French Civil Code and customary Germanic law all played significant roles. The unification of Germany in the nineteenth century paved the way for the creation of the *Bürgerliches Gesetzbuch* (German Civil Code) in 1896, which incorporated elements from both Roman and native Germanic legal traditions. This German code served as a model for legal systems in various parts of the world, including Austria, Nordic countries, Japan, Brazil and pre-revolutionary China (Merryman 1985; Mattila 2006).

In the domain of legal discourse, the French language played a prominent role. In France, the use of French for legal and administrative purposes gradually replaced Latin from the thirteenth century onwards, although Latin continued to persist in certain domains, such as legal education in universities, until the eighteenth century. French, with its influence transcending linguistic boundaries, emerged as the language of treaties and diplomacy during the eighteenth and nineteenth centuries. The widespread adoption of the Code Napoléon further accelerated the incorporation of French legal concepts and terminology into legal systems across Europe and beyond. The Napoleonic occupation significantly influenced the legal and governmental institutions of countries like Belgium, Italy and Spain, leading to the establishment of French-inspired high courts, such as the *Cour de Cassation*, in various legal systems (Mattila 2006). The influence of French law and language extended far beyond Europe as a result of its colonial empire. Former colonies in sub-Saharan Africa embraced French as their language for legal and governmental affairs due to the diverse linguistic landscape of these regions. However, in northern Africa where Arabic is dominant, French is gradually being substituted. Despite this shift, the prevalence of legal bilingualism highlights the enduring influence of French law (ibid.).

The discourse surrounding language in the civil law framework reveals a noticeable trend—the growing preference, dating back to the Middle Ages, for expressing legal principles in languages that can be understood by those who are subject to them. During the thirteenth century, various German dialects emerged as means of legal expression, and this tendency gained momentum in the eighteenth and nineteenth centuries. Nations like Prussia and France, among others, took on the task of codifying their legal systems using their native languages, marking a departure from the traditional use of Latin or other specialised languages. This evolution has continued into modern times, with each civil law jurisdiction having its own unique legal vocabulary. While Latin and French laid the foundation for legal discourse, contemporary legal languages have developed into distinct variations of their respective national languages. This evolution not only reflects linguistic changes but also the broader societal and cultural shifts that influence legal practice and discourse in different jurisdictions (ibid.).

2.3 Legal Language and the Common Law Tradition

The origins of the common law can be traced back to England, where historical records primarily focus on the Celts as the earliest identifiable inhabitants, despite the long history of habitation in the British Isles. The Celts have left behind tangible historical evidence, and our knowledge of their legal system mainly comes from Wales and Ireland, where Celtic languages continue to be spoken in the present day. Nevertheless, the impact of Celtic law and its associated language on the development of English common law has been limited, as the legal traditions of England have largely evolved independently (Tiersma 2012). The Celts were part of the pre-literary legal cultures, which were characterised by the absence of written laws and the transmission of legal concepts through oral means (Gibbons 1994). Before the Roman conquest, the inhabitants of England were the Celts, who spoke an Indo-European language known as Celtic (Baugh and Cable 2002). The arrival of the Celts is a topic of historical debate, but it is reasonable to assume that Celtic was the original Indo-European language in England, which was later replaced by Latin during the Roman era. The legal system of the Celts relied on the use of proverbs and maxims, which were expressed in a semi-poetic and rhetorical language that featured alliteration. It is highly probable that poets played a role as adjudicators, ensuring that legal knowledge was preserved through oral tradition (Tiersma 1999). Jurists during this Celtic period were considered "artisans of a repetitive oral tradition" (Wagner 2006: 731), contributing to the fundamental aspects of legal proceedings through oral means. While justice was administered on an individual basis, its implementation took place through an assembly resembling a jury, responsible for resolving conflicts and ensuring the flexible application of the law.

Throughout history, powerful entities have consistently harnessed the power of language to extend their influence, with the goal of enforcing their linguistic standards on the conquered lands. The reorganisation of legal systems, crucial for societal governance, has always been intertwined with such linguistic pursuits, serving as a key tactic for emerging powers. The Roman Empire serves as a prime example of this phenomenon, as the Romans effectively disseminated their legal principles and the Latin language, thus consolidating their dominance over medieval Europe. This dissemination was notably facilitated by the administrative structures of the church. After Julius Caesar's conquest of what is now England, it is reasonable to assume that Roman legal norms were imposed on the local population. However, the impact on the indigenous Celtic communities appears to have been limited and disappeared after the Romans withdrew from the island in the fifth century amidst their struggles to maintain their declining empire. While the Romans did leave behind a linguistic legacy, mainly in the form of place names and a small vocabulary of Latin terms, none of these elements were particularly relevant to legal discourse (Mellinkoff 1963).

Following the departure of Roman legions, the previously peaceful Celts became vulnerable to attacks from the Picts and Scots, leading them to seek assistance from Germanic tribes to safeguard their territories (Baugh and Cable 2002). Consequently, in 450 A.D., England experienced a significant transformation with the arrival of various groups such as the Angles, Jutes, Saxons and Frisians. These groups, collectively known as the "Anglo-Saxons", played a crucial role in reshaping the socio-political landscape by settling in different regions and asserting control over the land (Blake 1996). The entry of the Anglo-Saxons into England marked a pivotal moment in the island's history, as these distinct Germanic tribes not only enriched the cultural diversity but also influenced the political dynamics of the area. The strategic partnership forged with the Celts against external threats highlighted the complex geopolitical realities of that era (Baugh and Cable 2002: 49). As the Anglo-Saxons established themselves, they introduced a mixture of traditions, languages and governance systems, contributing to the development of a new societal framework in England. This migration and settlement, as highlighted by Blake (1996), took place in the mid-fifth century and had long-lasting effects that shaped the medieval foundations of England. The intricate interplay of geopolitical circumstances, cultural interactions and power struggles during this period set the stage for the evolving identity of England and its inhabitants.

The term "Anglo-Saxons" finds its roots in the Celtic designation "Saxons", originally employed to denote Germanic invaders indiscriminately. Subsequently, Latin scholars adopted this term to characterise the populace of England (Baugh and Cable 2002). These incoming peoples spoke cognate tongues, collectively termed "Anglo-Saxon" or Old English, which served as the written medium in England from the withdrawal of the Roman legions until the Norman conquest (Burnley 2000). Before the year 600, the legal landscape among the Anglo-Saxons was chiefly marked by a lack of literacy, with customary laws prevailing. Legal decisions often transpired within popular assemblies, known as moots. In cases of harm or fatality, aggrieved parties or their kin possessed the right to seek retribution, though the payment of compensation could absolve the wrongdoer. The amount of compensation hinged upon the severity of the injury and the social standing of the victim. Oaths held significant sway in legal proceedings, demanding precise recitation without falter, as any lapse could lead to an adverse outcome. Furthermore, various legal transactions, including wills and land transfers, relied on the meticulous recitation of specific verbal formulas, often imbued with poetic elements to aid memory and reinforce their legal validity (Tiersma 1999). This legal framework illuminates a society where oral tradition and communal assemblies played central roles in adjudication and legal transactions, reflecting the socio-political milieu of early Anglo-Saxon England.

The arrival of Christian missionaries in 597 was a pivotal moment in English history, leading to significant changes in laws and legal terminology. Christianity's influence spread throughout society, leading to the creation of churches and monastic communities. These religious institutions quickly became centres of education and knowledge, playing a key role in the spread of Latin, the language of the Church (Blake 1996). Under the guidance of the Church, Latin became not only prevalent in religious circles but also began to be used in law and literature, becoming the common language of justice and written communication. This cultural fusion marked the beginning of a new era, with the emergence of the earliest English laws. The combination of Christian teachings and legal principles laid the groundwork for a developing legal system, shaping the future of Anglo-Saxon jurisprudence. The introduction of Latin terms into legal discussions during this period was not just superficial; it represented a significant linguistic change that still influences modern legal English vocabulary. The lasting impact of this cultural blend highlights the enduring effect of Christianity on the legal and linguistic aspects of Anglo-Saxon society.

Despite the absence of well-defined legal professions, the Anglo-Saxons cultivated a legal language, some aspects of which can still be found in modern English. Examples include the terms *witness* and *will*, originating from this period, along with certain structural features of legal language still evident in contemporary English. The ritualistic and formulaic repetition characterising legal language can be traced back to the medieval period when words held a mystical and evocative power linked to divine intervention. Another feature from the Anglo-Saxon era, still discernible in modern legal English, is alliteration, once common in poetic language and employed in the legal domain to aid oral recitation in pre-literate societies (Tiersma 1999). While not as widespread in contemporary legal English, traces of this linguistic phenomenon endure in binomial expressions. In these constructions, two parallel elements, usually nouns or adjectives, are connected by the conjunctions "and" and "or". Despite the absence of alliteration, these expressions establish parallelism, enhancing the rhetorical impact of the statement (Gotti 2005). An illustrative example is the renowned formulation "to tell the truth, the whole truth, and nothing but the truth". The evolution of political and administrative structures in the Anglo-Saxon era prompted the gradual codification of laws. The first laws with conditional subordinates (if-then) emerged during this period (Tiersma 1999). It is noteworthy that despite some writings in Anglo-Saxon pertaining to practical life, such as place names and aspects of lifestyle codified through law, Latin remained synonymous with writing for the educated, and extensive works in English seemed unconventional (Blake 1996). Latin, albeit with adaptations, persisted as the primary written language, particularly in legal fields, maintaining a link with traditional legal practices.

During the ninth and tenth centuries, the British Isles experienced a series of Viking invasions, primarily originating from present-day Denmark. A significant number of Vikings chose to establish settlements in England, particularly in the region known as the Danelaw, which was governed by Danish laws. As time passed, the Scandinavian settlers gradually assimilated into the existing Anglo-Saxon population, leaving behind distinct linguistic imprints on the English language. This influence is evident in the incorporation of various legal terms such as *gift*, *loan*, *sale*, *trust* and even the very term *law* itself, which originally denoted "that which is laid down". The impact of the Scandinavian presence on English language and legal terminology has been significant (Tiersma 1999).

Legal English is a reflection of the linguistic amalgamation that has contributed to the formation of the English language as a whole. Yet, in particular, modern legal English is indebted to French and Latin influences. The Norman invasion of 1066, in particular, marks a crucial turning point in the ongoing development of legal English. Prior to the Normans' arrival, England already possessed an established legal system and an associated linguistic code. However, it was the Normans, a population of Nordic origin who settled in Normandy, that introduced significant changes to the existing legal framework. They brought about the systematisation of legal professions, the centralisation of justice and the introduction of novel legal concepts and procedures (Gibbons 1994). In addition to consolidating the British administrative system, the Normans organised the management of justice and implemented structural modifications to the linguistic code used in legal contexts. Following the conquest, French made headways in England, albeit not uniformly across the entire territory and population (Blake 1996).

During the medieval period, French emerged as the primary language used in legal documents, as is discussed in scholarly works such as those by Mellinkoff (1963) and Tiersma (1999). Mellinkoff (1963) posits that the prevalence of French in legal discourse was a result of the exclusive nature of the legal profession, where the use of a specialised language created a barrier to entry, thus forcing non-experts to depend on legal professionals for interpretation. This elitist structure perpetuated a linguistic hierarchy, which strengthened the authority of legal practitioners. On the other hand, Tiersma (1999) offers a more practical viewpoint, suggesting that the adoption of French made legal documents more accessible to practitioners as it reflected the language of the nobility and was commonly spoken among members of Parliament.

Furthermore, Baugh and Cable (2002) highlight the significance of the marriage between Henry III and Eleanor of Provence in 1236, which played a crucial role in strengthening the dominance of the French language in England's administrative and legal domains. This union brought a greater number of French speakers into these spheres, further solidifying French as the prevailing language in legal contexts. The growing cultural importance of French in Europe, combined with the establishment of a centralised system of royal justice, contributed to its rise as the language of legislation. Additionally, the emergence of a professional class of lawyers during the mid-thirteenth century firmly established French as the primary medium for legal discourse, ensuring its continued usage through intergenerational transmission within legal apprenticeships.

This specialised variation of French, commonly known as "legal French" (Tiersma 1999), was employed to exclude the general population from legal matters, thereby reinforcing the authority of legal professionals. The resistance to linguistic evolution within legal discourse highlights the conservative nature of the legal profession, preserving its dominance over legal interpretation and practice. While the rationale for safeguarding the public from misinterpretations of laws justified the preservation of French as the language of the law, alternative approaches, such as translating into English supplemented by French technical terms, could have increased accessibility without compromising legal precision.

Legal French has long been highly regarded for its eloquence and precision, but its lack of transparency to the laypeople highlighted the necessity for change. Mellinkoff (1963) astutely observes that elements of Old English legal language, characterised by fused clauses and poetic devices such as alliteration, persisted within legal French, influencing the stylistic norms of legal English. However, as legal discourse has evolved, the demand for bilingual terminology has diminished. Over time, the opacity of legal French to non-experts prompted calls for simplification and accessibility in legal language. As Mellinkoff (1963) explains, the archaic features inherited from Old English, while adding a certain aesthetic quality to legal discourse, have contributed to its esoteric nature, alienating those outside the legal profession. In response to these challenges, the reform of legal language has become an increasingly urgent concern. The progression of legal discourse towards greater clarity and inclusivity has resulted in a gradual departure from the dual-language conventions of the past. While traces of Old English stylistic elements may still persist in contemporary legal English, the trend towards unity and simplification reflects a broader societal push for transparency and comprehensibility in legal communication.

The transition from English to French occurred gradually, resulting in a dual linguistic system where French became the language of power, distinct from English, which was spoken among the lower social classes. This variant of French, known as "Anglo-Norman", was employed predominantly within the clergy and nobility (Blake 1996). Latin, alternating with English, continued to be employed in legal documents, contributing to the dominance of Latin in legal texts (Tiersma 1999). The Norman conquest established Latin as the official language for matters of law and justice, displacing English within this domain. The first statute drafted in French dates back to 1275, and from 1310 onwards

French gradually gained significance as the official written language, eventually replacing Latin. Despite its diminishing usage, French resurfaced as the language of the law during the fourteenth century, creating an artificial phenomenon during the thirteenth and fourteenth centuries (Baugh and Cable 2002). Despite the widespread use of French as the legal language in England, Latin has remained a cornerstone of legal expression, not only in English but also in other legal systems. The decision to use Latin for legal documents was driven by the need for a standardised language with structural and lexical rules that could be understood throughout the country, in contrast to the fragmented Old English dialects. This adaptation of Latin to the needs of English law gave rise to *Law Latin*, which contained elements from both languages, including the modification of English terms into Latin forms (Tiersma 1999). Latin continued to be used for expressing legal maxims, providing dignity and timelessness to legal rules, and in various expressions like *in personam* or *mens rea*, many of which have entered common usage. Furthermore, its influence can also be seen in a number of words and phrases such as *ad hoc*, *de facto*, *bona fide*, *inter alia* and *ultra vires*, which remain in current use in legal writing.

The development of legal English can be attributed to a combination of influences from French, Anglo-Saxon and Latin languages during the Norman period. This linguistic diversity, although demonstrating the adaptability and complexity of legal language, also resulted in inefficiencies and hindered the smooth functioning of the legal system (Maley 1994). However, the fourteenth century marked a significant shift towards the increasing use of English as the predominant language for legal proceedings. In particular, in 1356, the municipal authorities in London mandated the use of English in legal deliberations within the jurisdictions of London and Middlesex (ibid.). The culmination of this momentum came with the promulgation of the Statute of Pleading in 1362, which officially recognised English as the language of legal proceedings, while still requiring records to be kept in Latin. This statute criticised the use of French and highlighted the communication challenges faced by parties involved in legal disputes. Despite the requirement for English to be used in court, the statute itself was paradoxically written in French. Legal practitioners, however, largely ignored this law and continued to use French in their professional activities. In 1650, during the restoration of the monarchy, there was a setback when a law was passed making English the official legal language in Great Britain. However, this legislation was later repealed, leading to a resurgence of alternating usage among French, Latin and English in legal documentation. It was only in the eighteenth century, with the formal abrogation of the use of French and Latin by Parliament in 1731, that English firmly established its hegemony as the language of jurisprudence (Tiersma 1999).

The development of legal culture paralleled the linguistic transformations of its time, undergoing a shift from a preliterate to a literate stage. This transformation unfolded gradually, marked by the transition from oral tradition to written documentation, a change notably discernible during the late Anglo-Saxon period (Mattila 2006). Initially, the written records were not accorded the status of authoritative legal texts but rather were seen as mere transcriptions of oral communication (ibid.). Nonetheless, as time elapsed, written documentation asserted itself with autonomy and authority, evolving into independent legal reference materials (ibid.). The introduction of printing in the seventeenth century emerged as a pivotal moment, which was instrumental in standardising legal documentation and facilitating its wider dissemination, thereby contributing significantly to the formalisation of legal language (ibid.). However, this advancement also introduced complexities into legal discourse, such as increased lexical density, the use of nominalisations and the persistence of archaic expressions, among other challenges (ibid.).

2.4 Plain Language

The language of the law has long been recognised as archaic and verbose, a characteristic that has significantly contributed to its inaccessibility for those not trained in legal discourse. Scholars such as Mellinkoff (1963) have highlighted the considerable distance between legal language and everyday communication, drawing attention to the barriers that this creates for the general public. Tiersma (1999) and Bhatia (2010) further elaborate on this issue by pointing out the linguistic complexities that pervade legal texts, which serve to reinforce this distance and alienate non-specialists. Legal language is characterised by various features including nominalisation, passive constructions, long sentences, syntactic discontinuities and the use of embeddings (Tiersma 1999: 77–79; Williams 2004: 113–114; Coulthard and Johnson 2010: 10). While these features may ostensibly serve the purpose of enhancing precision and comprehensiveness in legal contexts, they often result in texts that are exceedingly difficult for the layperson to comprehend. This complexity has led to growing calls for simplifying legal language, culminating in the plain language movement. This movement advocates for a clearer, more accessible style in legal writing, aiming to bridge the gap between legal professionals and the public.

The complexities of legal language are deeply rooted in specific linguistic features that have become entrenched over centuries of legal drafting and interpretation. One of the primary characteristics of legal discourse is nominalisation, a process in which verbs are transformed into abstract nouns, resulting in a formal and often distant tone. For instance, legal phrases such as "the application of the law" tend to replace simpler expressions like "applying the law", which would be more direct and accessible to non-specialists (Williams 2004: 115). This stylistic choice obscures the subject's action, adding unnecessary abstraction to the text and making it more challenging for the reader to grasp its meaning. Another prominent feature of legal language is the preference for passive constructions. While the passive voice can serve a purpose in certain legal contexts by emphasising the action rather than the actor, its overuse frequently leads to ambiguity. For example, in a phrase like "it is agreed", the reader is left uncertain about who exactly is agreeing. In contrast, an active construction such as "the parties agree" would provide much greater transparency (Williams 2004: 114). This tendency towards passive phrasing reflects the historical inclination of the legal profession to distance the actor from the action, ostensibly to maintain neutrality and objectivity; however, this approach often comes at the expense of clarity, leaving readers confused about essential details.

In addition to passive constructions, legal texts are often characterised by long sentences that incorporate intricate syntactic structures. This complexity often results in sentences that include numerous embedded clauses and conditions, rendering them difficult and tedious to comprehend. Although these syntactic intricacies may aim to deliver thorough and detailed legal arguments, they place considerable cognitive strain on readers (Williams 2004: 113–114). Legal drafters commonly incorporate exceptions, qualifications and conditions within a single sentence, which creates multiple layers of meaning that can be difficult to interpret, even for individuals familiar with legal terminology. For instance, a single sentence might delineate a primary obligation while concurrently presenting various conditions that must be satisfied, which can lead to ambiguity regarding the overall purpose.

The lack of punctuation further compounds the difficulty of interpreting such texts. In many legal documents, punctuation is either minimal or strategically placed to serve the needs of the drafters rather than the understanding of the readers. This situation can result in readers lacking essential indicators to navigate through long, complex sentences, thus adding to the opacity of legal discourse (Williams 2004: 113). The absence of clear punctuation can obscure the relationships between different parts of a sentence, making it difficult for readers to discern where one thought ends and another begins.

Furthermore, legal language frequently employs deictic expressions—pronouns and adverbs that refer to concepts or individuals mentioned earlier or later in the text. This requires readers to constantly revisit prior content or predict forthcoming information to comprehend the references accurately (Abate 1998: 14–16; Bhatia 2010: 28). For example, a statement like "above mentioned" requires the reader to remember earlier parts of the text to fully understand its significance. Such reliance on contextual cues can be particularly challenging for those unfamiliar with the text or its structure.

Although these features may enhance precision in certain contexts—allowing detailed stipulations and subtle arguments—they contribute significantly to the perception that legal language is unnecessarily complex and inaccessible to laypersons. The cumulative effect of long sentences, sparse punctuation and deictic expressions creates a barrier that not only alienates laypersons but also complicates communication even among legal professionals. This complexity underscores the pressing need for reform towards clearer, more straightforward legal writing that prioritises understanding without sacrificing necessary detail.

Another issue is the male-gendered nature of legal discourse, which has long been a point of contention, especially due to its reliance on masculine generics and gendered suffixes. Traditionally, legal texts have predominantly used terms like "he" or "his" to refer to individuals regardless of their gender. This practice reflects the historical exclusion of women from the legal profession and reinforces male dominance in the legal sphere (Griffith 1988: 135; Leonardi 2021). By using masculine generics, legal documents not only marginalise women and non-binary individuals but also create ambiguity when the gender of a subject is unknown or irrelevant.

Efforts to address this bias have led to a growing movement towards gender-neutral language in legal drafting. This shift advocates replacing terms like "he" with neutral alternatives such as "they" or "their" to eliminate gender bias and make legal texts more inclusive. Gender-neutral language also improves clarity, a key goal of the plain language movement, by removing the confusion that can arise from the use of masculine generics.

In addition to pronouns, gender bias in legal discourse is also reflected in compound nouns and suffixes. Terms like "chairman," "policeman" and "fireman" carry implicit male bias, suggesting that these roles are inherently male. Similarly, the use of gendered suffixes such as "-ette", "-ess" and "-trix"—as in *suffragette*, *actress* or *executrix*—creates distinctions that feminise certain roles, often implying a lesser or secondary status for women. These suffixes are not only unnecessary but also perpetuate outdated gender norms that no longer reflect modern views of gender equality. In modern legal drafting, there is a growing movement towards adopting gender-neutral language, which is seen as more inclusive and accurate.

Legal texts are often prone to ambiguity and vagueness, features that, while frequently regarded as drawbacks, are sometimes intentionally employed by legal drafters. One remarkable example is the modal verb "shall", which has sparked considerable debate regarding its interpretation. It can denote both obligation and futurity, leading to uncertainty about its precise function in various contexts (Tiersma 1999; Williams 2023: 84). This duality creates confusion, as the same term may imply different legal obligations depending on the surrounding text. Moreover, legal drafters may deliberately introduce vagueness to afford flexibility in interpretation. This flexibility allows judges to apply laws in ways that best serve justice in individual cases, thus adapting the law to fit unique circumstances (Christie 1964: 911; Endicott 2000: 190–191). For instance, a statute that employs broad language can enable a judge to interpret its application based on the specific facts of a case, which may be beneficial in achieving fair outcomes. However, this intentional vagueness can also result in unpredictability, as it leaves room for varying interpretations that may lead to inconsistent applications of the law. The strategic use of vagueness is often seen as a necessary tool within legal frameworks. It allows the accommodation of unforeseen situations and complexities that rigid language might fail to address. However, this approach raises concerns about clarity and certainty in legal communication. Critics argue that such ambiguity can undermine the rule of law by making it difficult for individuals to understand their rights and obligations fully. The balance between necessary flexibility and the need for clear legal standards remains a contentious issue within legal discourse, thus reflecting broader debates about the role of language in law and its implications for justice and accountability.

A further barrier to understanding legal texts is the use of archaic expressions, many of which are derived from Latin and French, reflecting the historical development of English law. Terms such as *ab initio* and *habeas corpus*, while possessing specific legal meanings, are often unfamiliar to most modern readers and are rarely explained within the text itself (Laster 2001: 246; Bhatia 2010: 26–29). This reliance on outdated terminology can alienate individuals who lack legal training, as they may struggle to grasp the significance of these terms in contemporary contexts. The persistence of such expressions, despite the availability of more accessible English equivalents, exemplifies a remarkable resistance to change within legal drafting practices. The cumulative effect of these linguistic features is that legal documents—ranging from contracts and powers of attorney to writs, judgments and statutes—are often difficult for the average person to understand without specialised training. This complexity not only hinders public comprehension but also raises concerns about transparency and accountability within the legal system.

As a response to these challenges, there has been a growing movement towards plain language in legal writing. This movement aims to reduce the complexity and archaic nature of legal texts by advocating for clearer, more straightforward language that is accessible to all individuals, regardless of their background or expertise. The push for plain language is not merely about simplifying legal jargon; it also seeks to enhance the effectiveness of communication between legal professionals and the public. By eliminating unnecessary complexity, proponents argue that legal texts can become more inclusive, ultimately fostering a better understanding of rights and obligations among citizens. The plain language movement has gained traction in various jurisdictions, leading to legislative reforms that prioritise clarity and accessibility in legal documentation. However, despite these advancements, challenges remain in fully integrating plain language principles into all areas of legal practice.

The plain language movement, which gained traction in the 1970s and 1980s, emerged as a response to the growing recognition that legal language was alienating to the general public (Williams 2023: 3). This movement seeks to simplify legal language to enhance accessibility, particularly for individuals lacking legal expertise (Wydick 1978; Williams 2008; Tessuto 2008a, 2008b; Maci 2014; Gotti 2016). Advocates of plain language, sometimes referred to as "plainers" or "plain language proponents", argue that legal texts should be understandable to the average reader without necessitating legal counsel (Adler 2016: 67; Williams 2023: 4). The principles of plain language encompass several key strategies aimed at increasing clarity.

One of the most significant recommendations is the avoidance of archaic words and Latinisms, which are viewed as unnecessary barriers to comprehension. Legal drafters are encouraged to replace obscure terms with their modern English equivalents, thus improving the accessibility of the text (Williams 2004: 117–123). Another important principle is the reduction of sentence length. Long sentences, especially those containing multiple clauses and legal qualifiers, are a hallmark of traditional legal drafting, but they can be overwhelming for readers. Proponents of plain language argue that shorter, simpler sentences are easier to understand and that breaking complex ideas into smaller, more manageable units does not necessarily sacrifice legal precision (Williams

2004:117–123). Related to this is the emphasis on using active voice instead of passive constructions. As noted earlier, passive voice obscures agency and can make it unclear who is responsible for an action. Active voice, by contrast, is more direct and transparent, which aligns with the goals of plain language (Williams 2004: 114). Other strategies promoted by the plain language movement include writing a clear "purpose" heading before each section or clause, avoiding unnecessary jargon, and eliminating redundancies. Bhatia (2010: 26–28) suggests that legal drafters should avoid binomials and trinomials such as "from time to time" and formulaic phrases like "Now therefore this agreement witnesseth". These phrases, while traditional in legal drafting, often serve no functional purpose and can be replaced with simpler, more direct language. For example, the phrase "this clause does not" could replace the more convoluted "nothing in this clause", and "until" could substitute for "until such time as" (Bhatia 2010: 28). Similarly, Duckworth and Spyrou (1995) argue that long lists of nouns like "heirs, executors, administrators, successors, and assigns" should be replaced with a single term such as "party". This not only reduces the length of the text but also eliminates redundancy and potential confusion (Duckworth and Spyrou 1995:39). They also recommend simplifying binomials that contain Latin expressions, as in replacing "null and void" with "of no legal effect" (Duckworth and Spyrou 1995: 57).

The plain language movement has had a significant impact on legal drafting practices, particularly in the area of consumer law and statutory drafting. According to Williams (2023), there has been a noticeable "shift in style" in British legislation, where plainer language has gradually been adopted in statutes, making the law more accessible to the public (Williams 2023: 86). This shift is most evident in consumer-facing documents such as online terms and conditions, which have been rewritten in a more straightforward manner to ensure that ordinary readers can understand their rights and obligations. However, the movement's influence has been less pronounced in judicial contexts. While some court judgments have adopted a plainer style since the 2010s, the highly technical and precedential nature of judicial writing has meant that *legalese* continues to dominate (Williams 2020, 2023: 123). Judges must balance the need for clarity with the requirement for precision in their legal reasoning, and this often necessitates the retention of traditional legal terminology and structures.

The principles of plain language have also been embraced in international contexts, particularly within the European Union. The European Commission's *Clear English Guidelines* and *English Style Guide* (European Commission 2014, 2023) advocate for plain language in legislative drafting, and the European Parliament's *Joint Practical Guide* (2015) emphasises the importance of clarity in legal expression. It suggests that legal drafters should break down complex concepts into simple terms and prioritise clarity over stylistic concerns.

Despite these advancements, there remains significant resistance to the widespread adoption of plain language in legal discourse. Critics of the movement argue that simplification can sometimes come at the cost of legal precision. Tessuto (2008a: 26) questions whether plain language can truly convey the complexity of legal concepts to ordinary readers, suggesting that some degree of intricacy is necessary to reflect the multifaceted nature of the law. Solan (1993) similarly contends that while simplification may increase accessibility, it risks creating inaccuracies. He argues that legal language is deliberately complex to allow the ambiguity and nuance required in legal interpretation. Vagueness and flexibility are integral to legal reasoning, as they provide judges with the latitude to interpret statutes in ways that best serve justice (Christie 1964: 911; Endicott 2000: 190–191). This perspective aligns with Ződi's (2019) view that the complexity of legal language is a reflection of the complexity of the legal subject matter itself. Even if the language is simplified, the underlying legal concepts may remain too intricate for the layperson to fully understand. Bennion (2007) supports this view, particularly in the context of statutory drafting. He argues that the primary function of legislation is to state the law clearly, not to explain it in simple terms. Any attempt to simplify legislative language, he warns, could result in misinterpretation or a loss of the precision necessary to enforce the law effectively.

In the field of legal translation, the issue of simplification becomes even more complex. Giampieri and Harper (2023) advise against using plain language in translations when the source text employs complex legal jargon. They argue that a plain-language translation may not accurately convey the legal meaning of the original text, leading to potential misunderstandings in cross-jurisdictional contexts.

In summary, the plain language movement represents a significant shift towards making legal language more accessible to the general public. While it has undoubtedly succeeded in simplifying certain types of legal documents, such as consumer contracts and terms of service, its application in more complex legal texts, such as statutes and court judgments, remains contentious. Critics of the movement argue that the inherent complexity of legal concepts requires a level of linguistic intricacy that plain language cannot accommodate. As legal discourse continues to evolve, the challenge for legal drafters will be to strike a balance between clarity and precision, ensuring that the law remains accessible without sacrificing the detail and nuance necessary for its proper interpretation and application.

2.5 Concluding Remarks

The legal traditions of civil law and common law have experienced significant changes throughout history, influenced by various historical, cultural and linguistic factors that have shaped their evolution into the intricate systems we recognise today. In the civil law tradition, the impact of Roman law remains profound and enduring, as it not only introduced a systematic classification of legal concepts but also established a fundamental framework that continues to resonate in legal systems worldwide. The *Corpus Juris Civilis*, an extensive compilation initiated under Emperor Justinian and later rediscovered and revitalised in Europe, serves as evidence of the lasting legacy of Roman legal principles. This comprehensive codification played a vital role in disseminating Roman legal principles and, in turn, exerted a significant influence on the emergence and development of legal systems across the continent. Latin, as the language of Roman law, held a central position in legal education and practice, permeating the discourse of legal professionals and contributing significantly to a coherent conceptual language shared among European legal systems.

In contrast, the common law tradition, which originated in England, follows a distinct historical development, characterised by organic growth and development. Shaped by a variety of influences, including Celtic, Anglo-Saxon, Norse and Norman cultures, as well as the infusion of Christian doctrine and the adoption of Latin, the development of English legal language reflects a dynamic amalgamation of diverse linguistic and cultural elements. French, which was introduced by the Norman conquerors, emerged as a dominant language in legal discourse and coexisted alongside Latin and English for centuries until English officially established itself as the primary legal language in the eighteenth century.

Legal language has consistently held a significant position in upholding and spreading legal principles over the course of history. It serves as a crucial medium for transmitting legal norms and values across different generations and jurisdictions. Despite the separate historical trajectories of civil law and common law, both have made valuable contributions to the complex landscape of legal language. As a result, this has influenced the application and understanding of law within diverse legal systems worldwide. Additionally, it is important to acknowledge the significant milestone in the formalisation of legal language that occurred with the transition from oral to written legal documentation, facilitated by the emergence of printing. This advancement, however, also introduced new complexities, such as increased lexical density and the persistence of archaic expressions, among other challenges, that serve as enduring reminders of the conservative nature inherent in legal discourse.

In light of these historical developments, the plain language movement represents a critical response to the challenges posed by traditional legal language. Emerging in the 1970s amid growing recognition that such language was alienating to the general public, this movement seeks to simplify legal language to enhance accessibility for individuals lacking legal expertise. Advocates argue that legal texts should be comprehensible to average readers without necessitating professional assistance.

The principles underlying plain language emphasise clarity through various strategies, including avoiding archaic words and Latinisms that create unnecessary barriers to comprehension. By encouraging drafters to replace obscure terms with modern English equivalents, proponents aim to improve accessibility while maintaining essential legal concepts. This movement not only seeks to empower individuals but also fosters greater trust between legal professionals and the public.

In conclusion, while both civil law and common law traditions have rich historical foundations that contribute to their complexity, movements like that of plain language highlight an essential shift towards making legal discourse more inclusive. As societies evolve and expectations around communication change, embracing clearer language within legal frameworks becomes increasingly vital for ensuring that justice is accessible to all individuals—regardless of their background or expertise.

Nevertheless, it is important to acknowledge that the plain language movement is not universally accepted within the legal community. Some critics argue that traditional legal terminology carries established meanings that are crucial for precision and clarity in legal contexts. They contend that simplifying language may lead to ambiguity and misinterpretation, potentially undermining the law's integrity. This ongoing debate reflects a tension between the need for clear communication and the necessity of preserving the nuances inherent in legal language. The challenge will be balancing necessary precision with clarity in a manner that respects both tradition and contemporary needs within our diverse legal landscapes.

Bibliography

Abate, Salvatore C. 1998. *Il documento legale anglosassone*. Milan: Hoepli.

Adler, Mark. 2016. The Plain Language Movement. In *The Oxford Handbook of Language and Law*, ed. Peter M. Tiersma and Lawrence M. Solan, 67–83. Oxford: Oxford University Press.

Baugh, A. C., and T. Cable. 2002. *A History of the English Language*. Abingdon: Routledge.

Bennion, Francis. 2007. Confusion Over Plain Language Law. *The Commonwealth Lawyer* 16:63–68.

Bhatia, V. 2006. Legal Genres. In *Encyclopedia of Language and Linguistics*, ed. K. Brown, 1–7. Amsterdam: Elsevier.

Bhatia, Vijai K. 2010. *Textbook on Legal Language and Legal Writing*. New Delhi: Universal Law Publishing Co.

Blake, N. F. 1996. *A History of the English Language*. New York: Palgrave.

Burnley, D. 2000. *The History of the English Language: A Sourcebook*. 2nd ed. London: Routledge.
Christie, George C. 1964. Vagueness and Legal Language. *Minnesota Law Review* 48:885–911.
Coulthard, Malcolm, and Alison Johnson. 2010. Introduction. In *The Routledge Handbook of Forensic Linguistics*, ed. M. Coulthard and A. Johnson, 1–16. London and New York: Routledge.
Duckworth, Mark, and Arthur Spyrou. 1995. *Legal Words: 30 Essays on Legal Words and Phrases*. Sydney: Centre for Plain Legal Language, University of Sydney.
Endicott, Timothy. 2000. *Vagueness and Law*. Oxford: Oxford University Press.
European Commission. 2014. *Clear English. Tips for Translators*. https://commission.europa.eu/system/files/2020-06/clear-english-tips-translators_en.pdf.
European Commission. 2023. *English Style Guide*. https://commission.europa.eu/system/files/2023-03/styleguide_english_dgt_en.pdf.
European Parliament. 2015. *Joint Practical Guide of the European Parliament, the Council and the Commission for Persons Involved in the Drafting of European Union Legislation*. https://eur-lex.europa.eu/content/techleg/EN-legislative-drafting-guide.pdf.
Giampieri, Patrizia, and Martin Harper. 2023. *Legal Translation: From Dictionary to Corpus*. Brienza: Le Penseur.
Gibbons, J., ed. 1994. *Language and the Law*. New York: Longman.
Gotti, M. 2005. *Investigating Specialized Discourse*. Bern: Peter Lang.
Gotti, Maurizio. 2016. Linguistic Features of Legal Texts: *Translation Issues*. *Statute Law Review* 37 (2): 144–155.
Griffith, Mary E. 1988. Sexism, Language, and the Law. *West Virginia Law Review* 91 (1): 125–151.
Hooker, M. B. 1978. *Adat Law in Modern Indonesia*. Kuala Lumpur: Oxford University Press.
Laster, Kathy. 2001. *Law as Culture*. Annandale: The Federation Press.
Leonardi, Vanessa. 2021. United in Diversity and Trapped in a Paradox: (Il)legal Gender Equality in the EU Legal Documents and Their Translations. In *Gender Issues: Translating and Mediating Languages, Cultures and Societies*, ed. Eleonora Federici and Maci Stefania, 243–266. Berlin: Peter Lang.
Maci, Stefania. 2014. What Does He Think This Is? The Court of Human Rights or the United Nations?. (Plain) Language in the Written Memories of Arbitral Proceedings: A Cross-Cultural Case Study. *European Journal of Law Reform* 16 (3): 572–596.

Maley, Y. 1994. The Language of the Law. In *Language and the Law*, ed. J. Gibbons, 11–50. New York: Longman.

Mattila, H. E. S. 2006. *Comparative Legal Linguistics*. Translated by C. Goddard. Aldershot: Ashgate.

Mellinkoff, David. 1963. *The Language of the Law*. Boston, MA: Little, Brown and Company.

Merryman, J. H. 1985. *The Civil Law Tradition*. 2nd ed. Stanford, CA: Stanford University Press.

Robinson, O. F., T. D. Fergus, and W. M. Gordon. 2000. *European Legal History*. 3rd ed. Oxford: Oxford University Press.

Solan, Lawrence M. 1993. *The Language of Judges*. Chicago, IL: The University of Chicago Press.

Tessuto, Girolamo. 2008a. Drafting Laws in UK Settings: Implementing Plain Language and Discourse? *Atti del Convegno Internazionale Il Drafting Internazionale*, Dipartimento di Diritto Costituzionale Italiano e Comparato della Facoltà di Giurisprudenza dell'Università degli Studi di Napoli Federico II.

Tessuto, Girolamo. 2008b. Discourse System in English Arbitration Award. In *Legal Discourse Across Cultures and Systems*, ed. Vijai K. Bhatia, Christopher Candlin, and Jan Engberg, 181–197. Hong Kong: Hong Kong University Press.

Tiersma, P. M. 1999. *Legal Language*. Chicago: University of Chicago Press.

Tiersma, P. M. 2012. A History of the Languages of law. In *The Oxford Handbook of Language and Law*, ed. P. M. Tiersma and L. M. Solan, 13–26. Oxford: Oxford University Press.

Wagner, A. 2006. Law on Language. In *Encyclopedia of Language and Linguistics*, ed. K. Brown, 2nd ed., 731–737. Amsterdam: Elsevier.

Williams, Christopher. 2004. Legal English and Plain Language: An Introduction. *ESP Across Culture* 1:111–124.

Williams, Christopher. 2008. Legal English or legal Englishes? Differences in Drafting Techniques in the English-speaking World. Federalismi.it. *Rivista di Diritto Pubblico Italiano, Comunitario e Comparato* 1:1–13.

Williams, Christopher. 2020. Court Judgments and Plain Language: Some Recent Developments in Canada and the United Kingdom. In *Communicating English in Specialised Domains: A Festschrift for Maurizio Gotti*, ed. Stefania Maci, Michele Sala, and Cinzia Spinzi, 106–125. Newcastle upon Tyne: Cambridge Scholars Publishing.

Williams, Christopher. 2023. *The Impact of Plain Language on Legal English in the United Kingdom*. London and New York: Routledge.
Wydick, Richard C. 1978. Plain English for Lawyers. *California Law Review* 66 (4): 727–765.
Ződi, Zsolt. 2019. The Limits of Plain Legal Language: Understanding the Comprehensible Style in Law. *International Journal of Law in Context* 15 (3): 246–262.

3

Corpora and Linguistic Analysis

3.1 What is a Corpus?

According to John Sinclair (1991), a corpus is a "collection of naturally occurring language text, chosen to characterize a state or variety of a language" (ibid.: 171). Corpora, therefore, are databases of texts which are used to study and analyse language over time. Corpora can be classified as either "large" or "small". A corpus is generally considered "large" when it contains several thousands of words (Bowker and Pearson 2002: 10) The size of a corpus, however, is closely connected to the intended purpose and the particular field of study being examined. As Laviosa and Falco (2023: 9) observe, the key elements that characterise corpora include authenticity (since they contain samples of "authentic" language), electronic format and representativeness (as they sufficiently mirror their genre or sub-genre) (Biber 1993; Bernardini and Ferraresi 2022: 208). Corpus texts are considered authentic because they are based on real language, which, as highlighted, is "naturally occurring" (Sinclair 1991: 171). In other words, corpora are not designed using materials tailored for second language (L2) learners; rather, they include genuine texts collected with the purpose of representing specific varieties of language or

V. Leonardi, P. Giampieri, *Legal English through the Ages*,
https://doi.org/10.1007/978-3-032-02172-4_3

particular genres (Bowker and Pearson 2002; O' Keeffe et al. 2007). Consequently, the materials (i.e., the texts) that form part of a corpus are selected according to specific criteria (Bowker and Pearson 2002: 9–10).

The availability of electronic corpora enables researchers to carry out fast and accurate research. The development of the World Wide Web has facilitated the easy creation of DIY (do-it-yourself) corpora (Zanettin 2002b) as well as the rapid collection of large-scale electronic texts (McEnery and Hardie 2012: 57). Furthermore, online electronic interfaces provide users with access to corpora, thereby improving the efficiency of both the consultation process and the retrieval of results (McEnery and Hardie 2012: 59).

The searched term in a corpus is known as a "node word" (Sinclair 2004: 143; Zanettin 2012: 124) and is typically positioned at the centre of a concordance line (Gatto 2014: 24). Concordances (or concordance lines) present node words within their immediate context. This arrangement aids linguistic analyses by allowing users to observe Key Words in Context (KWiC), which are the words that precede or follow the node word (Sinclair 2004; Zanettin 2012: 124; Gatto 2014: 5 and 107).

The individual words within a corpus are referred to as either "tokens" or "word types" (Bowker and Pearson 2002; McEnery and Hardie 2012; Zanettin 2012). The latter are concerned with "a particular, unique, wordform" (McEnery and Hardie 2012: 50), thus representing "each individual word" (Bowker and Pearson 2002: 13) in a corpus. Tokens, by contrast, denote the number of "running words" (Zanettin 2012: 14) within a corpus, thus encompassing all the words and non-words (such as punctuation marks) that comprise the dataset.

Corpora and corpus interfaces offer numerous features that facilitate linguistic analyses and terminological searches. One of the primary functions of these tools is to quantify word occurrences or frequencies based on the number of retrieved concordances for each searched term (or node word). This approach enables users to explore whether a specific word or language pattern recurs within a corpus, a phenomenon referred to as "corpus evidence" (Sinclair 2004: 28). In practical terms, the frequency of occurrence helps determine the linguistic role of a word or group of words (Sinclair 2004: 28–29). Word frequency is a crucial aspect when analysing, translating or studying a language, as it provides insights into word usage and occurrences within a particular language or sector (Gatto 2014: 19). This analysis ultimately reveals patterns in language use (O'Keeffe et al. 2007: 60).

Ultimately, as previously highlighted, corpora are assembled according to specific criteria that vary depending on the language under investigation and the objectives for which the corpus was established. In this regard, it is essential that a corpus accurately reflects the diversity and variability of the language or genre it aims to analyse (McEnery and Hardie 2012: 10). This representativeness is crucial, as it ensures that the corpus can provide meaningful insights into linguistic patterns, usage and trends (Biber 1993). Corpus representativeness is addressed in detail in a later section of this chapter. By carefully selecting texts that embody a wide range of linguistic features, researchers can create a more comprehensive and detailed understanding of the language in question.

3.2 Brief Historical Development of Corpora

The first electronically available corpus was the *Brown Corpus of Standard American English*, developed at Brown University in the United States during the early 1960s. Compiled by W. Nelson Francis and Henry Kučera, this pioneering corpus comprises approximately one million words sourced from texts published in 1961, all written in American English. To ensure that it accurately represented the language, the *Brown Corpus* was meticulously divided into various sub-corpora, encompassing genres such as fiction, journalism and hobbies, among others. At the time of its creation, the *Brown Corpus* was considered both large and comprehensive, serving as a solid foundation for the analysis and validation of language use. The *Brown Corpus* was significant not only for its size but also for its innovative approach to linguistic research. It was created in an era when many linguists were focused on theoretical frameworks that often-overlooked actual language data. In contrast, Francis and Kučera aimed to capture a wide array of linguistic phenomena through empirical evidence, challenging prevailing paradigms in American linguistics. The corpus was made available on computer tape as early as 1964, thus marking a significant technological advancement for its time.

Following the establishment of the *Brown Corpus*, larger corpora were developed to further enhance linguistic research. In 1987, the *Collins Cobuild English Language Dictionary* was produced based on a corpus containing approximately 20 million words. This related corpus, known as the COBUILD (*Collins-Birmingham University International Language Database*), was implemented under the direction of Professor John Sinclair. During this period, advancements in optical character recognition (OCR) technology facilitated the scanning of printed texts, significantly streamlining the corpus construction process.

By the 1990s, further progress was made with the creation of the *British National Corpus* (BNC). Developed by a consortium that included Oxford University Press, Longman (now Pearson Education), Larousse Kingfisher Chambers, along with research centres from Oxford and Lancaster Universities and the British Library's Research and Innovation Centre, the BNC comprises an impressive 100 million words representing both written and spoken variations of English. Its breadth and scope have established it as a landmark in corpus development.

In recent years, corpora have expanded dramatically, now encompassing hundreds of millions of words across various fields. For instance, the *Covid-19 Open Research Dataset* (CORD-19) is accessible via the Sketch Engine platform and consists of over 200 million words from medical articles specifically related to the coronavirus pandemic (Wang et al. 2020). This corpus serves as an invaluable resource for researchers investigating aspects of the global health crisis. Another prominent corpus is the *Corpus of Contemporary American English* (COCA), developed by Professor Mark Davies in 2008. COCA contains more than one billion words collected from diverse sources between 1990 and 2020. The texts within this corpus encompass materials from magazines, web pages, conversations and more, thus serving as a comprehensive source for research exploring language patterns across multiple registers or genres. The extensive variety of texts enables researchers to gain insights into language use in various contexts.

The evolution of corpora from the *Brown Corpus* to contemporary datasets illustrates not only technological advancements but also a growing recognition of corpora as essential tools for linguistic analysis and research across disciplines. As the field of linguistics has progressed, the role of corpora has expanded beyond mere collections of texts to become foundational resources that inform several academic disciplines, including sociolinguistics, psycholinguistics and applied linguistics among others. Researchers now use corpora to investigate language change over time, explore regional dialects and analyse the impact of social factors on language use. The ability to conduct large-scale quantitative analyses has transformed how linguists approach questions about grammar, vocabulary and discourse patterns. Furthermore, the increasing accessibility of corpora through digital platforms has democratised linguistic research, thus allowing scholars from diverse backgrounds and institutions to engage with these resources. This shift has fostered collaborative projects that cross geographical and disciplinary boundaries, leading to richer insights and more comprehensive understandings of language phenomena.

In addition to academic research, corpora have found applications in language education, artificial intelligence and natural language processing. Language teachers use corpora to develop materials that reflect authentic language use, while developers of AI systems rely on extensive datasets to train algorithms for tasks such as translation and sentiment analysis. This multifaceted utility underscores the importance of corpora in both theoretical exploration and practical application.

The overall path of corpus development illustrates a wider movement towards empirical research methods within the field of linguistics. As researchers place greater emphasis on data-driven strategies, the importance of meticulously designed corpora is expected to increase, influencing the future of linguistic research and deepening our comprehension of human language in its full complexity.

3.3 Types and Features of Corpora

Broadly speaking, there are various types of corpora, each designed to serve specific purposes within the field of linguistic research.

A first important distinction is made between monolingual and multilingual corpora. Monolingual corpora consist of texts in a single language, and they are particularly useful for providing "valuable insights into conventional language usage within specific contexts" (Liu et al.

2023: 136; see also Bernardini et al. 2003). These corpora offer significant benefits for language acquisition and translation research, as they facilitate a more profound comprehension of idiomatic phrases and the subtle use of language within a specific linguistic community (Liu et al. 2023: 136; Bowker 1998; Laviosa and Falco 2023). On the other hand, multilingual corpora (Zanettin 2012) consist of texts in two or more languages, and they serve as essential tools for comparative language analysis (Barrière 2016: 105). Multilingual corpora can be further divided into comparable and parallel corpora.

Comparable and parallel corpora are two distinct types of corpora used in linguistic and translation research (Sinclair 1991: 23ff). Comparable corpora are compiled in different languages, each independent of the other, yet addressing the same subject matter (Rossini Favretti et al. 2007; Zanettin 2012: 150). For instance, the *Bononia Legal Corpus* (BoLC) (Rossini Favretti et al. 2007) is divided into two sub-corpora: one in Italian and the other in English, both focusing on civil and criminal judgments, parliamentary acts, appeal court judgments and other legal texts. Scholars acknowledge the practical utility of comparable corpora, particularly for hands-on experience in the translation process or as a tool for reflecting upon translation practices (Biel 2017; see also Giampieri 2019b). For example, Liu et al. (2023: 137) underline that comparable corpora provide access to authentic language samples in both the source and target languages, which in turn helps to reduce potential occurrences of "translationese". However, these corpora do not fully capture the complexities of the translation process, as they lack examples of actual language transfer or rendering (McEnery and Xiao 2007). In contrast, parallel corpora consist of original texts alongside their translations into other languages (Gatto 2014: 16). These corpora, therefore, contain both source texts and their corresponding target texts across various languages (Gatto 2014: 16; Zanettin 2012: 11). Parallel corpora, offering translations made by professional translators (Zanettin 2002a: 11), serve the purpose of enabling language comparison. As such, they are particularly valuable for studying lexis, syntax and stylistic features across languages (Liu et al. 2023: 137). Liu et al. (2023: 155) inform about the pedagogical usefulness of parallel corpora in translator training. Amongst others, they find that a balance should be kept between translation skills and corpus acquaintance. If the latter is too strongly emphasised, users may develop an uncritical reliance on corpus data, thus compromising their assessment skills on the appropriateness of certain translation options.

The first parallel corpus, the *Canadian Hansard Corpus* (Tognini-Bonelli and Sinclair 2006), comprised parliamentary proceedings in both English and Canadian French. Since then, parallel corpora have been increasingly compiled and used worldwide. A notable example today is the *European Parliament Proceedings Parallel Corpus* (Europarl) (Koehn 2005; Tiedemann 2012), which includes translations of European parliamentary proceedings into all official EU languages.

Bowker and Pearson (2002) categorise potential users of parallel corpora into three groups: language teachers and learners, translators and computational linguists (ibid.: 94). For the first group, parallel corpora function as contextualised dictionaries. For translators, they provide a means of reflecting on translation decisions, while for computational linguists, parallel corpora are useful when developing alignment software. Indeed, for effective consultation, parallel corpora need to be sentence-aligned (Bowker and Pearson 2002: 107, 120; Gatto 2014: 16), which enables users to search for a word in one language and view its translations in another.

The distinction between comparable and parallel corpora, however, has become increasingly blurred in recent years (Zanettin 2012: 149). Institutions within the European Union have developed multilingual databases and corpora where it is often difficult to distinguish source texts from target texts (Fantinuoli and Zanettin 2015: 3–4). Nevertheless, both types of corpora remain invaluable for language analysis. Scholars debate the completeness and usefulness of both comparable and parallel corpora in translation training, professional practice and second language learning (Bernardini 2011; Zanettin 2014; Giampieri 2018; Doval and Sánchez Nieto 2019). For instance, Zanettin (2014) notes that they enable users to "compare and contrast regularities of languages" (ibid.: 178), while Bernardini (2011: 2) argues that they provide complementary insights into translation norms.

In her research, Giampieri (2018) suggests that both Europarl and BoLC can be consulted in tandem "to dispel doubts and produce satisfactory legal translations" (ibid.: 149), particularly when English functions as a *lingua franca*. Biel (2010) posits that comparable corpora allow translation students to become familiar with sector-based conventions, while parallel corpora shed light on translation processes and techniques. Machniewski (2006) proposes three settings in which parallel and comparable corpora can be used. Parallel corpora are helpful in understanding past translators' choices, thus assisting in overcoming translation challenges, whereas comparable corpora facilitate a deeper understanding of language nuances in both source and target texts. In this way, both types of corpora contribute to the development of translation skills and help reduce L1 interference in translators. Furthermore, they are beneficial during the translation revision process.

Sinclair (1996) highlights the advantages of comparable corpora by arguing that they mitigate the language distortion inherent in parallel corpora and claims that "[t]he possibilities of a comparable corpus are to compare different languages or varieties in similar circumstances of communication, but avoiding the inevitable distortion introduced by the translations of a parallel corpus" (Sinclair 1996: online). In other words, both comparable and parallel corpora offer significant value in linguistic research and translation studies. While they serve distinct purposes, they are complementary resources that provide unique insights into language use, translation norms and linguistic structure. Their combined use in educational and professional contexts enhances both language comprehension and translation proficiency.

Another distinction is made between online and offline corpora. Online corpora represent a significant advancement in linguistic research, offering users the ability to consult vast databases of text through an internet interface. These corpora allow users to search for specific terms, and retrieve concordance lines. In contrast to offline corpora, which are accessed via specific software solutions such as *AntConc* or *TextSTAT*, online corpora are available through web-based platforms, providing more immediate and accessible consultation. Such web interfaces or platforms enable users to perform complex linguistic searches which can involve querying single or multiple words, listing collocations, conducting Key Word in Context (KWiC) searches or performing lemmatised and POS-tagged searches. Such functionalities allow for a detailed exploration of linguistic patterns, thus making online corpora a useful tool for both linguists and professionals. Nevertheless, in order to fully exploit the capabilities of these platforms, users should possess a thorough understanding of the search syntax employed by each platform. Although there may be slight variations among different interfaces, the underlying patterns generally remain consistent. The standardisation of these platforms enables a smoother transition among different platforms, thus allowing users to interact with multiple corpora with considerable ease.

There are various types of corpora available online, ranging from general corpora, which aim to represent language in its entirety, to specialised corpora, which focus on specific sectors or fields. General corpora represent a language as a whole and are primarily employed to make "general observations" (Bowker and Pearson 2002: 12) about the language being examined. These corpora are intended to provide a broad overview of a language, allowing researchers to assess language usage across a wide spectrum of contexts.

Examples of general corpora are the COCA and the BNC, which encompass a wide range of language data and genres, including fiction, magazines, newspapers and spoken language, which allow comprehensive linguistic analyses across different registers and styles of language use. The BNC, in particular, "aims to represent the universe of contemporary British English [and] to capture the full range of varieties of language use" (Aston and Burnard 1998: 5). The comprehensiveness of general corpora enables them to function as reference corpora (see Tamburini 2002), serving as standardised benchmarks against which linguistic variation and change can be evaluated.

Specialised corpora, also referred to as "special purpose corpora" (Bowker and Pearson 2002: 12), are focused on specific fields of study or particular language phenomena. These corpora are designed to cater to particular domains, languages or genres, making them valuable resources for focused academic research and professional practice (Jensen et al. 2012: 24). For instance, they are beneficial in academic research and professional settings, such as translator training (see Lee and Swales 2006; Farr and O'Keeffe 2019), where precise, domain-specific data are required. Academic corpora such as the *British Academic Written English* (BAWE), developed at the Universities of Warwick, Reading, and Oxford Brookes, and the *British Academic Spoken English* (BASE), developed at the University of Warwick and the University of Reading, both provide insight into academic discourse and language use in educational settings. Another example of a specialised corpus is the *British Law Report Corpus* (BLaRC), which includes judicial decisions from British courts and tribunals issued between 2008 and 2010, with approximately nine million words. This corpus serves as an invaluable resource for legal research and linguistic analysis of legal discourse. Other instances of such corpora are the *Hong Kong Financial Services Corpus* (HKFSC) and the *Hong Kong Engineering Corpus* (HKEC), which are tailored to the financial and engineering domains, respectively.

Finally, there exist learner corpora, which consist of texts produced by individuals learning a second language (L2 learners (Zanettin 2012: 12). Learner corpora have gained significant importance in the fields of language education and acquisition. Granger (2002: 7) observes that these corpora are generally compiled for particular language learning objectives, frequently aimed at evaluating common errors, interlanguage phenomena and the progression of language acquisition. Learner corpora provide invaluable data for language teachers and researchers, enabling them to identify patterns in L2 learners' performance and tailor instructional strategies accordingly (Bernardini and Ferraresi 2022: 490). Several of these corpora can be accessed free of charge on platforms like Lextutor (Cobb 2004), facilitating comprehensive analysis of learner language.

In contrast to online corpora, offline corpora are compiled and consulted offline, either by individual users or by other scholars. These corpora are often created on a case-by-case basis, tailored to meet the specific needs of a research or translation task. As Sánchez-Gijón (2009: 115) explains, offline corpora are frequently compiled "for the sole purpose of providing information—either factual, linguistic, or field-specific—for the purpose of completing a translation task". This highlights their customisation and direct application to specialised linguistic and professional contexts, making them highly adaptable for specific research requirements. One of the distinguishing features of offline corpora is that computer literacy is essential for their effective use. Users need to be acquainted with the search syntax of offline concordancers, which can be more complex than their online counterparts (Varantola 2002: 69). This requirement implies that offline corpora demand a certain degree of technical proficiency, as users need to manually organise and query the data through specialised software solutions. Despite the initial difficulties users may face when using offline corpora, they provide a level of flexibility in their composition and content that standardised online corpora often lack. Another significant difference lies in the size of offline corpora. Unlike the large-scale datasets often found in online corpora, offline corpora need not be extensive to be effective. As argued by Williams (1999: 516) and Zanettin (2001: 178), even small, domain-specific corpora can yield valuable insights. A corpus composed of just a dozen texts can still be deemed representative and reliable for specialised research (Giampieri 2019a). This makes offline corpora particularly useful for research where resources are limited or where only a small, specialised dataset is needed. In terms of practical use, offline corpora resemble DIY corpora, offering the benefit of flexibility in terms of the selection of texts and their composition. Scholars and translators can compile their own corpora from a range of texts that are directly relevant to their work, enhancing the specificity and precision of their analyses. However, this customisation comes with additional effort in terms of data compilation, cleaning and tagging, requiring users to have a higher level of technical expertise than is typically needed for online corpora.

DIY corpora are frequently described as "on the fly" (Gallego-Hernández 2015) or "disposable" (Zanettin 2002b), as they are created by the user and discarded once a language or translation project is concluded, or when they are no longer required. DIY corpora can be accessed either online or offline, depending on the user's information and communication technology (ICT) skills or preferences. For those opting for online access, platforms such as Sketch Engine (Kilgarriff et al. 2004) provide interfaces that enable the uploading and consultation of corpus texts. Conversely, offline users may rely on concordancers like *AntConc* or *TextSTAT* to consult their corpora.

One of the primary challenges associated with DIY and offline corpora is that their compilation is a time-consuming process (Zanettin 2002b: 245; Wilkinson 2006; Aston 2009: ix-x), often leading to the conclusion that the effort required to create them outweighs their benefits (Vintar 2008: 50). This considerable investment of time and resources may discourage prospective users from engaging in corpus compilation. To address these challenges, scholars have developed specific software programmes designed to crawl the web and retrieve documents automatically. For instance, BooTCaT (Baroni and Bernardini 2004) is a free software tool that enables users to create corpora either automatically or semi-automatically. Users simply insert a set of keywords, referred to as "seeds" and the software handles all necessary tasks, including document retrieval and file storage in designated folders. Some researchers prefer using fourth-generation concordancers, which facilitate the creation of a corpus online by allowing users to input keywords. Alternatively, users have the option to upload their own electronic documents to these concordancers, thus enabling them to perform consultations and linguistic analyses on their custom-made corpora. A further difficulty encountered by numerous DIY and offline corpus creators is the tendency to discard these corpora after the completion of a project. This is largely attributed to the inability to share them with other researchers, translators or users due to copyright issues (McEnery and Hardie 2012: 43–44). As a result, fourth-generation concordancers are regarded as valuable tools since they allow users to avoid copyright infringement and facilitate the exchange of corpora among researchers.

A further distinction is made between written and spoken language corpora. Written corpora typically consist of texts from various genres, such as academic prose, literary works or journalistic writing, from specific authors or historical periods. These corpora provide a rich resource to analyse formal and structured language. Conversely, spoken corpora consist of transcriptions of oral communication, including a wide range of discourse types such as casual conversations, televised discussions, political debates or academic presentations and lectures. Spoken corpora are essential to explore natural language use, intonation and interactional dynamics, which are often absent from written language data.

Another key differentiation in corpus linguistics is between synchronic and diachronic corpora. Synchronic corpora capture language at a specific point in time, thus offering insights into language use within a specified temporal framework. These corpora serve as valuable tools to analyse language as it currently exists or within a particular historical context. Conversely, diachronic corpora cover extensive timeframes, thus enabling researchers to investigate the changes and evolution of language over time

(Zanettin 2012: 45). This temporal examination is essential to understand linguistic trends, variations in vocabulary and the development of new linguistic forms.

The diverse types and features of corpora reflect the complex nature of linguistic research. Each type fulfils specific functions, enabling researchers to explore different aspects of language usage across a range of contexts and disciplines. This classification of corpora not only enhances our understanding of language complexities but also strengthens the practical applications of corpus linguistics in fields such as education, translation and computational linguistics.

3.3.1 Lexical and Syntactic Searches

Consulting corpora is beneficial as it uncovers and highlights language patterns, contextual word usages, multi-word expressions, which are also referred to as "lexical phrases" (O'Keeffe et al. 2007: 63), collocations and colligations. Multi-word expressions or lexical phrases consist of groups of words that frequently appear together and are often specific to particular registers or genres (ibid.: 210). O'Keeffe et al. (2007) assert that "language is available for use in ready-made chunks" (ibid.: 60), which corpora tend to reveal. For example, in spoken language, phrases such as "you know what" and "you know what I mean" are particularly prevalent (O'Keeffe et al. 2007: 66).

Closely related to lexical phrases are collocations and colligations. Collocations refer to patterns of language usage (Sinclair 1991) and concern the likelihood of co-occurrence among lexical items (Lehecka 2015). According to Sinclair (1991), "[a] word which occurs in close proximity to a word under investigation is called a collocate of it" (ibid.: 170). Collocations are words that "go together" and are often "found in each other's company" (Bowker and Pearson 2002: 32). Not only do they frequently occur together, but they can also convey specific meanings when placed in close proximity. Firth (1935) posits that the meaning of a word depends significantly on how it combines with other words, i.e., its collocates. Numerous linguists have provided examples of collocations; for instance, in 1966, Halliday noted that the term tea is typically described as "strong", whereas engines are characterised as "powerful", rarely the other way around (see also Sinclair 2004: 29). Common verbs like "turn" and "go" exhibit preferred proximities, such as "turn/go grey/brown/white" or "go mad/insane" (O'Keeffe et al. 2007: 59–60). Consequently, lexical phrases and collocates play pivotal roles in language learning and translation training and practice (O'Keeffe et al. 2007; Laviosa and Falco 2023). Colligations represent the co-occurrence of grammatical classes (Firth 1957). Thus, it can be inferred that "what collocation is on a lexical level of analysis, colligation is on a syntactic level" (Römer 2005: 13). Sinclair (2004: 38) provides compelling examples of the colligations associated with the noun "place", showing that this term is generally preceded by a possessive adjective—most commonly "my". In second left position, there is usually a preposition—frequently "to"—and in third left position, an adverb of place such as "back", "up" or "down". Furthermore, constructions such as "the… of" (e.g., "the true feelings of people") exemplify colligational patterns (ibid.).

It is important to note that, for the effective derivation of colligations, the concordancing programme must assign a word class to each node word (Sinclair 2004:142). In this context, Part Of Speech (POS) tagging is employed. A corpus can be annotated for parts of speech, which involves assigning grammatical labels to all words based on their grammatical class (Bowker and Pearson 2002: 83–84). Therefore, annotation entails "adding interpretative linguistic information to a corpus" (Leech 2005: 25). This process enhances the accuracy and speed of corpus searches by facilitating easier identification of collocations and colligations.

Many corpus interfaces also enable users to search for lemmas. A lemma serves as a headword encompassing all its inflected forms (Sinclair 1991: 41–42). It is defined as "a set of lexical forms having the same stem and belonging to the same major word class, differing only in inflection and/or spelling" (Francis and Kučera 1982: 1). For example, if the verb "be" is regarded as a lemma, its inflected forms include "is", "are", "was", "were" and "being" (Sinclair 2004: 231). In certain corpora, the asterisk symbol (*), referred to as the "wildcard character" (Bowker and Pearson 2002: 18; Zanettin 2012: 57; Gatto 2014: 91), facilitates lemma searches. The wildcard character can also replace any character, whether alphanumeric or non-alphanumeric (Zanettin 2012: 124). For instance, searching for "said* *ly*" retrieves adverbs ending in -ly that follow the verb "said" (ibid.: 190; 2012) whereas searching for "print*" predominantly yields results like "print", "printer", "printers", "printing", "prints", among others. (Bowker and Pearson 2002: 18). The wildcard can also be positioned between words to obtain specific terms or phrases; thus, searching for "who is a * member of the" may reveal modifiers such as "founding" and/or "retired", among others (Zanettin 2012: 57).

3.3.2 Corpus Representativeness

One of the most crucial characteristics of corpora is their representativeness (Biber 1993). As Leech (1991) acknowledges, a corpus is considered representative when "the findings based on its contents can be generalised to a larger hypothetical corpus" (ibid.: 27). In other words, a corpus is deemed representative when it can be used to conduct general observations about a particular language (Bowker and Pearson 2002: 12). This implies that the corpus should accurately reflect the language of the genre or sub-genre it aims to represent (Biel 2010; McEnery et al. 2010; Prieto Ramos 2019). The concept of representativeness is a subject of considerable debate within the field of corpus linguistics, as the more representative a corpus is, the deeper the insights it provides into language.

Nevertheless, it is important not to assume that a larger corpus necessarily equates to greater representativeness (Zanettin 2012: 45). It has been argued, indeed, that corpora may reach a saturation point, beyond which the addition of new words or terms does not yield any further linguistically relevant information (Jensen et al. 2012: 24; Zanettin 2012: 47). Therefore, even small but well-constructed, *ad hoc* corpora can achieve a high degree of representativeness. In this context, corpora should be specifically tailored to the particular sector or field that users are interested in. Zanettin (2012: 46) raises critical questions regarding "according to whom" and "of what" a corpus should be representative. This emphasises the need for representative corpora to include a sufficient range of language examples from the relevant genres or fields of study. For instance, Liu et al. (2023: 137) assert that "the effectiveness of comparable corpora relies heavily on the careful selection of representative and authentic texts". Consequently, representativeness is not merely a question of size but one of careful selection, ensuring that the corpus mirrors the essential features of the language it intends to represent.

3.4 Concordancers

To consult a corpus, users require a platform or software programme, often referred to as a concordancer. This software interface enables users to search and retrieve linguistic data from a corpus by generating concordances. A concordance (as mentioned, also known as a concordance line) is essentially a string of text that contains the searched term within its context (Zanettin 2012: 143). Concordancers are software tools or interfaces that display these concordances (Bernardini and Ferraresi 2022: 207). As Bowker and Pearson (2002) explain, "[a] concordancer allows the user to see all the occurrences of a particular word in its immediate contexts" (ibid.: 13). This functionality is crucial for studying word usage, collocations and contextual meanings in linguistic research among others.

The evolution of electronic concordancers has occurred over four distinct generations, as acknowledged by McEnery and Hardie (2012: 37ff), each representing advancements in both functionality and accessibility. The first generation of concordancers (McEnery and Hardie 2012: 37–39) was installed on mainframe computers and could only be accessed at a specific physical location. These early tools had very limited capabilities, primarily displaying KWiCs (Key Words in Context), where the searched word was shown within an extract of its surrounding context. Additional functions, such as frequency analysis or collocation analysis, required separate programmes. An early example of this kind of tool was the CLOC concordance package (Reed 1978), developed at the University of Birmingham. Due to the lack of flexibility and remote access, these tools were restricted in scope and usability. The second-generation concordancers (McEnery and Hardie 2012: 39–40) emerged in the 1980s and could be used in any IBM-compatible personal computers. These tools, while more accessible due to their compatibility with home PCs, still offered only basic KWiC functionalities, much like their predecessors. Furthermore, the memory limitations of early PCs meant that the corpora being consulted had to be relatively small. While the shift from mainframes to personal computers increased the availability of these tools, their practical application in linguistic analysis remained constrained by the hardware capabilities of the time. Third-generation concordancers (McEnery and Hardie 2012: 40–43) represent a significant leap forward in terms of functionality and accessibility. Software programmes such as *AntConc* (Anthony 2023) and *TextSTAT* (Hüning 2008) fall into this category. These programmes can be installed locally on a PC, thus allowing users to consult corpora offline. With these tools, users are no longer restricted to simple KWiC analysis. Instead, they can conduct complex linguistic analyses, including lemmatisation (grouping words by their base forms), collocation (the study of word combinations) and n-grams listing (the identification of word sequences of a particular length), among many other features. However, it is important to note that some third-generation software solutions may not run on all operating systems, thus limiting their cross-platform usability. The most recent evolution in concordancing tools, fourth-generation concordancers (McEnery and Hardie 2012: 44ff), have shifted to web-based interfaces. These tools are no longer installed on individual PCs but are accessed and run online, thus allowing users to consult corpora irrespective of their operating system. This approach is known as a client/server architecture, where the actual language analyses are performed on remote servers, offering users faster and more complex query capabilities. In addition to improving functionality, fourth-generation concordancers have addressed copyright issues, which had previously hindered the sharing of corpora. Prior to these developments, it was often impossible for researchers to make corpora publicly available due to potential copyright infringements. Fourth-generation tools address this concern by presenting only brief excerpts of the original text in their concordance results. This limited display makes it difficult to reconstruct the full original text, thus protecting the copyright of the source material.

The evolution of concordancers across various generations mirrors the rapid technological advancements of the digital age, fundamentally transforming corpus analysis into a powerful, user-friendly and highly accessible tool for linguistic research. Each generation of concordancers has built upon the previous one, enhancing functionality and usability while addressing critical challenges such as copyright issues and data management. Consequently, corpora have been reinforced as invaluable resources for linguists, translators and researchers across a wide range of disciplines. The capacity to conduct detailed analyses using expansive datasets has enriched academic inquiry and facilitated practical applications in language education and translation studies. Furthermore, through continuous adjustments to meet the needs of researchers and address ethical issues, contemporary concordancers have made corpus analysis a vital component of linguistic research, enhancing understanding of the complexities and subtleties of language in its various forms.

3.5 Legal Corpora

In the last fifty years, there has been a significant increase in academic focus on legal language, driven by advancements in applied linguistics and social sciences. This growing interest marks a substantial shift in perspective, as the examination of legal language has evolved from relying solely on authors' instincts and qualitative insights, exemplified by Mellinkoff's pioneering research from 1963. Investigations into legal language, indeed, were initially and predominantly influenced by the personal perspectives of authors and qualitative evaluations (Alcaraz 1994; Tiersma 1999; Borja 2000). The analysis of legal communication largely depended on the intuitive understanding of language users within the legal field. Although this early approach provided valuable insights, it was inherently limited by subjectivity and the absence of systematic, data-driven methodologies.

As corpus linguistics has developed and diverse corpora have become more accessible, the landscape of legal language research has transformed dramatically. Researchers now employ sophisticated tools and methodologies to analyse legal discourse based on naturally occurring data. This evolution has broadened the scope and depth of studies in legal language, thus allowing for more comprehensive and empirically grounded insights. The application of corpus linguistics enables the systematic examination of language patterns, usage and evolution within various legal contexts.

Researchers can explore vast quantities of data across different registers, ranging from court judgments and statutes to contracts and legal opinions, each reflecting distinct linguistic features and communicative functions. This variety allows scholars to investigate how legal language adapts to different audiences, purposes and contexts. For instance, the analysis of courtroom discourse may reveal specific linguistic strategies employed by lawyers to persuade juries or judges, while examination of legislative texts might uncover patterns that reflect the formalities and conventions unique to statutory drafting. Furthermore, corpora can facilitate comparative studies across jurisdictions, enabling researchers to identify variations in legal terminology and phraseology that may arise from cultural or procedural differences.

The shift towards data-driven analyses has not only enhanced the rigour of research methodologies but has also facilitated a more detailed understanding of the complexities inherent in legal communication. Researchers can now use extensive datasets to measure word frequencies, collocations and co-occurrences, thus shedding light on the linguistic expression of legal concepts. For example, examining the frequency of specific terms or phrases can provide insights into evolving legal practices or societal attitudes towards certain issues.

With regard to the corpus-based analyses undertaken in this study, three diachronic legal corpora—CHELAR, BLaRC and BoLC—were selected to examine the features of legal language. The focus was particularly on identifying instances of *legalese* and sexism within legal discourse and their linguistic trends over time. This comprehensive approach enables the detection of significant patterns and changes in legal discourse, thus making a significant contribution to the field of legal linguistics and enhancing the understanding of how legal language mirrors societal changes. Each corpus—CHELAR, BLaRC and BoLC—provides unique insights that, when considered collectively, offer a comprehensive framework for exploring legal English across various historical periods.

3.5.1 The *Corpus of Historical English Law Reports* (CHELAR)

The *Corpus of Historical English Law Reports* (CHELAR) encompasses the timeframe from 1535 to 1999, focusing on the language employed in law reports within the British Common Law system. It was developed by the Variation, Linguistic Change, and Grammaticalization (VLCG) research unit, headed by Teresa Fanego at the University of Santiago de Compostela. The project began in 2011, with the first version of the corpus being released in 2016 and an upgraded version in 2018, which included TEI-XML format files for improved accessibility. CHELAR includes 463,326 words extracted from 369 law reports, which are organised into nine chronological periods and it provides interesting insights into the evolution of legal discourse and its linguistic features.

Fanego et al. (2017) explore the evolution and structure of law reporting in England, highlighting the distinct features that distinguish modern law reports from earlier versions, such as the Year Books. They observe that modern law reports are characterised by their comprehensiveness, including key terms, case summaries and references to prior cases, which make them more accurate and detailed than the earlier English Reports (Bhatia 1993). The authors explain that the format of the modern law report serves as a "faithful record" of case facts, judicial arguments and reasoning, which is crucial to the judicial system of the UK, as courts depend on precedents established in prior judgments (ibid.).

In their work, Fanego et al. (2017) make use of Bhatia's typology, which classifies legal writing into three primary genres: academic writing, which includes research journals and legal textbooks; juridical writing, encompassing law reports and judgments; and government-related texts (Bhatia 1987). The authors assert that the growing interest in legal English stems from advancements in linguistics and applied linguistics, particularly regarding language use in real-world contexts and the development of language support courses (Bhatia 1993). The corpus enables diachronic analyses, allowing researchers to observe changes in language use over nearly five centuries. The examination of the language used in law reports provides two significant advantages: it uncovers both changes in linguistic patterns and the evolution of legal principles as well as the communication methods used by the judiciary. The authors trace the historical roots of English law reporting back to the Year Books, which were concise manuscript notes published annually from 1268 to 1535. These notes were originally composed in Latin or French before being translated into English (Tiersma 1999). They also examine the transition to printed editions that began in 1535, ultimately resulting in the creation of the Law Reports, which are now regarded as the most authoritative series for England and Wales. Furthermore, Fanego et al. (2017) highlight the difficulties and the challenges encountered in compiling a balanced corpus of legal texts, as evidenced in the construction of CHELAR, which aims to record the development of legal English from 1535 to 1999 (Rodríguez-Puente 2011).

One of the key strengths of CHELAR lies in its focus on legal reports as a distinct genre, which is critical to understand the formalisation of legal language and the progressive standardisation of legal terminology. The corpus enables researchers to trace the emergence and evolution of significant legal terms, syntactic structures and rhetorical conventions over time, thus making it a valuable resource for diachronic studies. Several studies have used the CHELAR corpus to identify significant linguistic trends, such as a reduction in the frequency of passive verb constructions and a rise in the use of first-person pronouns. This shift suggests a transition towards a more subjective and personalised style in legal writing. These changes are particularly associated with the establishment of the *Incorporated Council of Law Reporting for England and Wales*, which regulated the production and publication of law reports (Fanego and Rodríguez-Puente 2019).

In particular, Biber and Gray (2019) compared the linguistic features of law reports with those found in scientific research articles, newspapers and works of fiction from 1700 to 1999, concluding that law reports maintain a more conservative linguistic style, thus displaying a greater resistance to historical linguistic change when compared to other written registers. Rodríguez-Puente (2019) focused on variations in the use of personal pronouns, noting a significant rise in first-person pronouns from the nineteenth century onwards, a trend that correlates with the increased regulation of law report production. In another study,

Rodríguez-Puente (2020a) examined the prevalence of active versus passive voice in law reports, confirming the dominance of passive constructions up until the late twentieth century, with a marked decline in their use from the mid-nineteenth century. Furthermore, Rodríguez-Puente (2020b) analysed the distribution of the derivational suffixes "-ity" and "-ness" across various registers, finding that their usage in law reports more closely resembles that found in formal documents than in informal texts. Another study by Blanco-García (2018, cited in Rodríguez and Fanego 2020) explored the marking of concession in CHELAR, specifically comparing the usage of "notwithstanding" with that of "although" and "though", highlighting the association of the term with official and bureaucratic language.

Although CHELAR is an invaluable resource to analyse the historical developments in legal language, it is worth acknowledging certain limitations associated with its use. Its exclusive focus on law reports means that it does not offer a broader perspective on legal discourse in its entirety, such as the language used in statutes, legal contracts or more informal legal documents. Nevertheless, the detailed annotation of the corpus, including part-of-speech (POS) tagging, enables accurate linguistic analysis of temporal variation, genre-specific features and lexical patterns. Overall, CHELAR stands as a pioneering resource in the field of legal linguistics, significantly enhancing understanding of the complex relationship between law, language and societal developments over time while encouraging further research into the linguistic features and stylistic shifts that define this distinctive genre of writing.

3.5.2 The *British Law Report Corpus* (BLaRC)

The *British Law Report Corpus* (BLaRC) is a specialised legal English corpus compiled by Mª José Marín Pérez and Camino Rea Rizzo at the University of Murcia. It consists of 8.5 million words extracted from 1,228 British law reports published between 2008 and 2010 in the UK. The choice to focus exclusively on judicial decisions, as noted by Marín Pérez and Rizzo (2012), stems from their role in recording judicial decisions and rulings. Due to their varied nature, which covers various legal domains and includes references to numerous legal documents, such as statutes and contracts, law reports hold significant importance within the British legal system, thus serving as the foundational element for this specialised corpus (ibid.).

The design of the BLaRC corpus posed several key challenges, primarily ensuring that it was representative of the legal language used in British courts. According to linguistic principles such as those outlined by Douglas Biber (1993), as acknowledged by Marín Pérez and Rizzo (2012), a corpus must be representative of the full range of linguistic variability within its target domain. Therefore, sampling strategies and corpus structure were carefully considered in order to include texts that accurately represent the communicative function of legal discourse (ibid.). BLaRC focused exclusively on judicial decisions, given their relevance and comprehensiveness in covering a wide range of legal issues. To reflect the diversity within legal practice, the corpus was structured to include reports from different areas of law, such as criminal, civil and commercial law. This allowed the researchers to study terminological variations across different legal fields. Furthermore, the reports came from a variety of courts and tribunals within the UK, thus ensuring that the corpus captured different levels of legal hierarchy and geographical regions (Marín 2017). The question of optimal corpus size was one of the most debated aspects of its design. The initial target was set at 8.5 million words, based on guidelines from established linguists like Sinclair (1991), who recommended that specialised corpora should contain between 10 and 20 million words to ensure comprehensive analysis. Other studies, like those by Pearson (1998) and Kennedy (1998), however, suggest that while larger corpora may offer more data, they are not necessarily better for all purposes, especially in specialised fields (Marín 2017; see also Jensen et al. 2012: 24; Zanettin 2012: 47). To further refine the corpus, the researchers followed the method of type/token ratio analysis—a statistical technique used to determine how many new terms emerge as the corpus grows. By studying the appearance of new terms (types) relative to the total number of words (tokens), they found that after reaching approximately 2.6 million words, the rate of new term emergence significantly declined. This suggested that a smaller corpus might still have been sufficient for the objectives of the study. Nevertheless, the decision was made to continue with an 8.5-million-word target to ensure coverage of legal terminology across various subfields (ibid.).

Marín Pérez and Rizzo employed Automatic Term Recognition (ATR) methods to extract the terminology for their analysis. The main tool used was Drouin's TermoStat (2003), a well-regarded software for identifying specialised terms in a corpus. This tool automatically extracted candidate terms, which were then validated against a legal English glossary containing over 10,000 terms. By progressively adding sub-corpora to BLaRC, they were able to monitor the type/term ratio and observe how new terms emerged, leading to insights into the frequency and distribution of legal terms within the corpus (Marín 2017). The results showed that once the corpus exceeded 6.78 million words, the emergence of new terms became negligible, confirming that the corpus had reached a sufficient size for comprehensive terminological analysis. The ATR method was found to be highly effective, identifying 88% of legal terms from the top 200 candidate terms extracted automatically (ibid.).

The distribution of texts within BLaRC was uneven, largely influenced by the geographical and hierarchical distribution of UK courts. Higher courts, such as the Court of Appeal or High Court of Justice, contributed more texts due to their binding precedent role. In contrast, some tribunals and lower courts were underrepresented, either due to their limited jurisdiction or because they had only recently been established or disbanded (ibid.). Marín Pérez and Rizzo established the word target for each category in proportion to the number of texts available for that court or tribunal during the period from 2008 to 2010 in order to ensure representativeness. For instance, the Court of Appeal (Civil Division) accounted for 15.89% of the total texts, which resulted in a word target of 956,398 words. In contrast, smaller entities such as the Patents County Court contributed only 0.08%, leading to a corresponding word target of 15,242 words (ibid.).

Therefore, the BLaRC corpus serves as a comprehensive and representative resource for the study of legal English. Its careful design, large size and focus on terminological diversity make it a valuable tool for both linguistic and legal researchers.

3.5.3 The *Bononia Legal Corpus* (BoLC)

The *Bononia Legal Corpus* (BoLC) is an extensive research project aimed at developing multilingual comparable machine-readable legal corpora, with a particular emphasis on English and Italian legal texts. Launched in 1997 at the University of Bologna, this project seeks to advance cross-linguistic research and improve comprehension of legal terminology across varying legal systems. The corpus is specifically designed to include European Community documents, particularly directives and judgments, which are vital to understand the transnational legal framework and its implications for member states (Rossini Favretti et al. 2007).

A preliminary pilot corpus was created as the first step in compiling the BoLC. This pilot corpus served as a foundational dataset for the analysis of European legislation, thus enabling researchers to enhance their methodologies and develop a conceptual framework for the larger corpus. The documents selected for the pilot corpus were carefully chosen to include a wide variety of legal texts, with a focus on directives and judgments issued between 1968 and 1995. These documents were chosen because they reflect modern legal language and are essential to understand the transnational nature of law within the European Union (ibid.). The pilot corpus included:

- 2232 Directives: 6,500,000 words,
- 1798 Directives: 5,800,000 words,
- 4472 Judgments: 13,700,000 words,
- 4471 Sentenze: 12,300,000 words.

The final version of the BoLC was encoded using SGML (Standard Generalized Markup Language) ISO-Latin-1, which facilitates platform independence and ensures that the corpus can be accessed and processed across various computer systems. This encoding standard is particularly significant in handling multilingual documents, as it allows for the correct display of characters, including accents in Italian, which may not be properly rendered on all systems. The use of SGML also aids in the standardisation of document formatting, thus facilitating data management and retrieval. Such rigorous encoding standards ensure that the legal texts in the BoLC corpus are not only clean and error-free but also accessible to researchers across jurisdictions and languages, thus facilitating broader legal and linguistic analysis.

In terms of data retrieval and access, the project developed two key software applications: the Corpus Universal Examiner (CUE) and its Java counterpart, the Java Corpus Universal Examiner (JCUE). CUE, originally written in C++ for UNIX systems, employs complex indexing schemes, such as inverted indexing, to facilitate rapid data retrieval and access. It also incorporates compression methods, like Huffman coding, to minimise the storage space required for the corpora. JCUE, on the other hand, is a client-server application that allows users to retrieve documents from remote locations, thus improving accessibility for researchers working on various platforms, including Windows and Macintosh systems.

The primary objective of the BoLC is to provide contrastive information regarding legal terminology and usage, which can assist lexicon developers in creating accurate and effective tools for translation and other applications. Rossini Favretti et al. (2007) highlight the importance of corpus evidence in examining large text samples and identifying typical features of various text types and genres. The findings from the BoLC are expected to enhance understanding of the linguistic differences rooted in the distinct socio-institutional systems, thus providing valuable insights for legal translation and linguistic analysis.

As the development of specialised corpora continues to evolve, the BoLC is expected to play an increasingly vital role within the field of corpus linguistics. It will offer empirical data for semantic analysis while contributing to a broader understanding of legal language across different jurisdictions. This research project not only enriches academic discourse but also serves practical applications within legal translation, linguistics and comparative law studies.

3.6 Concluding Remarks

Corpora have proven to be invaluable resources in linguistic research, particularly in the analysis of legal language. Beginning with a broad overview of the development and role of corpora, this chapter illustrated the shift from intuition-based approaches to data-driven methodologies, highlighting the importance of empirical research. This transition is especially critical in the study of legal discourse, where linguistic precision and complexity necessitate systematic exploration on a larger scale.

Corpora, as repositories of naturally occurring language, provide the empirical foundation to explore linguistic patterns and trends. Their key features, such as authenticity, representativeness and electronic accessibility, among others, make them essential for in-depth linguistic analyses. Concordancers play a central role in corpus analysis, providing tools that allow researchers to retrieve specific words or phrases in their natural contexts. This function is particularly relevant for legal language, where the meaning and use of terms depend heavily on their precise context. The evolution of concordancing software applications, from basic keyword-in-context (KWiC) tools to more advanced, web-based platforms, has enhanced the ability to conduct in-depth analyses, including frequency counts, lemmatisation and the study of collocations and colligations. These advancements allow a more detailed exploration of legal discourse, thus shedding light on how legal phrases and structures are used and how they evolve over time.

The application of corpus linguistics to legal studies undoubtedly represents a significant methodological advancement. By providing access to large datasets of naturally occurring legal texts, corpora enable more objective and replicable analyses of legal discourse. Three diachronic legal corpora, in particular, are central to this approach, namely CHELAR, BLaRC and BoLC.

The *Corpus of Historical English Law Reports* (CHELAR) will be consulted to explore the evolution of legal language from 1535 to 1999. This corpus serves as a key resource to understand the formalisation of legal language over centuries. Both the *British Law Report Corpus* (BLaRC) and the *Bononia Legal Corpus* (BoLC), with their focus on more modern terminology and contexts, provide an overview of contemporary legal English and serve as valuable resources to examine recent linguistic trends in legal discourse from a comparative perspective. More specifically, these corpora will provide the foundation to analyse two critical aspects of legal discourse, namely *legalese* and linguistic sexism. The study of *legalese* will examine whether legal language has become more accessible over time or if traditional formalities still dominate, whereas the investigation of gendered language will explore how legal texts reflect and/or perpetuate gender biases.

Although corpus-based methods offer significant advantages, it is crucial to acknowledge their fundamental limitations. No corpus, regardless of its scope or design, can entirely encapsulate the extensive and complex nature of legal discourse, which encompasses a wide range of genres and text types beyond law reports, including statutes, contracts, judicial opinions and administrative documents, among others. Each of these legal genres possesses distinct linguistic features, thus making it challenging to achieve comprehensive coverage. Nevertheless, despite these limitations, these three legal corpora have been carefully selected for their representativeness and relevance. It is hoped that they will nonetheless shed light on key patterns of linguistic change, thus offering valuable insights into the evolution of legal language over time and across different contexts.

Bibliography

Alcaraz Varó, Enrique. 1994. *El Inglés Jurídico: Textos y Documentos*. Madrid: Ariel Derecho.

Anthony, Laurence. 2023. AntConc (Version 4.2.4) [Computer Software]. Tokyo, Japan: Waseda University. https://www.laurenceanthony.net/software.

Aston, Guy. 2009. Foreword. In *Corpus Use and Translating. Corpus Use for Learning to Translate and Learning Corpus Use to Translate*, ed. A. Beeby, P. Rodríguez-Inés, and P. Sánchez-Gijón, ix–x. Amsterdam: John Benjamins.

Aston, Guy, and Lou Burnard. 1998. *The BNC Handbook*. Edinburgh: Edinburgh University Press.

Baroni, Marco, and Silvia Bernardini. 2004. BooTCaT: Bootstrapping Corpora and Terms from the Web. *Proceedings of LREC 2004*.

Barrière, Caroline. 2016. *Natural Language Understanding in a Semantic Web Context*. Bern: Springer International Publishing.
Bernardini, Silvia. 2011. Monolingual Comparable Corpora and Parallel Corpora in the Search for Features of Translated Language. *Synaps* 26:2–13.
Bernardini, Silvia, and Adriano Ferraresi. 2022. Corpus Linguistics. In *The Routledge Handbook of Translation and Methodology*, ed. Federico Zanettin and Christopher Rundle, 207–222. New York: Routledge.
Bernardini, Silvia, Dominic Stewart, and Federico Zanettin. 2003. Corpora in Translator Education: An Introduction. In *Corpora in Translator Education*, ed. Federico Zanettin, Silvia Bernardini, and Dominic Stewart, 1–13. Manchester: St. Jerome.
Bhatia, Vijay K. 1987. Language of the Law. *Language Teaching* 20 (4): 227–234.
Bhatia, Vijay K. 1993. *Analysing Genre. Language Use in Professional Settings*. Harlow, Essex: Pearson Education.
Biber, Douglas. 1993. Representativeness in Corpus Design. *Literary and linguistic computing 8* (4): 243–257.
Biber, Douglas, and Bethany Gray. 2019. Are Law Reports an 'Agile' or an 'Uptight' Register? Tracking Patterns of Historical Change in the Use of Colloquial and Complexity Features. In *Corpus-based research on variation in English legal discourse*, ed. T. Fanego and P. Rodríguez-Puente, 149–169. Amsterdam: John Benjamins.
Biel, Łucja 2010. Corpus-Based Studies of Legal Language for Translation Purposes: Methodological and Practical Potential. In *Reconceptualizing LSP. Online proceedings of the XVII European LSP Symposium 2009*, eds. Carmen Heine and Jan Engberg. http://www.asb.dk/fileadmin/www.asb.dk/isek/biel.pdf
Biel, Łucja. 2017. Enhancing the Communicative Dimension of Legal Translation: Comparable Corpora in the Research-informed Classroom. *The Interpreter and Translator Trainer* 11 (4): 316–336.
Borja Albí, Anabel. 2000. *El Texto Jurídico en Inglés y su Traducción*. Barcelona: Ariel.
Bowker, Lynne. 1998. Using Specialised Monolingual Native-language Corpora as a Translation Resource. *Meta* 43 (4): 631–651.
Bowker, Lynne, and Jennifer Pearson. 2002. *Working with Specialized Language: A Practical Guide to Using Corpora*. London/New York: Routledge.
Cobb, Tom. 2004. The Compleat Lexical Tutor. *v.4. TESL-EJ* 8:3. http://www.tesl-ej.org/wordpress/issues/volume8/ej31/ej31m2/?wscr

Davies, Mark. 2008. The Corpus of Contemporary American English (COCA): 520 Million Words, 1990–Present. http://corpus.byu.edu/coca/

Doval, Irene, and Maria T. Sánchez Nieto. 2019. *Parallel Corpora for Contrastive and Translation Studies: New Resources and Applications*. Amsterdam/Philadelphia: John Benjamins.

Fanego, Teresa, and Paula Rodríguez-Puente, eds. 2019. *Corpus-Based Research on Variation in English Legal Discourse*. Amsterdam: John Benjamins.

Fanego, Teresa, Paula Rodríguez-Puente, María José López-Couso, Belén Méndez-Naya, Paloma Núñez-Pertejo, Cristina Blanco-García, and Iván Tamaredo. 2017. The Corpus of Historical English Law Reports 1535–1999 (CHELAR): A resource for analysing the development of English legal discourse. *ICAME Journal* 41:53–82.

Fantinuoli, Claudio, and Federico Zanettin. 2015. Creating and Using Multilingual Corpora in Translation Studies. In *New Directions in Corpus-based Translation Studies*, ed. Claudio Fantinuoli and Federico Zanettin, 1–10. Berlin: Language Science Press.

Farr, Fiona, and Anne O'Keeffe. 2019. Using Corpora to Analyse LANGUAGE. In *Routledge Handbook of English Language Teacher Education*, ed. Steve Walsh and Steve Mann, 268–282. London: Routledge.

Firth, John R. 1935. The Technique of Semantics. *Transactions of the Philological Society* 34:36–72.

Firth, John R. 1957. A Synopsis of Linguistic Theory 1930–55. *Studies in Linguistic Analysis, Philological Society, Oxford.* Reprinted in: Palmer, F. R. (ed.) (1968). *Selected Papers of J. R. Firth 1952–59*, pp. 168–205. Longmans, London.

Francis, Nelson W., and Henry Kučera. 1982. *Frequency Analysis of English Usage: Lexicon and Grammar*. Boston: Houghton Mifflin.

Gallego-Hernández, Daniel. 2015. The Use of Corpora as Translation Resources: A Study Based on a Survey of Spanish Professional Translators. *Perspectives* 23 (3): 375–391.

Gatto, Maristella. 2014. *Web as Corpus: Theory and Practice*. London: Bloomsbury.

Giampieri, Patrizia. 2018. Online Parallel and Comparable Corpora for Legal Translations. *Altre Modernità* 20 (11): 237–252.

Giampieri, Patrizia. 2019a. Manual and and Automatic Corpus Compilation: A Case Study for Legal translations. *International Journal of Language Studies* 13 (3): 1–16.

Giampieri, Patrizia. 2019b. The BoLC for Legal Translations: A Trial Lesson. *Comparative Legilinguistics* 39:21–46.

Granger, Sylviane. 2002. A Bird's Eye View of Learner Corpus Research. In *Computer Learner Corpora, Second Language Acquisition and Foreign Language Teaching*, ed. Granger Sylviane, Hung Joseph, and Petch-Tyson Stephanie, 3–33. Amsterdam: John Benjamins.

Halliday, Michael A. K. 1966. Lexis as a Linguistic level'. In *Memory of J. R. Firth*, ed. C. Bazell, J. Catford, M. A. K. Halliday, and R. Robins, 148–162. London: Longman.

Hüning, Matthias. 2008. TextSTAT (version 2.9). http://neon.niederlandistik.fu-berlin.de/en/textstat/.

Jensen, Vigdis, Birthe Mousten, and Anne Lise Laursen. 2012. Electronic Corpora as Translation Tools: A Solution in Practice. *Communication & Language at Work* 1 (1): 21–33.

Kennedy, Graeme. 1998. *An Introduction to Corpus Linguistics*. New York: Longman.

Kilgarriff, Adam, Pavel Rychlý, Pavel Smrž, and David Tugwell. 2004. Itri-04-08 the Sketch Engine. Information Technology. http://www.sketchengine.eu.

Koehn, Philipp. 2005. Europarl: A Parallel Corpus for Statistical Machine Translation. *MT Summit X*, http://homepages.inf.ed.ac.uk/pkoehn/publications/europarlmtsummit05.Pdf

Laviosa, Sara, and Gaetano Falco. 2023. Corpora and Translator Education: Past, Present, and Future. In *Corpora and Translation Education, Advances and Challenges*, ed. Jun Pan and Sara Laviosa, 9–34. Singapore: Springer Nature Singapore.

Lee, David, and John Swales. 2006. A Corpus-based EAP Course for NNS Doctoral Students: Moving from Available Specialised Corpora to Self-compiled Corpora. *English for Specific Purposes* 25:56–75.

Leech, Geoffrey. 1991. The State of the Art in Corpus Linguistics. In *English corpus Linguistics: Studies in Honour of Jan Svartvik*, ed. K. Aijmer and B. Altenberg. London: Longman.

Leech, Geoffrey. 2005. Adding Linguistic Annotation. In *Developing Linguistic Corpora: a Guide to Good Practice*, ed. M. Wynne, 25–39. Oxford: Oxbrow Books.

Lehecka, Tomás. 2015. Collocation and Colligation. In *Handbook of Pragmatics Online*, ed. J. O. Östman and J. Verschueren, 1–20. Amsterdam: John Benjamins.

Liu, Kanglong, Yanfang Su, and Li Dechao. 2023. How Do Students Perform and Perceive Parallel Corpus Use in Translation Tasks? Evidence from an Experimental Study. In *Corpora and Translation Education, Advances and*

Challenges, ed. Jun Pan and Sara Laviosa, 135–160. Singapore: Springer Nature Singapore.

Machniewski, Maciej. 2006. Analysing and Teaching Translation Through Corpora: Lexical Convention and Lexical Use. *Poznań Studies in Contemporary Linguistics* 41:237–255.

Marín, M. J. 2017. Legalese as Seen Through the Lens of Corpus Linguistics. An Introduction to Software Tools for Terminological Analysis. *International Journal of Language and Law (JLL)* 6:18–45.

Marín Pérez, M. J., and Rea Rizzo, C. 2012. Structure and design of the British Law Report Corpus (BLRC) : a legal corpus of judicial decisions from the UK. Journal of English Studies, 10, 131–145. https://doi.org/10.18172/jes.184

McEnery, Tony, and Andrew Hardie. 2012. *Corpus Linguistics: Method, Theory and Practice*. Cambridge: Cambridge University Press.

McEnery, Tony, and Richard Xiao. 2007. Parallel and Comparable Corpora: What is Happening? In *Incorporating Corpora*, ed. Gunilla Anderman and Margaret Rogers, 18–31. London: Multilingual Matters.

McEnery, Tony, Richard Xiao, and Yukio Tono. 2010. *Corpus-based Language Studies: An Advanced RESOURCE BOOK*. LONDON: Routledge.

Mellinkoff, David. 1963. *The Language of the Law*. Boston, MA: Little, Brown and Company.

O'Keeffe, Anne, Michael McCarthy, and Ronald Carter. 2007. *From Corpus to Classroom: Language Use and Language Teaching*. Cambridge: Cambridge University Press.

Pearson, Jennifer. 1998. *Terms in Context*. Amsterdam: John Benjamins.

Prieto Ramos, Fernando. 2019. The Use of Corpora in Legal and Institutional Translation Studies: Directions and Applications. *Translation Spaces* 8 (1): 1–11.

Reed, Alan. 1978. *CLOC User Manual*. Birmingham: University of Birmingham.

Rodríguez-Puente, Paula. 2011. Introducing the Corpus of Historical English Law Reports: Structure and Compilation Techniques. *Revista de Lenguas para Fines Específicos* 17:99–120.

Rodríguez-Puente, Paula. 2019. Interpersonality in Legal Written Discourse. A Diachronic Analysis of Personal Pronouns in Law Reports, 1535 to Present. In *Corpus-based Research on Variation in English Legal Discourse*, ed. T. Fanego and P. Rodríguez-Puente, 172–199. Amsterdam: John Benjamins.

Rodríguez-Puente, Paula. 2020a. Historical Legal Discourse: British Law Reports. In *The Routledge Handbook of Corpus Approaches to Discourse Analysis*, ed. Ericson Friginal and Jack Hardy, 499–517. New York: Routledge.

Rodríguez-Puente, Paula. 2020b. Register Variation in Word-Formation Processes: The Development of -ity and -ness in Early Modern English. *International Journal of English Studies* 20 (2): 147–169.

Rodríguez-Puente, Paula, and Teresa Fanego. 2020. Developing and exploiting the *Corpus of Historical English Law Reports 1535–1999* (CHELAR). *Nexus AEDEAN* 2020 (2): 39–43.

Römer, Ute. 2005. *Progressives, Patterns, Pedagogy: A Corpus-driven Approach to English progressive Forms, Functions, Contexts and Didactics*. Amsterdam: John Benjamins.

Rossini Favretti, Rema, Fabio Tamburini, and Enrico Martelli. 2007. Words from Bononia Legal Corpus. In *Text Corpora and Multilingual Lexicography*, ed. Wolfgang Tuebert, 11–30. Amsterdam: John Benjamins.

Sánchez-Gijón, Pilar. 2009. Developing Documentation Skills to Build do-ityourself Corpora in the specialised Translation Course. In *Corpus use and Translating. Corpus Use for Learning to Translate and Learning Corpus Use to Translate*, ed. Allison Beeby, Patricia Rodríguez-Inés, and Pilar Sánchez-Gijón, 109–127. Amsterdam: John Benjamins.

Sinclair, John. 1991. *Corpus, Concordance, Collocation*. Oxford: Oxford University Press.

Sinclair, John. 1996. *EAGLES Preliminary Recommendations on Corpus Typology EAG—TCWG—CTYP/P*. http://www.ilc.cnr.it/EAGLES96/corpustyp/corpustyp.html

Sinclair, John. 2004. *Trust the Text: Language, Corpus and Discourse*. London/New York: Routledge.

Tamburini, Fabio. 2002. A Dynamic Model for Reference Corpora Structure Definition. In *Proceedings of the Third International Conference on Language Resources and Evaluation (LREC'02)*, Las Palmas, Canary Islands – Spain, pp. 1847–1850. European Language Resources Association (ELRA). http://www.lrec-conf.org/proceedings/lrec2002/pdf/29.pdf.

Tiedemann, Jörg. 2012. Parallel Data, Tools and Interfaces in OPUS. In *Proceedings of the Eight International Conference on Language Resources and Evaluation (LREC'2012)*, European Language Resources Association, Istanbul, N. Calzolari et al.. 2214–2218. http://www.lrec-conf.org/proceedings/lrec2012/pdf/463_Paper.pdf.

Tiersma, Peter. 1999. *Legal Language*. Chicago: The University of Chicago Press.

Tognini-Bonelli, Elena, and John Sinclair. 2006. Corpora. In *Encyclopedia of Language and Linguistics*, ed. K. Brown, 216–219. Amsterdam: Elsevier.

Varantola, Krista. 2002. Disposable corpora as intelligent tools in translation. *Cadernos de Tradução* 1 (9): 171–189.

Vintar, Špela. 2008. Corpora in Translation: A Slovene Perspective. *The Journal of Specialised Translation* 10:40–55.

Wang, Lucy Lu, Kyle Lo, Yoganand Chandrasekhar, Russell Reas, Jiangjiang Yang, Darrin Eide, K. Funk, Rodney Michael Kinney, Ziyang Liu, W. Merrill, Paul Mooney, Dewey Murdick, Devvret Rishi, Jerry Sheehan, Zhihong Shen, Brandon Stilson, Alex D. Wade, Kuansan Wang, Christopher Wilhelm, Boya Xie, Douglas M. Raymond, Daniel S. Weld, Oren Etzioni, and Sebastian Kohlmeier. 2020. CORD-19: The Covid-19 Open Research Dataset. *ArXiv*. https://aclanthology.org/2020.nlpcovid19-acl.1.pdf.

Wilkinson, Michael. 2006. Compiling Corpora for Use as Translation Resources. *Translation Journal* 101. http://www.translationdirectory.com/article910.htm

Williams, Ian A. 1999. Corpus-based Contrastive Analysis and the Translation of Specialized Texts. In *Lengua y cultura: Estudios en torno a la traducción*, ed. Miguel Ángel Vega and Rafael Martín Gaitero, 515–522. Madrid: Universidad Complutense.

Zanettin, Federico. 2001. Swimming in Words: Corpora, Translation, and Language Learning. In *Learning with corpora*, ed. G. Aston, 177–197. Houston, TX: Athelstan.

Zanettin, Federico. 2002a. Corpora in Translation Practice. In *Third International Workshop on Language Resources for Translation Work, Research & Training*, Italy, 10–14.

Zanettin, Federico. 2002b. DIY Corpora: the WWW and the Translator. In *Training the Language Services Provider for the New Millennium*, ed. Belinda Maia, Johann Haller, and Margherita Ulrych, 239–248. Porto: Universidade do Porto.

Zanettin, Federico. 2012. *Translation-Driven Corpora: Corpus Resources for Descriptive and Applied Translation Studies*. London: Routledge.

Zanettin, Federico. 2014. Corpora in Translation. In *Translation: A Multidisciplinary Approach*, ed. Juliane House, 178–199. Palgrave Macmillan.

4

Analytical Framework for Corpus-Based Examination of Legal English

4.1 What is *Legalese*?

Legalese refers to a formal and specialised mode of communication predominantly used in legal contexts, such as contracts, statutes, court pleadings and judicial rulings. While it serves a distinct purpose in ensuring legal precision and addressing potential ambiguities, its dense structure and technical vocabulary can make it challenging for the general public to interpret. Several key aspects contribute to the complexity of *legalese*. Legal language must be precise to avoid misinterpretation; therefore, legal documents are drafted with extreme caution, aiming to cover all foreseeable scenarios. Lawyers and judges often rely on established legal principles, precedents and statutory language to ensure consistency in interpretation. This heavy reliance on established terminology ensures that certain legal concepts remain stable over time, despite changing social and linguistic norms. Much of *legalese* can be traced back to historical sources, including Latin and Norman French, which have significantly influenced English legal vocabulary. Terms such as "habeas corpus", "pro bono" and "de facto" remain in use, even though the average person may be unfamiliar with their meanings.

V. Leonardi, P. Giampieri, *Legal English through the Ages*,
https://doi.org/10.1007/978-3-032-02172-4_4

Furthermore, *legalese* often retains older forms of English, incorporating words like "hereinafter" or "aforesaid". While these terms may be clear to trained legal professionals, they can confuse readers unfamiliar with such archaic vocabulary. Legal documents are characterised by their rigid structure and formal style. This formality is not merely for appearance; it reflects the necessity for documents to be taken seriously in legal settings. For instance, contracts must be written in ways that leave little room for misinterpretation. As a result, legal writers frequently employ long sentences, complex clauses and technical jargon to achieve this aim. However, this structure often leads to convoluted sentences that hinder readability.

The intention behind *legalese* is to be unambiguous and exhaustive. Legal writers anticipate various interpretations and ensure that all possibilities are addressed within the document. However, this intention can result in texts that are far from user-friendly. While law aims for precision, the consequence is that the average person may struggle to interpret legal documents without expert assistance. Consequently, *legalese* has been criticised for alienating those who need to engage with law but lack the necessary education or training.

In recent years, there has been a growing movement towards "plain language" initiatives advocating for legal writing that is both clear and concise. Governments, legal institutions and scholars increasingly promote the use of plain language in legal documentation, striving for a balance between precision and accessibility. Advocates argue that legal documents can retain their clarity and robustness while being more readable for the general public, thereby improving access to justice.

Legalese is also shaped by the need for lawyers and judges to interpret laws in various contexts. Given the complexity of human affairs, laws must be adaptable to different circumstances; thus, certain words or phrases are intentionally left open to interpretation. While this flexibility is crucial in legal settings, it may add to the complexity of the language, necessitating clarification from legal professionals. In other words, while *legalese* arguably plays a vital role in maintaining the accuracy, consistency and predictability of legal texts, it poses significant challenges for those outside the legal profession. Efforts to simplify legal language without sacrificing precision are ongoing and reflect a broader attempt to make law more accessible to the general public. Nevertheless, the persistence of *legalese* largely reflects the intricate and evolving nature of law itself.

4.1.1 Complex Prepositional and Adverbial Phrases

Complex prepositional and adverbial phrases are integral elements of legal discourse, characterised by semantic precision that aims to avoid vagueness. Coulthard and Johnson (2010: 11) explain that complex prepositions, as opposed to simpler ones, tend to offer greater specificity in meaning, which is particularly important in legal contexts where clarity is essential to prevent multiple interpretations. For this reason, complex prepositional phrases frequently appear in legal documents.

Biel (2015), in her examination of legal multi-word units, explores the differences between simple prepositions like "by" and "on", compound prepositions such as "hereafter" and "hereto" and more intricate complex prepositions like "subject to" or "in relation to". The distinction between these types is key to understanding how legal language operates. Compound prepositions like "hereafter" and "hereto" are also commonly referred to as "pronominal adverbs", a term explored in works such as Bhatia (2010: 16) and Williams (2023: 32). Biel (2015) highlights how complex prepositions tend to dominate British legislation, as well as EU directives and regulations, revealing distinct preferences in the legal language of these two systems. For example, UK legislation frequently employs terms like "in relation to" and "for the purpose(s) of", while EU legal discourse often favours expressions such as "in accordance with". These differences show how legal language can vary not only across jurisdictions but also depending on the legislative style and intent behind particular legal systems.

Pontrandolfo (2023: 126) introduces a critical distinction between "legal phraseology" and "phraseology in legal language", making a distinction between multi-word patterns that produce specific legal effects and those that do not carry any particular legal significance. Legal phraseology refers to terms or patterns of words that have a direct legal implication, such as "dismiss the appeal", which implies a specific judicial action.

In contrast, the latter category, "phraseology in legal language", includes complex prepositions and adverbial phrases that pertain more to linguistic structure than legal effect. For instance, phrases like "without prejudice to" do not carry a direct legal outcome but are commonly used in legal writing for clarification or limitation purposes.

Giampieri (2024) further notes that some complex multi-word phrases may even introduce a level of vagueness or approximation, which appears paradoxical given the typical insistence on precision of the legal system itself. Phrases such as "or otherwise" and "of any nature whatsoever", for instance, exemplify this phenomenon. (ibid.: 75, 80). These expressions, while semantically broad, are sometimes employed in legal writing to ensure comprehensiveness, capturing a range of possibilities or scenarios, even at the expense of clarity.

Furthermore, there is a notable persistence of archaic expressions in legal language that are rarely found elsewhere. This includes not only complex phrases but also antiquated adverbs such as "whosoever", "howsoever" and "whatsoever", which have been criticised for their redundancy. The Plain language and The Law Report (Law Reform Commission of Victoria 2017: 131), for instance, argue that these types of archaic adverbs contribute little to meaning and should therefore be eliminated from legal texts in favour of clearer alternatives.

This call for simplification aligns with the broader plain language movement, which seeks to make legal language more accessible to non-specialists. Nevertheless, in spite of these criticisms, these outdated forms have demonstrated a notable resilience to alteration, continuing to appear in numerous legal documents to this day. The complexity and persistence of prepositional and adverbial phrases in legal language are further exemplified by a list of expressions commonly found in such texts, including "any such", "as such", "by virtue of", "for and concerning", "for and during", "for and in the name (of)", "for and on behalf of", "in respect of", "in the event of", "irrespective of", "no(t) more than", "other than", "pursuant to", "to wit", "until such" and "without prejudice" (Duckworth and Spyrou 1995; Bhatia 2010; Giampieri 2016). These expressions play an essential role in legal drafting and interpretation, often serving to introduce conditions, clarify relationships between legal provisions or limit the application of specific rules. Analysing these complex prepositions and adverbs not only aids in understanding their function within legal texts but also sheds light on the historical continuity and evolving nature of legal discourse. Such analysis highlights how certain patterns of phraseology persist across time and legal genres, even as other aspects of legal language evolve to meet modern needs. This balance between tradition and innovation is a defining feature of legal language, making it both a reflection of legal history and a tool for contemporary legal practice.

4.1.2 Deixis

Deixis refers to linguistic elements that are inherently tied to the context in which they are used, serving to point to specific persons, times, places or situations (Levinson 1983: 62). As explained by Allott (2010: 54), deixis involves linguistic items that reflect an awareness of the surrounding context. This concept encompasses various types of deixis, including personal deixis, which pertains to the ways individuals are referred to or addressed, and is often linked to what is also termed "social deixis" (ibid.: 59). Social deixis concerns markers that encode social relationships or status differences among participants in a conversation. Place deixis involves spatial references, highlighting the proximity or distance of objects or locations relative to the speaker, while temporal deixis deals with time-related expressions that depend on the situation or context for clarity. Pronouns such as "you" and "we", demonstrative adjectives like "this" and "that" and other spatial and temporal markers such as "here", "there", "now" and "then" are all examples of deictic expressions (ibid.: 55).

In legal documents, personal deixis plays a particularly prominent role, especially in contracts and agreements. Rather than addressing individuals by their first or last names, legal texts often refer to parties by their roles or positions. For example, instead of naming specific people, contracts will refer to them as "Lessor" or "Lessee", as noted by Coulthard and Johnson (2007: 44) and Pavlíčková (2008: 89). This practice not only enhances clarity but also generalises the relationship between the parties involved, making the contract applicable to different persons without needing to alter the text. Giampieri (2024: 119) underscores how the use of personal deixis in legal language contributes to the formality and standardisation of legal discourse.

As far as spatial deixis is concerned, Tiersma (1999: 91) notes that terms in legal language are often used anaphorically, meaning they refer to something previously mentioned. Words like "said", "aforesaid" and "aforementioned" are common in this regard, though their use dates back to Middle English. Duckworth and Spyrou (1995: 80) point out that these terms are considered antiquated; while they add a certain formality to legal texts, they may obscure meaning. The authors argue that such expressions "sacrifice clarity for gravity", suggesting that simpler alternatives might serve the purpose more effectively. Abate (1998: 14–15) also explores the relationship between spatial deixis and the use of adverbs prefixed with "there-" or "here-". According to Abate, "there-" adverbs typically refer to elements not immediately present, whereas "here-" adverbs relate to aspects within the same paragraph or document. Pavlíčková (2008: 94–96) lists various deictic adverbs such as "herein", "hereto", "hereunder" and "thereat", which are common in legal writing but contribute to its complexity. Adams (2024), among others, criticises the continued use of these multi-word expressions, arguing that they introduce ambiguity and are largely archaic.

Temporal deixis encompasses terms that anchor statements in a particular time frame, often indicating a shift in the legal or factual situation. For example, words like "henceforth", meaning "from now on", or phrases like "at the time of", which refer to specific moments, are frequently used in legal texts (Giampieri 2024: 63, 81). Pavlíčková (2008: 94–96) notes that adverbs with temporal connotations, such as "hereinafter", "heretofore" and "thereafter", are integral to legal documents in establishing timelines and sequencing events. These terms are particularly important for specifying when obligations begin or end and help structure the legal responsibilities of parties over time.

The presence of deictic elements in legal discourse highlights how language functions to reference other parts of the text or the real-world context to which the document applies. Terms such as "above mentioned", "aforementioned" and "aforesaid" serve as pointers to earlier portions of the document, ensuring clarity in reference (Bhatia 2010: 26). These elements, while potentially confusing to non-legal professionals, play a vital role in legal documents by maintaining internal coherence and minimising ambiguity. Abate (1998: 15) identifies additional examples of deictic tools such as "hereinafter" (meaning "from now on"), "hereof" ("of this document"), "heretofore" ("before now") and "hereunto" ("to this document"), all of which serve specific referential functions in legal texts. Terms like "the said" are also used to indicate a previously mentioned person or item, ensuring that references remain clear throughout the document (Duckworth and Spyrou 1995: 81; Tiersma 1999: 89–91; Giampieri 2016: 436). Moreover, deictic expressions such as "therein", which means "inside this document" or "regarding this document", are widely used in legal discourse alongside other related forms such as "thereinafter", "thereinbefore", "thereof", "thereunder", "thereupon", "therewith", "wherefore" and "whereof" (Abate 1998: 14–15; Giampieri 2022; Williams 2023).

The significance of these terms lies in their role in preserving textual cohesion, enabling legal documents to refer to themselves in a systematic and formal manner. This ensures that readers can comprehend their logical flow and internal connections. Although the use of deixis in legal texts may be unclear to those outside the legal profession, it is an essential component of legal language, facilitating accurate and contextually relevant references within intricate legal documents.

4.1.3 Vagueness

Vagueness, as explained by Tiersma (1999: 128), is a fundamental aspect of language itself, and legal language, despite its attempts at precision, is not exempt from the inherent vagueness and ambiguity present in everyday English (ibid.: 109). The very nature of language involves a degree of indeterminacy, making it difficult to fully eliminate imprecision. Endicott (2005: 28) emphasises that vagueness plays a crucial role in the functioning of norms, as it allows legal standards to guide conduct in a flexible manner. Bajčić (2018) further explores the issue of language indeterminacy, noting that ambiguity in legal language stems from the need to relate abstract legal concepts to real-world facts in order to regulate actual events. This practical necessity means that legal terms often need to be adaptable enough to apply to a variety of situations, leading to vagueness.

Dickerson (1986) suggests that this approximation or vagueness in legal discourse is not entirely negative, as it brings certain benefits, particularly in terms of flexibility. According to Dickerson, vague language allows for adaptability in legal texts, giving them the capacity to evolve alongside changing circumstances without requiring constant revision. Christie (1964: 911) and Endicott (2005) also share this view, asserting that vague language can enhance the versatility of legal documents in certain contexts, ensuring that they remain accurate across a range of different applications. This flexibility is particularly advantageous for judges, who, as Endicott (2000: 190–191) argues, are afforded the freedom to interpret laws and administer justice more effectively due to the malleability provided by vague language. Soames (2014) supports this point, contending that legal drafters intentionally employ vague language to grant judicial authorities the discretion needed to resolve complex or unusual cases. In this sense, vagueness becomes a tool that empowers judges to tailor their decisions to the unique circumstances of each case, thereby promoting fairness and justice.

Nevertheless, not all scholars agree regarding the merits of vagueness in legal language. Solan (2012: 92–95) presents a contrasting viewpoint, arguing that vagueness can lead to significant interpretative challenges during court trials. He highlights the tension between the need for approximation—allowing legal norms to be broadly applicable—and the requirement for precision, which ensures clarity in the interpretation of statutes. According to Solan, this conflict arises because judges must often decide whether to prioritise the flexible, vague meanings of words or focus on a more literal interpretation to ensure fidelity to the law. At the same time, judges must balance this decision with their own legal values and principles, which can further complicate their interpretative task (Solan 2012: 95). Canale (2017) echoes this concern, noting that while judges are tasked with interpreting the intentional content of statutes to compensate for the inherent indeterminacy in legal language, they must also work to minimise vagueness—particularly in borderline cases. Through careful interpretation, judges can reduce ambiguity in legal texts, ensuring that laws are applied consistently and predictably.

Despite these efforts to curb vagueness, there are risks associated with allowing too much interpretative flexibility. Scotto di Carlo (2013) warns that excessive vagueness can open the door to manipulation or misinterpretation—particularly in politically charged situations. She references UN Resolutions concerning the Second Gulf War as an example, arguing that excessive approximation in these resolutions may have contributed to the escalation of the Iraqi conflict. In her view, had the language of these resolutions been more precise, it might have facilitated a diplomatic solution rather than military intervention. This highlights the potential dangers of leaving too much room for interpretation in legal and diplomatic contexts where precision can be critical for maintaining peace and stability.

In legal contracts, examples of vague expressions include phrases like "of any nature whatsoever", "any other damage whatsoever" and "whatsoever suffered and howsoever incurred" (Giampieri 2024: 80, 157, 174). These phrases are intentionally broad, allowing them to cover a wide range of potential scenarios. Bajčić (2018) provides another instance of vagueness within EU labour law where the term "worker" serves as a cornerstone of the principle of freedom of movement. Despite its importance, the definition of "worker" is left somewhat ambiguous in EU law, necessitating interpretation by the Court of Justice of the European Union to clarify its meaning.

This reliance on case law to address statutory vagueness underscores the role of courts in refining and interpreting legal language, ensuring that it remains functional in regulating real-life events. The vague terms addressed in this work include expressions such as "howsoever", meaning "in any manner", "whatsoever", meaning "at all", "whomsoever" and "whosoever", which both translate to "whoever" or "anyone", and "wheresoever", which means "in any place". Another term, "soever", conveys a general sense of "of any kind" (Bhatia 2010; Giampieri 2016).

These expressions contribute to the flexibility of legal language but also pose interpretative challenges due to their expansive meanings, which can result in ambiguity. Nevertheless, vagueness is a fundamental aspect of legal language, as it enables laws to be flexible, multifaceted and relevant in a constantly changing society. This dual nature of vagueness—serving both to facilitate and to complicate—renders it an intriguing and intricate element of legal discourse.

4.1.4 Complex or Archaic Verbs

Complex and archaic verbs are a significant feature of legal English, contributing to the complexity and formality of legal discourse. One such example is the verb "darraign", which means "to clear a legal account or settle an accusation or controversy" (Williams 2004: 112). According to Bhatia (2010: 28), some of these complex verbs could be replaced by simpler and more contemporary alternatives. For instance, the phrase "fails to" should ideally be substituted with the clearer expression "does not", whereas "implement" could simply be replaced by more straightforward verbs, such as "carry out" or "fulfil". Furthermore, legal language often features cases of nominalisation, where a verb-noun combination is used instead of a single verb, making sentences unnecessarily complex (Williams 2023: 32, 83). Bhatia (2010: 28) highlights examples such as "make payment" (instead of "pay") and "make an application" (instead of "apply")—a pattern echoed by Williams (2023: 83).

Legal texts are also marked by verbal doublets and triplets, sequences of verbs that appear redundant. Garner (2002) critiques this tendency, arguing that legal prose is burdened by an excess of verbs, which often makes it difficult for readers to navigate the text smoothly. He describes the experience as being "sucked into verbal quicksand" (Garner 2002: 68). An example of such a doublet is "aid and abet", commonly used to describe participation in a crime. The term "aid" derives from Old French *aider* (meaning "help"), whereas "abet" comes from the Latin *abeter*, meaning "to entice" (Duckworth and Spyrou 1995: 10). Garner (2004: 214) adds that the binominal expression "counsel and procure" serves as a synonym for "aid and abet", with both phrases indicating assistance or facilitation in committing a crime. Other examples of tautological doublets include "transfer and assign", which has been used in statutory and private legal documents since the late seventeenth century. "Transfer" originates from the Latin *transferre*, whereas "assign" derives from Old French *assigner* (Duckworth and Spyrou 1995: 89).

Jackson's (1995: 122) analysis brings to the fore longer sequences of verbs such as "release, discharge and agree", as well as combinations of modal verbs such as "can, shall, or may". Bhatia (2010: 29) mentions further examples of legal doublets and triplets, such as "give, devise, and bequeath" in wills and testaments, "indemnify and hold harmless" in indemnification clauses, "keep and maintain" in tenancy or lease agreements, among others, and "remise, release, and quitclaim" used in quitclaims to renounce current and future legal claims or rights to land. Each of these expressions could be replaced by simplexes (i.e., single verbs), such as "give", "indemnify", "maintain" and "release", respectively, which would streamline the language without losing meaning.

Another stylistic feature of legal language is the tendency to separate verbs or verb phrases by inserting additional expressions or clauses, creating syntactical discontinuities (Williams 2023: 31). This pattern often complicates the interpretation of both individual verbs and entire paragraphs for the reader.

Nevertheless, one of the most criticised aspects of legal English is, perhaps, the use of the modal verb "shall", which introduces vagueness into legal documents. As Tiersma (1999: 85, 105) and Williams (2023: 32) point out, "shall" is problematic because it can express both futurity and obligation. This dual function can cause confusion, as "shall" may establish prohibitions or binding actions and, at the same time, it lays down necessary conditions or a new state of things (Felici 2012).

Some complex or archaic (modal) verbs analysed in this book include the following:

- Shall: indicating future actions or obligations (Tiersma 1999: 105–106; Bhatia 2010: 28; Williams 2023: 159).
- Deem: meaning "consider to be" (Duckworth and Spyrou 1995: 13).
- Endeavour: meaning "try" (Bhatia 2010: 28).
- Estop: meaning "prevent" (Bhatia 2010: 28).
- Fail to: a more complex way of saying "does not" (Bhatia 2010: 28).
- Resolve: meaning "decide" or "reaffirm" (Giampieri 2022: 30).
- Vested in: meaning "officially given or acquired" (Longinotti 2009: 19).

These examples illustrate how the complex and archaic nature of legal terminology can hinder accessibility and lead to possible misinterpretations. Substituting these terms with more straightforward and contemporary alternatives can enhance the clarity and approachability of legal documents while maintaining legal accuracy.

4.1.5 Archaic Nouns

Archaic nouns are a distinguishing feature of legal language, persisting even in modern legal documents and contracts despite the evolving nature of general language use. Scholars widely recognise this as an enduring characteristic of legal English. For instance, Bhatia (2010: 28–29, 77) points out that terms such as "instrument" and "chattel" are commonly used, though modern equivalents like "document" and "goods" could be employed instead. Similarly, "deed" often appears in legal contexts where "document" could more aptly convey the intended meaning without losing legal precision.

Tiersma (1999: 104) provides a detailed analysis of the term "these presents", which can be interpreted as "the present writing". This expression is found in numerous legal documents, such as powers of attorney, and exemplifies how legal language often retains outdated phrases that could be expressed in more straightforward, modern terminology. Duckworth and Spyrou (1995: 50–51) examine the term "malice", which originates from the Latin word *malitia*, meaning "spite". Over the years, "malice" has acquired negative implications associated with ill intent or spitefulness, suggesting that it could be substituted with more transparent alternatives like "ill-will". Another significant aspect highlighted by Tiersma (1999: 131) is the restricted use of pronouns within legal texts. The absence of pronouns results in the repetitive use of the same nouns throughout legal documents, thereby diminishing the diversity of legal language. Although this intentional repetition aims to eliminate ambiguity, it often results in a formal and occasionally awkward writing style. Coulthard and Johnson (2007: 44) also address this issue, observing that the persistent use of nouns, instead of incorporating synonyms or pronouns, prioritises clarity at the expense of linguistic variety.

The situation is further complicated by what Garner (2002: 69) describes as the "noun plague", which is a tendency in legal writing to combine several nouns to modify additional nouns. This practice leads to lengthy chains of nouns used together, frequently resulting in complex and elaborate expressions. Coulthard and Johnson (2007) provide examples such as "financial assistance reduction", a compound noun phrase that includes nominalised verbs but lacks an explicit subject. This stylistic choice, known as nominalisation, is a hallmark of legal writing. Kelley (2018: 181) explains that by converting verbs into nouns, writers can obscure the action that the verbs convey, thereby weakening the vitality and clarity of sentences. He suggests that such practice drains the "life" from the writing, making it more difficult to follow and less engaging.

Furthermore, Coulthard and Johnson (2007: 44–45) highlight another complexity associated with nouns, specifically through the use of gerund phrases that feature constructions such as "including all/any", followed by a noun. These phrases are commonly found in legal contracts, exemplified by phrases like "including any actual loss or expense incurred" or "including all common parts, the internal decorations and the fixtures". Such constructions serve a clear legal function, as they seek to encompass a broad spectrum of possibilities and contingencies; however, they also contribute to the complexity and length of legal documents.

An examination of the specific archaic nouns discussed in this context uncovers several significant examples. "Chattel" denotes "goods" (Bhatia 2010: 29), a term frequently encountered in property law. Another instance is "deed", which means "legal document" (Mellinkoff 1963; Bhatia 2010: 77). The term "escrow" refers to property held in trust, specifically defined as "a legal document or property delivered by a promisor to a third party to be held by the third party for a given amount of time" (Duckworth and Spyrou 1995: 16; Garner 2004: 1649). The term "malice", as previously indicated, corresponds to "spite" or "ill-will" (Duckworth and Spyrou 1995: 51). "Instrument" is used to mean "writing" or "document" (Duckworth and Spyrou 1995: 42; Bhatia 2010: 28). Lastly, "presents", as in "these presents", is another term for "the present writing" (Tiersma 1999: 104).

The continued use of archaic nouns in legal writing can be attributed to tradition, precision and the authoritative tone they convey. Nevertheless, contemporary legal scholars promote the adoption of clearer and more accessible alternatives. Such changes would enhance the comprehensibility of legal documents for the general public and diminish the interpretative ambiguities frequently associated with outdated terminology. Although legal language tends to be conservative, a gradual evolution towards simplicity could prove beneficial, provided that it does not compromise the essential precision required in legal practice.

4.1.6 Law Latin

As previously mentioned, Latin has had a profound influence on the development of legal terminology. Its impact is evident in numerous terms and phrases that remain essential in contemporary legal documents and discussions. Latin was introduced to England during the Roman conquest (Tiersma 1999: 9); however, its effect on the indigenous population and legal customs at that time was limited, and Roman law did not establish a lasting influence. The revival of Latin in England began with the arrival of Christianity in 597, particularly through the establishment of canon law. This body of ecclesiastical law, which addresses matters related to religion, such as family and marriage, was heavily reliant on Latin (Tiersma 1999: 16). The proliferation of Latin during this period not only shaped legal language but also left an enduring mark on the English vocabulary.

Many of the Latin terms introduced during this period are still used today. Words like "client", "conviction" and "legitimate" are prime examples of Latin-derived terms that have been fully assimilated into legal English (Tiersma 1999: 16; Williams 2023: 29). Over the years, Latin established itself as a *lingua franca* (Mattila 2013: 161; Williams 2023: 117), a common language that transcended regional dialects and national languages, particularly among the educated classes and within the legal profession. This phenomenon gave rise to what is commonly referred to as "Law Latin" (Tiersma 1999: 25; Williams 2004: 112).

The influence of Latin extended beyond mere vocabulary. The Anglo-Saxon language, which served as the foundation for Old English, incorporated a range of stylistic elements, including alliteration. Alliteration, defined as the recurrence of the same sound or letter at the beginning of adjacent or closely related words, continues to be a characteristic of legal language today. Instances of this can be seen in phrases such as "hold harmless", "assuming arguendo" and "part and parcel" (Tiersma 1999: 15). Furthermore, alliteration patterns frequently appear in binomial and trinomial expressions, which often consist of words of different origins. Examples include well-known legal phrases such as "aid and abet", "appropriate and proper" and "rest, residue, and remainder" (Duckworth and Spyrou 1995: 10; Tiersma 1999: 15; Bhatia 2010: 266). Duckworth and Spyrou (1995: 48) further emphasise this concept with the phrase "last will and testament", highlighting its representation of a bilingual English/Latin style that was prevalent during a specific historical era (Mellinkoff 1963: 121).

Williams (2023: 30) argues that Latin expressions remain prevalent in legal discourse, primarily due to the characteristics of the legal profession. Legal terminology, which encompasses Latin phrases and terms, acts as a specialised language that contributes to the exclusivity of the profession. Lawyers frequently use such terminology as a marker of membership within their professional community and as a means of in-group communication (Tiersma 1999: 69, 107). This emphasises that Latin fulfils both a practical function and a symbolic role, forging a connection between contemporary legal practitioners and the rich historical tradition of legal practice.

Various scholars have extensively analysed the presence of Latin in contemporary legal English. These include Duckworth and Spyrou (1995), Laster (2001), Williams (2004, 2023), Bhatia (2010), Saha (2010) and Giampieri (2016). Among the Latin terms still used in legal English are head nouns like *culpa*, *dolus*, *caveat*, *ex parte* and *actus reus* (Saha 2010: 142). Some Latin formulae have also endured, such as *conditio sine qua non*, meaning "necessary condition" (Giampieri 2016: 429), and *pro bono*, which means "for the public good" or "for free" (Duckworth and Spyrou 1995: 64). Furthermore, certain idiomatic expressions, like *ignorantia juris non excusat* ("ignorance of the law is not an excuse") and *mala grammatica non vitiam chartam* ("bad grammar does not vitiate a deed"), continue to be relevant in legal contexts (Saha 2010: 144).

The Law Latin forms discussed in this book encompass a range of phrases that remain integral to legal discourse. For instance, *bona fide* means "in good faith" (Bhatia 2010: 29; Saha 2010: 142). This term is crucial as it denotes sincerity and honesty in transactions, ensuring that parties act with integrity, which is, for instance, fundamental in contract law. The phrase *a fortiori* translates as "all the more" or "even more so" (Laster 2001: 246; Giampieri 2016: 429). It is significant in legal reasoning, allowing practitioners to argue that if one situation is true, a related situation must also be true, thereby reinforcing logical deductions in legal arguments. Similarly, *de facto* means "in fact" (Laster 2001: 246; Saha 2010: 142). This term is important for distinguishing between what exists in reality versus what is legally recognised, particularly in discussions of governance or relationships that operate without formal recognition. The term *de jure* (or *de iure*) means "in law" or "in legal terms" (Laster 2001: 246; Saha 2010: 142; Giampieri 2016: 429). It serves to clarify legal rights and obligations, particularly in cases involving statutory interpretation and constitutional law. The abbreviation *et seq.*, which stands for *et sequentia*, means "and those following" (Bhatia 2010: 29). This abbreviation is commonly used in legal citations to refer to specific pages or sections of statutes and articles, promoting clarity and precision in legal documents by indicating that the referenced information continues in subsequent sections. *Ex parte* denotes legal proceedings "without notice" or "as the only interested party" (Saha 2010: 142; Giampieri 2016: 430). This term is vital for situations requiring urgent action where notifying the other party may not be feasible, thus allowing courts to make timely decisions while balancing fairness and due process. Other notable examples include *in re* ("against a thing", Garner 2004: 2324; Bhatia 2010: 375), which is often used when the subject matter itself is the focus rather than the parties involved. This underscores the principle that legal proceedings can revolve around specific issues rather than just individual litigants. The phrase *inter alia* means "among other things" or "amongst others" (Bhatia 2010: 29; Saha 2010: 142; Giampieri 2022: 29). It allows lawyers to reference multiple points without being overly verbose, maintaining clarity while acknowledging additional relevant factors. *Inter partes* translates as "between the parties" (Bhatia 2010: 300; Garner 2004: 2397). This term emphasises the adversarial nature of legal disputes, reinforcing the importance of both sides being heard in litigation contexts. Another commonly used Latin term is *ipso facto*, meaning "by that very fact" or "thereby" (Giampieri 2016: 430). This term serves as a powerful tool for establishing causation within legal arguments, allowing lawyers to assert that certain outcomes naturally follow from established facts. *Prima facie*, which means "at first glance", remains a central term in legal evaluations and preliminary assessments (Bhatia 2010: 29). It indicates that there is sufficient evidence to support a claim unless disproven by further evidence, guiding judges and juries in their evaluations of cases. Other terms include *pro bono* ("for free" or "for the public good", Duckworth and Spyrou 1995: 64) and *viva voce* ("by the living voice", Garner 2004: 3631, 4866), which further demonstrate the enduring vitality of Law Latin in today's legal vocabulary. The term *pro bono* is particularly significant as it embodies the legal profession's commitment to providing services without charge, thereby ensuring access to justice for those who cannot afford legal representation. This concept has become increasingly important in contemporary discussions about social responsibility within the legal field, highlighting the role of lawyers in serving the community and promoting equity. Similarly, *viva voce* reflects a procedural aspect of legal practice, referring to oral testimony given in court as opposed to written evidence. This term emphasises the importance of live testimony in establishing credibility and allowing for direct examination and cross-examination, which are crucial elements of the adversarial legal system.

The enduring role of Latin in legal English is rooted in its historical evolution, the formation of professional identity and the specific demands of legal communication. Latin has been a foundational element of legal discourse since the Roman era, establishing a framework that ensures contemporary legal language remains precise and meaningful. Despite calls from some scholars and practitioners for the simplification of legal terminology through the replacement of Latin expressions with modern alternatives, many Latin phrases continue to enhance the accuracy and continuity of legal language. Nevertheless, the reliance on Latin can create barriers for laypersons and those outside the legal profession, leading to confusion and misinterpretation. This situation underscores an ongoing debate within the legal field about balancing the preservation of legal tradition with the need for accessibility in legal communication. As discussions surrounding plain language gain momentum, it is essential for legal professionals to address this challenge. Although Latin adds a sense of authority and tradition, its use in legal contexts can create barriers to understanding for those outside the profession. Consequently, it is vital to strike a balance between this traditional usage and the necessity for clear and accessible legal communication. Making legal language understandable to all parties involved promotes trust and encourages a more inclusive understanding of the law.

4.1.7 Law French

The influences of French in legal language can be traced directly to the Norman Conquest in 1066, which marked the start of a profound linguistic shift in England. After William the Conqueror's victory, the ruling class predominantly spoke Norman French, and this had a notable effect on legal and administrative language, as it became the language of governance, law, politics and religion (Tiersma 1999: 19; Williams 2023: 27). The introduction of Norman French into these sectors led to a transformation in the legal lexicon, with French terms becoming deeply embedded in the institutional language of the time (Burnley 1992: 423–432). Nevertheless, it is important to note that Latin remained the primary language of written documents. Consequently, from the early thirteenth century onwards, both Norman French and Latin were employed in regulating institutional and legal matters, resulting in a bilingual legal framework that relied on two foreign languages (Burnley 1992: 428; Tiersma 1999: 20; Williams 2023: 29). The dual usage of these languages highlights the complexity of medieval English legal discourse, where Latin was used for writing while French remained significant in oral pleadings. According to Burnley (1992: 428) "[i]n the law courts, it was not until 1362 that Parliament formally acknowledged the right of English in place of Latin or French". However, even with this change, French continued to influence the legal lexicon, particularly in the spoken form, which persisted until 1731 for formal pleadings (Baker 1998: 20–23). Despite the decline of French as a legal language, Law French evolved into a specialised form of legal jargon. This hybrid form combined elements of French, Latin and English, particularly in written documentation (Baker 1998: 23–24; Williams 2023: 29). As a result, Law French represents a distinct linguistic phenomenon that transcends mere translation, embodying a blend of languages that shaped English legal culture.

Due to these historical layers, the etymology of certain legal terms remains uncertain or contested. The term "escrow" (nowadays referring to a bond or a deed kept in custody by a third party), for instance, illustrates this complexity. It is derived from the Old French term *escro* (meaning "piece of parchment") and/or the Latin *scriptum* ("a piece of writing") (Duckworth and Spyrou 1995: 16). Similarly, the juxtaposition of legal terms from both Law Latin and Law French has led to the creation of synonymous doublets or triplets. These pairings, such as "null and void", "goods and chattels", "deem and consider" and "appropriate and proper", often combine terms of different linguistic origins to ensure precision and inclusivity. While individual words in these combinations, such as "goods" or "deem", may derive from Old English, the practice of pairing them with Law Latin or Law French terms reflects the blending of these languages within the legal tradition (Tiersma 1999: 28; Bhatia 2010: 266). These linguistic patterns continue to influence modern legal language, where precision and clarity are paramount, even if some terms seem repetitive to the layperson.

Many Norman French-derived terms are still used in both government and legal settings today. For instance, terms like "authority", "chancellor", "court", "crown", "magistrate" and "minister" are direct descendants of Norman French, while other terms like "judge" and "appeal" have become commonplace in both legal and general contexts (Tiersma 1999: 19; Williams 2004: 112). Nevertheless, some terms remain confined to the legal domain, such as "attainder", which refers to the loss of civil rights following a conviction for a serious crime (Williams 2004: 112). The continued use of such terms reflects the endurance of Law French and its integration into legal discourse over centuries. Even in modern European legal English, expressions like *acquis communautaire* maintain a French origin and illustrate the continued influence of French on legal terminology (ibid.).

Several terms derived from Law French will be closely examined in this study to demonstrate the extensive influence of French on English legal terminology. For example, the terms "attorney general" and "solicitor general" highlight how French has shaped the nomenclature of high-ranking legal positions. These titles reflect the hierarchical structure within the legal profession and underline the lasting legacy of Norman French in legal discourse. Terms such as "abut", which means to join at a border or boundary (Garner 2004: 32), and "appurtenance", which refers to something attached to something else (Garner 2004: 316), show the enduring relevance of French in property law. Similarly, "arrear(age)", which indicates the state of being behind in the payment of a debt (Garner 2004: 333), reflects the influence of French-derived terminology in financial and legal contexts. In the socio-political sphere, the term "burgess", meaning an inhabitant of a borough or town (Garner 2004: 592), shows the historical relationship between legal terminology and civic governance, as this term was vital for defining civic status in medieval English towns. Other expressions like "cestui que trust", which refers to a beneficiary (Duckworth and Spyrou 1995: 8), highlight the precision required in defining property rights and inheritance law. Furthermore, terms such as "commence(ment)", which signifies a start or an introductory clause (Garner 2004: 2413; Leonardi and Giampieri 2024), reflect the structured nature of legal procedure and the continued use of Law French in framing legal processes. The term "covenant", meaning a formal agreement or promise (Garner 2004: 1100), remains crucial in contract law, further demonstrating the enduring significance of French terminology in the regulation of legal agreements. In the field of property law, "demise", which refers to the passing of property by descent or death (Garner 2004: 1306), highlights how Law French terms have persisted in modern legal contexts concerning inheritance and leasehold property. Similarly, in criminal law, the term "embezzle(ment)", referring to the fraudulent taking of personal property (Garner 2004: 1580), shows the lasting impact of French on defining unlawful financial activities. The term "feoffment", although archaic, remains significant as it refers to the granting of land (Garner 2004: 1846). This concept provides insight into the medieval systems of land tenure and the historical formalisation of such rights. Finally, the term "presentment", which refers to the act of presenting or laying before a court or tribunal a formal statement (Garner 2004: 3749), underscores the procedural role of Law French in shaping the modern framework of English legal practice.

4.1.8 Formulaic Expressions

Formulaic expressions have a long-standing history in legal discourse and are deeply embedded in legal traditions. Originating primarily from Latin, these expressions have been preserved, adapted or, in some instances, abandoned as legal drafting has evolved over the centuries (Tiersma 1999; Williams 2023). Their endurance within modern legal language is often attributed to the ritualistic nature of law, where the repetition and formalism of specific phrases or expressions maintain a sense of authority, tradition and stability in legal procedures. The historical reason for the persistence of legal formulae is linked to the belief in their symbolic power. During the Middle Ages, these formulaic expressions were thought to carry talismanic powers, ensuring the success of legal proceedings and transactions when uttered correctly (Tiersma 1999: 13). This belief gave rise to a highly structured and formulaic legal language, where specific phrases were expected to be recited to satisfy both legal and ritualistic purposes. Over time, these expressions became ingrained in legal practices, and some, such as "tell the truth, the whole truth, and nothing but the truth", have persisted into modern legal proceedings (Tiersma 1999: 15). The Anglo-Saxon period further reinforced the use of repetitive word pairs and alliterations in legal texts, creating a rhythmic and mnemonic quality that endures to this day. Modern lawyers continue to use alliterations and formulae, particularly in closing arguments, to appeal to both the rhetorical and ceremonial dimensions of legal discourse.

Several scholars have argued that the inflexible, verbose and often formulaic nature of legal discourse can be attributed to the historical reliance on such expressions (Biel and Engberg 2013; Pontrandolfo 2023). Kopaczyk (2009) has pointed out that formulae, especially binomial multi-words (such as "null and void" or "aid and abet"), often contribute little semantically to the text but serve a primarily rhetorical and aesthetic function (Kopaczyk 2009: 95). The repetitive nature of these expressions can be seen as a way to ensure precision, as well as to uphold traditional stylistic standards. Pontrandolfo (2023: 135–136) refers to legal formulae as recurrent language clusters or prefabricated chunks that have become standardised over time. These formulaic clusters, often lengthy, have become an accepted part of legal texts globally, contributing to the uniformity and predictability of legal documents (Gotti 2012: 52). For instance, in modern contract drafting, *boilerplate clauses* are predominantly composed of such formulaic expressions, which fill a significant portion of the document and serve to protect legal interests while offering predictability in interpretation (Pontrandolfo 2023). Giurizzato (2008) explores the formulaic nature of legal oaths and affirmations, noting that the process of providing evidence in court is framed by highly structured, formulaic language. Before testifying, witnesses are required to swear an oath or affirm the truth of their statements in a manner that adheres to long-established legal phrasing, thus reinforcing the solemnity of their testimony. Nystedt (2000), in his study of EU legal texts, highlights how formulaic expressions are particularly prevalent in European Union documents, making them linguistically predictable but also reinforcing legal certainty across multiple jurisdictions.

The ongoing use of these formulaic expressions offers insight into the evolution of legal language, reflecting a broader tendency towards simplification and modernisation, while still maintaining an adherence to tradition. As legal language evolves, these expressions continue to serve various functions within legal documents, such as providing clarity, structure and formality, ensuring that legal language remains consistent and recognisable across jurisdictions and historical periods. To further illustrate the significance of formulaic expressions, several specific examples will be analysed in Chap. 5 in detail. These examples highlight how particular phrases continue to function in modern legal contexts, either as part of traditional legal ceremonies or in everyday legal documentation. One such expression is "In witness whereof", a classic phrase used to conclude deeds and formal documents. This expression is a direct translation of the Latin *in cujus rei testimonium*, and its continued use in modern legal contexts underscores the formal and ceremonial nature of legal transactions (Garner 2004: 2243; Giampieri 2022: 27). Similarly, "Know all men (by these presents)" often appears at the beginning of solemn legal documents, such as deeds. This phrase, translating the Latin *noverint universi per praesentes*, means "be it known" or "be it remembered", further highlighting its role in formalising legal notifications (Tiersma 1999: 93; Garner 2004: 2547).

Another common expression is "Nothing in this / the", frequently employed to clarify that a particular provision or document does not override or negate other legal obligations or rights (Bhatia 2010: 28). The use of "Now therefore" often marks the conclusion of negotiations, introducing the final agreement between the parties, for instance: "Now therefore, the parties hereto have agreed as follows" (Giampieri 2022: 27). This formula lends a sense of finality and mutual consent in the contractual terms. Furthermore, expressions like "Of the first part", "of the one part" or "on the one hand" are employed to distinguish and identify parties involved in legal agreements. These phrases ensure clarity when differentiating between the parties in documents such as contracts, making legal responsibilities and relationships explicit (Bhatia 2010: 28).

The persistence of such formulaic expressions illustrates their central role in maintaining the formal and ritualistic tone of legal documents. While some of these expressions might appear redundant or archaic in modern contexts, their continued use ensures consistency, precision and recognition in legal discourse across different legal systems. Their role is not merely decorative but serves practical functions such as confirming legal validity, clarifying party obligations and avoiding misinterpretation.

4.2 Sexist Language and Gender Bias

The roots of sexist language are deeply embedded in historical and cultural contexts. Many languages have evolved within patriarchal societies where male experiences and perspectives have been privileged. Consequently, language has developed to reflect these biases, often marginalising women and reinforcing traditional gender roles. As Spender (1980) notes, the English language, for example, is "man-made" and preserves ancient biases against women, which are reflected in its vocabulary and grammar. According to Leonardi (2007), discourse is greatly influenced by language, which acts as a powerful tool for manipulation. It functions as a reflective mirror, exposing the underlying ideological frameworks. This recognition of the manipulative potential of language highlights its inherent connection to ideology, as it serves as a medium through which dominant narratives are constructed and disseminated (ibid.). Thompson contends that the scrutiny of ideology primarily revolves around language, as it serves as the primary vehicle for conveying meaning, thereby upholding relationships of domination (Thompson 1984). Gruber supports this notion, asserting that ideology is expressed through linguistic structures and is shaped by language (Gruber 1990). Hall (1982) suggests that ideology functions as a replication of prevailing discourse. The study of linguistic sexism involves analysing language use and discourse to identify and understand how gender bias operates linguistically with implications for social attitudes, cultural norms and gender equality (Leonardi 2007).

The English language has faced considerable criticism regarding sexism, particularly influenced by the advent of early American feminism (Crystal 1987). This critique of English can be further dissected into two primary categories, centred on both grammatical structures (syntax and morphology) and vocabulary selection. The way sentences are structured and words are formed can inadvertently reinforce gender stereotypes or contribute to gender-neutral language practices. For instance, the use of masculine generics or the defaulting to male pronouns can subtly marginalise women and perpetuate a male-centric worldview. By dissecting the grammatical aspects of language, scholars aim to uncover and challenge these entrenched biases, advocating linguistic structures that promote inclusivity and gender equity. Moreover, the vocabulary employed in language reflects societal attitudes and norms towards gender. Lexical choices not only reflect existing power dynamics but also have the potential to shape and reinforce them. Words carrying gender-specific connotations or stereotypes can perpetuate inequality and discrimination. By scrutinising lexical choices, linguists aim to dismantle linguistic barriers and foster a more inclusive linguistic environment that embraces diversity and respects all genders.

Legal terminology is often perceived as precise and objective; however, it can also conceal instances of gender bias and discrimination. As a distinct form of communication with significant societal implications, legal language is susceptible to the influence of sexist connotations. The evolution of gender-neutral legal language dates back to the twelfth century, but recent changes were largely driven by the feminist movement of the 1970s, which challenged non-inclusive language. A key milestone was the 1980 publication of *The Handbook of Nonsexist Writing* (Miller and Swift 1980), which encouraged eliminating unconscious biases. Later, Strunk and White (2000) acknowledged that generic masculine pronouns could be limiting or offensive, suggesting alternatives. These shifts reflect broader social changes of the 1970s and 1980s, with increasing efforts to adopt gender-neutral terminology in definitions and examples.

The demand for gender-neutral legal language is growing, with more laypersons requesting documents in a gender-neutral format (Strzelczyk 2019). Discussions around gender and inclusive language are becoming more common, and many legal writing guides now recommend avoiding gendered generics and gendered suffixes to promote neutrality. Gender representation in legal systems is shaped by historical and cultural contexts, often misused in discriminatory ways, especially in family and marriage laws. Adopting gender-neutral language can lead to more inclusive legislation, enhancing protection and freedom. Legal experts emphasise its importance for clarity, professionalism and compliance with equality principles (Mossman 1994).

Since the 1980s, the U.S. has made significant progress in adopting gender-neutral legal language, with task forces established at state and federal levels to address gender bias in legal language. These efforts led to the integration of gender-neutral terms into constitutions and statutes, and inclusive language discussions began appearing in legal textbooks (Fischer 2009). However, many judges still use male-gendered generics, reflecting outdated communication styles. Recently, some states introduced gender-neutral jury instructions and court style manuals, as research shows that biased language reinforces the notion of men as the default standard (ibid.).

Canada is a leader in promoting inclusivity, especially since the enactment of the Canadian Charter of Rights and Freedoms in 1982, which strengthened protections for individual rights, including freedom of expression and equality. The Charter has played a key role in aligning legislation with these values, supporting language rights and advancing equality for minorities and disadvantaged groups (Canadian Charter I 1982). As far as gender-neutral legal language is concerned, the Canadian Department of Justice published guidelines on the use of the singular "they" to eliminate gender-specific language (Government of Canada 2020). Canadian federal agencies have also issued guidelines to avoid biased language, and the *Canadian Translation Bureau* provided several recommendations for gender-inclusive writing. These efforts demonstrate Canada's commitment to fostering equality through language.

Across Europe, Guarino (2023) investigates changes in EU secondary legislation from 1982 to 2022, assessing adherence to official guidelines. His study reveals significant progress, particularly in the decline of generic masculine pronouns and the growing adoption of gender-neutral terms. However, deeply rooted linguistic habits, resistance to change and the complexities of legal discourse continue to pose challenges. Through a diachronic analysis of legislative texts, Guarino evaluates the effectiveness of EU guidelines, shedding light on both achievements and the persistent difficulties in fully embedding inclusive language practices.

Buiatti (2022) critically analyses how different countries have approached gender-neutral legal language as a means of combating discrimination and promoting equality. Malta's Gender Identity, Gender Expression and Sex Characteristics Act stands as a landmark measure, allowing individuals to select an "X" gender marker on official documents, thus setting a precedent for inclusivity. Italy, by contrast, struggles with entrenched cultural norms that hinder widespread adoption, despite some regional legislative initiatives. Beyond Europe, the United States has made strides towards gender-neutral legal language, though inconsistencies persist across states. Canada has demonstrated particular commitment by integrating indigenous terms and fostering inclusivity within legal texts. Meanwhile, India and Mali illustrate how cultural and linguistic factors shape legal language, presenting both obstacles and opportunities for reform. While progress is evident across various jurisdictions, Buiatti argues that overcoming systemic biases requires sustained and coordinated efforts.

Heinemann's review (2022) of *Gender in Legislative Languages* by Cavagnoli and Mori offers further insight into the challenges of implementing gender-inclusive language within the EU. The review critiques the methodological limitations of this book and explores the evolution of legal language in French, Italian and Spanish, where feminisation is often favoured over neutralisation due to linguistic structures. Heinemann underscores the necessity of a broader comparative approach to tackling these complexities across different cultural and linguistic contexts. Examining the EU's multilingual landscape and national guidelines in the UK, Germany, France, Spain and Italy, the review acknowledges growing recognition of inclusive language's importance. However, as linguistic and cultural barriers persist, practical implementation remains a considerable challenge.

The evolution of gendered language in British legal discourse has undergone significant transformations, reflecting broader societal changes towards inclusivity and equality. Traditionally, legal writing in the UK relied heavily on masculine terms to refer to individuals, employing masculine pronouns such as he/him and man-compound occupational nouns. This practice not only reinforced gender stereotypes but also obscured the contributions and rights of women within legal frameworks. Such language practices were prevalent until the early twenty-first century, perpetuating a narrative that favoured male perspectives in legal discourse (Bailey 2020). A pivotal change occurred in 2007 when the UK government adopted a policy requiring the use of gender-neutral language in legislative drafting. This shift aimed to enhance clarity and inclusivity in legal texts, ensuring that all individuals are represented fairly and accurately. The move was part of a broader effort to modernise legal language and reflect contemporary values regarding gender equality (ibid.). Interestingly, prior to the mid-nineteenth century, it was relatively common for legislation to be drafted using gender-neutral terms. However, this practice changed dramatically with the passage of the 1850 Act, which stated that masculine terms would be deemed to include females. This legislative fiction allowed for the continued use of masculine pronouns and man-compounds to refer to all individuals, regardless of gender. The Interpretation Act of 1978 further entrenched this practice by reiterating that masculine terms should include females, a concept still reflected in many private law agreements today. By 2019, over a decade had passed since the government began adopting gender-neutral language in legislation. While this transition required some adjustment within the legal community, it has gradually become second nature in legal drafting. Increasing awareness of the benefits of gender-neutral language has also emerged across the wider legal sector, including among those responsible for drafting private law documents (ibid.). In response to this growing interest, a practical guide on gender-neutral writing was launched. This guide provides straightforward strategies for avoiding gender-specific pronouns by (1) repeating the noun, for instance, "a person is entitled to a benefit if the person…", (2) changing the pronoun using "they" or "their" in singular contexts, such as "a person fails to comply with their duty...", and (3) rewriting to avoid pronouns, for example, "it is an offence for a person to..." instead of "a person commits an offence if he...". This guide was developed by the *Office of the Parliamentary Counsel* and the *Government Legal Department*, with support from organisations like the *Interlaw Diversity Forum* and *Global Butterflies* (ibid.).

As far as the corpus-based analysis is concerned, several linguistic elements must be considered in order to effectively analyse the evolution of gender-inclusive language in legal English and evaluate the implementation of recent guidelines. The most commonly criticised suffixes have always included those in *-man* and *-ess*. Nevertheless, other interesting examples, especially in the context of legal discourse, are those related to suffixes ending in -trix.

The suffix *-trix* originates from Latin (*-trīx*) and has been used since the sixteenth century to form feminine agent nouns corresponding to the masculine form *-tor* (e.g., *executor/executrix*) (Marchand 1960). Several legal terms, such as *administratrix*, *executrix*, *inheritrix*, *proprietrix*, *testatrix* and *legislatrix*, have historically been derived using *-trix* (ibid.). Despite their historical significance, however, these *-trix* terms have largely fallen out of common usage in contemporary legal language. While they still occur sporadically in formal legal contexts, they are often regarded as outdated and unnecessary. This decline is indicative of a broader linguistic shift towards inclusivity and equality. The predominance of *-tor* forms, which are used to refer to both sexes, highlights how these masculine terms have gradually become entrenched as the default descriptors over time. This trend reflects not only a linguistic evolution but also a societal recognition of the need for gender-neutral terminology. In this context, the emergence of gender-neutral terms such as *personal representative* signifies a substantial departure from traditional gendered language (EIGE 2019). This term effectively replaces outdated forms like *executrix* and *administratrix*, which are increasingly viewed as relics of a bygone era that failed to adequately represent women's roles in legal contexts. The adoption of *personal representative* aligns with contemporary values that prioritise equality and representation within legal discourse. By using this term, legal practitioners and documents acknowledge that individuals in these roles can be of any gender, thereby promoting an inclusive environment that reflects modern societal norms. The shift towards gender-neutral language is further emphasised by the recognition that roles traditionally associated with women should not be defined by outdated suffixes that imply inferiority or secondary status. The term *personal representative* not only serves as a neutral alternative but also actively contributes to dismantling the stereotypes associated with historical *-trix* forms. This change is particularly significant in legal contexts where clarity and neutrality are paramount, as it ensures that all individuals, regardless of gender, are equally represented and recognised within the legal framework. Moreover, this evolution in terminology reflects ongoing efforts to reform legal language in a manner that is consistent with contemporary understandings of gender and equality. The move away from *-trix* forms towards terms like *personal representative* underscores a commitment to fostering an inclusive legal environment where all individuals can participate fully and equally, without being constrained by archaic linguistic conventions.

It is also worth noting the *-ette* suffix, which derives from French diminutive forms and was initially used to denote something smaller or of lesser importance, not just in size but also in stature or relevance. This suffix has historically been applied to words with feminine diminutive connotations, such as *suffragette*, which referred to women advocating for voting rights. While the term was originally coined to celebrate women's activism, its diminutive form has since fallen out of favour due to its patronising undertone, implying inferiority or trivialisation (ibid.). In contemporary usage, *-ette* is generally avoided because it reinforces stereotypes of diminutiveness and carries a strong bias against women, suggesting that their contributions are lesser or secondary compared to those of men (ibid.). The implications of using such diminutive forms extend beyond mere semantics since they reflect and perpetuate societal attitudes that undermine women's roles and achievements. As language evolves, there is a growing recognition that terms which imply inferiority can have detrimental effects on perceptions of women's capabilities and contributions in various fields, including law. Consequently, legal discourse has increasingly moved towards language that promotes equality and respect for all genders.

The emergence and formalisation of gendered legal terminology in English inheritance law, particularly the distinctions between *heirs male* and *heirs female*, reflect deeper socio-legal patterns rooted in the feudal structure and patriarchal assumptions of medieval society. Through instruments such as entails and inquisitions post mortem (IPMs), these terms acquired legal precision and became integral to the governance of land succession. Their development offers insights not only into the legal ordering of descent but also into contemporary understandings of gender and familial hierarchy. Inquisitions post mortem were formal inquiries conducted after the death of tenants-in-chief of the Crown to establish what lands they held, their value and the identity of their heirs. These records, preserved in the Calendar of Inquisitions Post Mortem (CIPM 1904), provide crucial evidence for understanding medieval inheritance practices and the practical application of gendered legal terminology in succession law. By the late thirteenth century, the common law rules of inheritance, founded on the principle of primogeniture, were largely settled (Simpson 1961). Under these rules, priority in inheritance was given to direct descendants over collateral relatives, and, crucially, male descendants were favoured over female ones. Within the same generational tier, only the eldest male could inherit; if no male issue existed, daughters would inherit jointly as co-heiresses. This structure effectively reinforced the transmission of land along the male line unless legal instruments specified otherwise. The operation of these principles can be observed in practice through contemporary records. The case of John Hadley of London, whose heirs were both his daughter Katherine and his grandson John, illustrates how a deceased descendant could be "represented" by their issue, sometimes modifying the strict operation of primogeniture (CIPM xix.723–7). Such examples demonstrate the complexity of inheritance patterns even within the established legal framework.

The gendered language of *heirs male* and *heirs female* became especially salient with the advent of entails, introduced through the *Statute De Donis Conditionalibus* of 1285. Entails enabled landowners to control succession more narrowly than the default common law allowed. Grants in fee tail could specify descent *in tail male* or *in tail female*, thereby excluding entire lines of potential heirs by virtue of gender (Biancalana

2001: 106–40). This specification curtailed the otherwise inclusive nature of common law descent that, albeit hierarchically, did admit daughters in the absence of sons. Such gender-specific entails were often used strategically to preserve estates within a preferred lineage, typically the paternal male line. The Beauchamp family's estate provides a compelling case study of these dynamics in operation. Earl Thomas (d. 1369) entailed his estates in tail male to prevent inheritance by the daughters of his deceased eldest son, ensuring instead that the lands passed to his male heir, Richard Beauchamp (Hicks 1998). Only when the male line failed with the death of Henry, Duke of Warwick, did the estate pass to his daughter Anne, who herself died a minor in 1449 (ibid.).

The IPMs relating to Anne Beauchamp interpreted her seisin as being in fee simple, thus allowing succession to her aunt Anne (Richard's daughter by his second wife), to the exclusion of her much older half-sisters, who were barred by the law of the half blood. This case encapsulates the interplay of entail, gendered succession and technical rules of blood relationship in the construction of inheritance patterns, demonstrating how legal technicalities could compound gender-based exclusions. Customary laws such as gavelkind in Kent diverged from primogeniture by permitting partible inheritance among male heirs, yet still privileged men over women. In borough or manorial customs favouring ultimogeniture, younger sons could inherit ahead of elder siblings, but again this flexibility rarely extended to female heirs (CIPM xix.941–2). Even when descent turned to collaterals, the preference for males remained: brothers before sisters, uncles before aunts, all within the full blood lineage (Wedd 2020).

Entailments specifying *heirs male* often ran counter to the identity of the common law heir, creating complex legal situations. Richard de la Pole, for instance, held Grafton in tail male with a remainder to his younger brother Thomas. Upon his death without issue, Thomas inherited under the entail, while other properties held in fee simple passed to the common law heir, Richard's elder brother Michael (CIPM xviii.336). This divergence underlines how gendered legal terms were not merely descriptive but functionally determinative in the hierarchy of succession. The increasing deployment of uses in the later medieval period further complicated the landscape. Uses enabled landowners to circumvent feudal obligations and to exercise greater discretion over succession, often through secret or conditional arrangements. Although the identity of the beneficiary (*cestui que use*) was not legally recognised in common law, IPMs occasionally recorded such arrangements, albeit selectively. They often reinforced or subverted gendered expectations, especially in the context of wills or delayed bequests conditioned upon the completion of religious or commemorative acts, such as the construction of the Beauchamp chapel at Warwick (Hicks 1998).

The persistence and legal entrenchment of *heirs male* and *heirs female* terminology shaped not only who could inherit but also how familial relationships were interpreted and valued. They reinforced a patrilineal ideal in which women were only contingently entitled, and only in the absence of suitable male heirs. However, as the Beauchamp and Despenser cases demonstrate, female claims could be advanced through representation or fee tail general, depending on the precise wording of settlements and the influence of interested parties such as Richard Neville, "Warwick the Kingmaker" (ibid.). While IPMs offer a vital window into these dynamics, they are not unproblematic. As Payling has observed, their evidentiary reliability varies, especially where entailments or enfeoffments are concerned, and jurors often relied on partial or strategic information (Payling 1986: 71). Nevertheless, IPMs remain one of the most significant sources for tracing the deployment of gendered legal language in the law of succession, particularly the rise and consolidation of the heirs male clause as a powerful instrument of exclusion.

The examination of feminine pronouns is also crucial when assessing gender bias in legal texts. An increase in pronouns such as "her", "hers" and "she" implies a positive trend towards recognising female subjects within legal contexts. This shift is significant as it reflects an acknowledgment of women's agency and presence in legal narratives that have historically been male-dominated. The use of feminine pronouns not only signifies the inclusion of women in legal discourse but also affirms their roles as active participants rather than passive subjects. This is particularly important in a field where language shapes perceptions and can influence the outcomes of legal processes. Conversely, the prevalence of masculine pronouns like "him", "his" and "he" can reveal persistent biases that marginalise female perspectives. The dominance of male pronouns as defaults often implies that male experiences are universal while female experiences are considered exceptions or secondary. This linguistic practice reinforces traditional gender hierarchies and perpetuates the notion that legal authority and expertise are inherently male attributes. Such biases can undermine the credibility and recognition of women's contributions within the legal profession, further entrenching systemic inequalities. Moreover, the historical context of pronoun usage in legal texts underscores these dynamics. As mentioned above, the 1850 Act passed by the British Parliament established a precedent whereby masculine terms were deemed to include females, thus sidelining women's identities and contributions. This legislative fiction has persisted over time, leading to a linguistic landscape where masculine pronouns dominate, often at the expense of gender inclusivity. The ongoing reliance on masculine language not only obscures women's roles but also diminishes the perceived legitimacy of their experiences within legal frameworks. In response to these issues, there has been a concerted effort within legal writing to adopt more gender-neutral language. Guidelines from various legal institutions advocate the use of singular, gender-neutral pronouns such as "they" to refer to unspecified individuals, thereby mitigating the need for gendered pronouns altogether. This approach not only enhances clarity but also promotes inclusivity by acknowledging the diversity of gender identities beyond the binary framework.

Phrases such as "if a man" or "if a woman" provide a lens through which it is possible to explore how hypothetical scenarios are framed in terms of gender issues in legal contexts. The use of these expressions may serve to highlight inherent biases in the representation of both men and women, thus reflecting societal attitudes that often privilege male experiences over female ones. For instance, when legal texts or discussions default to "if a man", it may imply that male experiences are the normative standard while female experiences are treated as exceptions or afterthoughts. This framing reinforces traditional gender roles and perpetuates the notion that men are the primary actors in legal scenarios, thereby marginalising women's contributions and perspectives. The implications of such gendered phrasing extend beyond mere representation as they can influence how laws are interpreted and applied. When legal language consistently centres around male pronouns and scenarios, it risks embedding patriarchal assumptions into the fabric of legal reasoning. This can lead to outcomes that fail to adequately consider the realities faced by women or other gender minorities, thereby perpetuating systemic inequalities. In other words, the prevalence of masculine language in law has historically contributed to a culture where women's rights and experiences are overshadowed by those of men, thus leading to biased interpretations and applications of the law. In response to these issues, focusing on neutral alternatives, such as "if a person" or "if someone" is crucial to progress towards inclusivity in legal discourse. The adoption of gender-neutral language not only promotes equality but also fosters an environment where individuals are recognised for their roles and contributions without being constrained by gendered assumptions. Such language choices reflect a broader commitment to dismantling biases that have long been entrenched in legal systems. The shift towards using neutral language is supported by various guidelines and recommendations from legal institutions advocating for gender inclusivity. Furthermore, the emphasis on neutral phrasing helps to create an inclusive legal environment where all individuals feel represented and valued. By consciously choosing language that avoids gender-specific references unless necessary, legal practitioners can contribute to a more equitable system that acknowledges the contributions of all genders. This linguistic evolution is essential not only for improving representation but also for ensuring that the law serves all members of society fairly and justly.

The frequency and context of the term "men" will also be analysed to determine its role as the default group in legal discourse. Historically, the term has often been used generically to represent humanity at large, thereby reinforcing the notion that male experiences and perspectives are universal. This linguistic practice can obscure the contributions and realities of women and gender minorities, effectively marginalising their presence in legal discussions. By examining how frequently "men" appears in legal texts compared to references to women may help detect if the legal framework is still predominantly oriented around male experiences, further entrenching gender biases within the law. Conversely, if "men" is often mentioned alongside discussions of inclusivity or equality, it may indicate an evolving understanding of gender roles within legal contexts. Similarly, examining how often women are mentioned can provide critical insights into their representation over time. An increase in references to women in legal texts could signify progress towards greater inclusivity. Nevertheless, it is also essential to consider not only the quantity but also the quality of these mentions. Are women portrayed as active participants with agency or are they relegated to passive roles? The nature of these representations can reveal much about societal attitudes towards gender and the extent to which women are recognised as equals within the legal system. Phrases like "men and women" reflect attempts to include both genders explicitly and warrant careful analysis to understand trends in inclusivity.

By recognising and addressing biases embedded in language, the legal profession can work towards creating a more equitable framework that reflects the diverse experiences and contributions of all individuals. This commitment to inclusive language not only enhances clarity but also fosters a culture of respect and equality within the legal system.

4.3 Concluding Remarks

In examining legal language, this chapter illustrated that its complexity stems from various interconnected linguistic characteristics, such as archaic terminology, formal structures and specialised legal jargon, often referred to as *legalese*. Legal discourse is characterised by a rigid formalism, rooted in historical traditions that continues to influence modern legal texts. These linguistic elements serve the purpose of precision and clarity within legal contexts but often render legal documents inaccessible to laypersons. Furthermore, the persistence of these features highlights the conservatism of legal language, reflecting the stability and predictability required in law, but also suggesting a resistance to change.

A key aspect of *legalese* is its reliance on complex prepositional and adverbial phrases, which are essential to achieve semantic precision. Legal writers frequently use these constructions to eliminate ambiguity and provide specific legal effects. However, the problem is that these multi-word phrases often result in complex sentences, which reduce and hinder the readability of legal documents. Furthermore, many of these expressions reflect the historic roots of legal English, with a noticeable influence from Latin and Norman French. This reliance on historical forms reinforces the perceived authority of legal texts, thus contributing to their inaccessibility for the general public.

Deictic elements, which depend on the context for interpretation, are also integral to legal writing. Temporal and spatial deixis are both equally important, as legal texts frequently refer to earlier sections of the document or legal timelines using terms such as "herein" or "thereafter". While these deictic features are necessary to maintain internal coherence in legal texts, they also contribute to the overall opacity of the language.

Vagueness is another inherent aspect of legal language, despite its intention to be precise. Legal standards often need to be flexible enough to apply to a wide range of real-world situations. This flexibility is achieved through the use of vague terms that allow for judicial discretion. Phrases such as "howsoever" and "whatsoever" capture this vagueness, providing legal drafters with tools to cover multiple contingencies without having to specify every possible scenario. Although this flexibility can be beneficial for the courts, it frequently results in interpretative difficulties, especially for those without legal training who are trying to grasp the core of legal documents.

The use of archaic verbs and nouns further complicates legal language. Many terms, such as "deem" or "endeavour", can be easily replaced by simpler, more modern equivalents without sacrificing legal precision. Despite this, these archaic forms remain pervasive in legal writing, often due to tradition and a perceived need to maintain the authoritative tone of legal documents. Likewise, nominalisation adds unnecessary complexity to sentences, thus contributing to what is often referred to as the "noun plague" in legal writing. This feature is particularly common in statutory texts, where phrases like "to make an application" are used instead of simpler alternatives like "to apply".

The chapter also highlighted the historical influence of Latin and French on legal English. Latin, in particular, left a lasting mark on legal terminology, with many phrases such as *bona fide* and *de facto* still in use today. These Latin terms serve a symbolic function, connecting modern legal practice to its historical roots and providing legal professionals with a shared vocabulary that transcends national boundaries. Similarly, the Norman Conquest introduced a wealth of French terms into legal discourse, many of which are still used today. Although these linguistic features lend authority to legal texts, they also reinforce the exclusivity of the legal profession, thus creating barriers for laypeople seeking to engage with legal matters.

The persistence of formulaic expressions in legal texts further underscores the ritualistic nature of legal language. These expressions, though seemingly redundant, play an important role in maintaining the formality and predictability of legal documents. Despite ongoing efforts to simplify legal writing through initiatives, such as the plain language movement, these formulaic expressions demonstrate an extraordinary resilience to transformation.

Finally, in exploring gender issues within legal discourse, it is evident that gender biases, stereotypes and inequalities significantly influence legal systems and their outcomes. Historical contexts reveal how language has perpetuated these biases, often leading to differential treatment and unequal access to justice for individuals based on their gender. The adoption of gender-responsive policies and language is crucial for promoting inclusivity and challenging traditional norms. This includes the use of gender-neutral terms in legal texts, which can help dismantle stereotypes and ensure that all individuals, regardless of gender, are treated with dignity and respect. Attempts to reform legal language reflect a broader commitment to achieving gender equality within legal frameworks, thus highlighting the importance of intersectionality in addressing the unique challenges faced by diverse gender identities.

In conclusion, ongoing efforts to simplify and modernise legal writing, including the pursuit of gender-neutral language, reflect a steadfast commitment to making legal texts more accessible and inclusive, while maintaining the essential precision and clarity intrinsic to the law. The forthcoming analysis will examine how legal language has evolved over time and assess the effectiveness of recent reforms aimed at enhancing clarity, comprehension and inclusivity.

Bibliography

Abate, Salvatore C. 1998. *Il documento legale anglosassone*. Hoepli.

Adams, Kenneth. 2024. *A Manual of Style for Contract Drafting*. 5th ed. Chicago, IL: ABA Publishing.

Allott, Nicholas. 2010. *Key terms in Pragmatics*. London: Continuum International Publishing.

Bailey, Diggory. 2020. *Breaking Down Gender Stereotypes in Legal Writing*. Civil Service publication.

Bajčić, Martina. 2018. Coping with Vague EU Legal Concepts. In *Transnational, European, and National Labour Relations. Europeanization and Globalization*, ed. G. Sander, V. Tomljenović, and N. Bodiroga-Vukobrat, 97–107. Cham: Springer Link.

Baker, John H. 1998. The Three Languages of the Common Law. *McGill Law Journal* 43:5–24.

Bhatia, Vijay K. 2010. *Textbook on Legal Language and Legal Writing*. New Delhi: Universal law publishing Co. Pvt. Ltd.

Biancalana, J. 2001. *The Fee Tail and the Common Recovery in Medieval England 1176–1502*. Cambridge: Cambridge University Press.

Biel, Łucja. 2015. Phraseological Profiles of Legislative Genres: Complex Prepositions as a Special Case of Legal Phrasemes in EU Law and National Law. *Fachsprache - International Journal of Specialized Communication 37* (3–4): 139–160.

Biel, Łucja, and Jan Engberg. 2013. Research Models and Methods in Legal Translation. *Linguistica Antverpensia, New Series - Themes in Translation Studies 12*:1–11.

Buiatti, M. V. 2022. Gender Neutral Legal Language: A Comparative Overview. *Comparative Law and Language* 1 (2): 33–54.

Burnley, David. 1992. Lexis and Semantics. In *The Cambridge History of the English Language Volume II 1066–1476*, ed. Norman Blake, 409–499. Cambridge: Cambridge University Press.

Calendar of Inquisitions Post Mortem. 1904. Great Britain. Public Record Office, London: Printed for H.M. Stationery Office.

Canale, Damiano. 2017. What Inferentialism Tells us About Combinatory Vagueness in Law. In *Pragmatics and Law. Perspectives in Pragmatics, Philosophy and Psychology*, ed. F. Poggi and A. Capone, vol. 10, 43–66. Cham: Springer Link.

Christie, George C. 1964. Vagueness and Legal Language. *Minnesota Law Review* 48:885–911.
Constitution Act, Part I, *Canadian Charter of Rights and Freedoms*, 1982.
Coulthard, Malcolm, and Alison Johnson. 2007. *An Introduction to Forensic Linguistics*. London / New York: Routledge.
Coulthard, Michael, and Alison Johnson. 2010. Introduction. In *The Routledge Handbook of Forensic Linguistics*, ed. Michael Coulthard and Alison Johnson, 1–16. London / New York: Routledge.
Crystal, David. 1987. *The Cambridge Encyclopaedia of Language*. Cambridge: Cambridge University Press.
Dickerson, Reed. 1986. *The Fundamentals of Legal Drafting*. 2nd ed. Boston: Little, Brown and Company.
Duckworth, Mark, and Arthur Spyrou. 1995. *Legal Words: 30 Essays on Legal Words and Phrases*. Sydney: Centre for Plain Legal Language, University of Sydney.
Endicott, Timothy. 2000. *Vagueness and Law*. Oxford: Oxford University Press.
Endicott, Timothy. 2005. The Value of Vagueness. In *Vagueness in Normative Texts*, ed. Vijay K. Bhatia, Jan Engberg, Maurizio Gotti, and Dorothee Heller, 27–48. Bern: Peter Lang.
European Institute for Gender Equality (EIGE). 2019. *Toolkit on Gender-sensitive Communication*. Luxembourg: Publications Office of the European Union.
Felici, Annarita. 2012. 'Shall' Ambiguity in EU Legislative Texts. *Comparative Legilinguistics* 10:51 66.
Fischer, Judith D. 2009. Framing Gender: Federal Appellate Judges' Choices About Gender-Neutral Language. *University of San Francisco Law Review* 43 (3): 473.
Garner, Bryan A. 2002. *The Elements of Legal Style*. 2nd ed. Oxford: Oxford University Press.
Garner, Bryan A. 2004. *Black's Law Dictionary*. 8th ed. St Paul, MN: Thomson/West.
Giampieri, Patrizia. 2016. Is The European Legal English Legalese-Free? *Italian Journal of Public Law* 8 (2): 424–440.
Giampieri, Patrizia. 2022. How (Un)readable are the European and UNESCO Cultural Conventions in the Digital Era? *IJLLD* 10 (2): 22–42.
Giampieri, Patrizia. 2024. *Corpus-based Translation of Private Legal Documents*. Amsterdam: John Benjamins.

Giurizzato, Antonella. 2008. Dificultad de reformulación de las fórmulas fraseológicas y léxicas en la traducción legal del inglés al español. In *Terminología, Traducción y Comunicación especializada. Homenaje a Amelia de Irazazábal, Actas del Congreso Internacional 11–12 de octubre 2007*, ed. Carmen Navarro, 231–246. Verona: Edizioni Fiorini.

Gotti, Maurizio. 2012. Text and Genre. In *The Oxford Handbook of Language and Law*, ed. Peter Tiersma and Lawrence M. Solan, 52–66. Oxford University Press.

Government of Canada, Department of Justice, Reports and Publications. 2020. *Legistics Singular "They"*.

Gruber, Helmut. 1990. Ein Gespenst geht um in Österreich. In *Sprache in der Politik: Politik in der Sprache. Analysen zum Öffentlichen Sprachgebrauch*, ed. R. Wodak and F. Menz, 191–207. Klagenfurt: Drava.

Guarino, Ornella. 2023. Gender-neutral Language in EU Secondary Legislation: The Case of the English Language. *Iperstoria* 21:412–432. https://doi.org/10.13136/2281-4582/2023.i21.1310.

Hall, Stuart. 1982. The Rediscovery of "Ideology: Return of the Repressed in Media Studies". In *Culture, Society and the Media*, ed. M. Gurevitch, T. Bennett, J. Curran, and J. Woollacott, 56–90. London and New York: Routledge.

Heinemann, E. 2022. Gender and Legal Language: Inclusive Drafting or Divisive Issue? An Old Debate, New Developments and a Review of "Gender in Legislative Languages: From EU to National Law in English, French, German, Italian and Spanish" by Stefania Cavagnoli and Laura Mori (eds.). Berlin, Frank and Timme 2019. ZERL-Zeitschrift für Europäische Rechtslinguistik.

Hicks, M. 1998. *Warwick the Kingmaker*. Oxford: Oxford University Press.

Jackson, Bernard S. 1995. *Making Sense in Law*. Liverpool: Deborah Charles Publications.

Kelley, Christopher R. 2018. An Essay on Legal Writing in plain English. *Kyiv-Mohyla Law and Politics Journal* 4:175–193.

Kopaczyk, Joanna. 2009. (Multi-word) Units of Meaning in 16th-century Legal Scots. In *Selected Proceedings of the 2008 Symposium on New Approaches in English Historical Lexis (HEL-LEX 2)*, ed. R. W. McConchie, 88–95. Somerville, MA: Cascadilla Proceedings Project.

Laster, Kathy. 2001. *Law as Culture*. Annandale: The Federation Press.

Law Reform Commission of Victoria. 2017. *Plain English and The Law report*. https://www.lawreform.vic.gov.au/wp-content/uploads/2022/04/Plain-English-and-the-Law-republished_forweb.pdf.

Leonardi, Vanessa. 2007. *Gender and Ideology in Translation: Do Women and Men Translate Differently? A Contrastive Analysis from Italian into English.* Bern: Peter Lang.

Leonardi, V., and P. Giampieri. 2024. Translating Employment Contracts: Insights from Corpus Linguistics. *Annali del Dipartimento di Metodi e Modelli per l'Economia, il Territorio e la Finanza*, 115–134.

Levinson, Stephen C. 1983. *Pragmatics*. Cambridge: Cambridge University Press.

Longinotti, Daniela. 2009. Problemi specifici della traduzione giuridica: Traduzione di sentenze dal tedesco all'inglese. *Quaderni di Palazzo Serra* 17:1–38. http://www.lcm.unige.it/ricerca/pub/17/longinotti.pdf.

Marchand, Hans. 1960. *The Categories and Types of Present-Day English Word Formation: A Synchronic-Diachronic Approach*. Wiesbaden: Otto Harrassowitz.

Mattila, Heikki E. S. 2013. *Comparative Legal Linguistics: Language of Law, Latin and Modern Lingua Francas*. 2nd ed. Translated by Christopher Goddard. London: Routledge.

Mellinkoff, David. 1963. *The Language of the Law*. Boston: Little Brown and Co.

Miller, Casey, and Kate Swift. 1980. *The Handbook of Nonsexist Writing*. Harper and Row.

Mossman, Mary Jane. 1994. The Use of Non-Discriminatory Language in the Law. *Canadian Bar Review* 73 (3): 347–371.

Nystedt, Jane. 2000. L'italiano nei documenti della CEE: le sequenze di parole. In *Linguistica giuridica italiana e tedesca. Atti del Convegno di studi 'Linguistica giuridica italiana e tedesca: obiettivi, approcci, risultati'*, ed. Daniela Veronesi, 273–284. Padova: Unipress.

Pavlíčková, Eva. 2008. Ways of Addressing in Legal Discourse. *Discourse and Interaction* 1 (1): 87–98.

Payling, S. J. 1986. Inheritance and Local Politics in the Later Middle Ages: The Case of Ralph. *Lord Cromwell, and the Heriz Inheritance, Nottingham Medieval Studies* 30:67–96.

Pontrandolfo, Gianluca. 2023. The Importance of Being Patterned. Old and New Perspectives on Legal Phraseology. In *Handbook of terminology*, ed. Łucjia Biel and Hendrik J. Kockaert, vol. 3, 124–151. Amsterdam: John Benjamins.

Saha, Tushar Kanti. 2010. *Textbook on Legal Methods, Legal Systems and Research*. New Delhi: Universal Law Publishing Co.

Scotto di Carlo, G. (2013). The language of the UN: vagueness in security council resolutions relating to the second gulf war. *International Journal for the Semiotics of Law-Revue Internationale de Sémiotique Juridique 26*(3), 693–706.

Simpson, A. W. B. 1961. *An Introduction to the History of the Land Law*. Oxford: Oxford University Press.

Soames, Scott. 2014. *Analytic Philosophy in America: And Other Historical and Contemporary Essays*. Princeton: Princeton University Press. https://doi.org/10.1515/9781400850464-015.

Solan, Lawrence M. 2012. Linguistic Issues in Statutory Interpretations. In *The Oxford Handbook of Language and Law*, ed. Peter Tiersma and Lawrence M. Solan, 87–99. Oxford: Oxford University Press.

Spender, Dale. 1980. *Man Made Language*. London: Routledge and Kegan Paul.

Strunk, William, and Elwyn Brooks White. 2000. *The Elements of Style*. New York: Allyn and Bacon.

Strzelczyk, Kati Pajak. 2019. How to Write Gender-neutral Contracts. *National Law Review* 9 (294): 1–3.

Thompson, John B. 1984. *Studies in the Theory of Ideology*. Cambridge: Polity.

Tiersma, Peter. 1999. *Legal Language*. Chicago: University of Chicago Press.

Wedd, I. K. (2020). *Gavelkind and the Land Market in Somerden Hundred, Kent, 1550–1700*. https://doi.org/10.17863/CAM.49923

Williams, Christopher. 2004. Legal Language and Plain Language: An Introduction. *ESP Across Culture* 1:111–124.

Williams, Christopher. 2023. *The Impact of Plain Language on Legal English in the United Kingdom*. London/New York: Routledge.

5

Corpus-Based Analyses: Findings and Discussion

5.1 Complex Prepositional and Adverbial Phrases

The examination of complex prepositional and adverbial phrases across these three legal corpora provides insights into the varying stylistic and functional choices embedded within each corpus. These differences likely reflect the specific historical, national or transnational contexts of the corpora as well as shifts in legal linguistic trends over time (Table 5.1).

In legal language, complex prepositional and adverbial phrases are fundamental, marked by their precise semantic meaning, which serves to prevent ambiguity. As previously acknowledged by Coulthard and Johnson (2010), complex prepositions, in contrast to simpler forms, provide more nuanced meanings, a quality that is particularly important in legal settings where clarity is essential to prevent varied interpretations. This theoretical stance is reflected in the common occurrence of specific complex prepositional phrases within legal texts, such as those used in EU legislation, where referential markers play a crucial role in ensuring legal consistency across different jurisdictions. For example, the phrase *any such* appears most frequently in BoLC, with 186.75 occurrences per

V. Leonardi, P. Giampieri, *Legal English through the Ages*,
https://doi.org/10.1007/978-3-032-02172-4_5

Table 5.1 Corpus analysis of prepositional and adverbial phrases

	CHELAR		BLaRC		BoLC	
Complex prepositions	No.	Freq. pmT	No.	Freq. pmT	No	Freq. pmT
Any such	54	100.12	795	79.21	10,231	**186.75**
As such	28	**51.92**	516	51.41	2,169	39.59
By virtue of	99	183.56	832	82.90	18,237	**332.88**
For and concerning	4	**7.42**	0	0.00	0	0.00
For and during	11	**20.40**	1	0.10	2	0.04
For and in the name	1	**1.85**	0	0.00	0	0.00
For and on behalf of	5	**9.27**	18	1.79	49	0.89
From time to time	32	**59.33**	261	26.01	3,124	57.02
In respect of	120	222.50	4,599	458.25	51,313	**936.62**
In the event of	13	24.10	298	**29.69**	1,193	21.78
Irrespective of	1	1.85	223	**22.22**	565	10.31
No(t) more than	8	14.83	554	55.20	3,430	**62.61**
Other than	52	96.42	1,242	123.75	15,157	**276.66**
Pursuant to	45	83.44	1,331	132.62	8,999	**164.26**
To wit	70	**129.79**	0	0.00	8	0.15
Until such [+noun]	7	**12.98**	50	4.98	406	7.41
Without prejudice	4	7.42	478	47.63	1,994	36.40

million tokens (pmT), aligning with Biel's (2015) observation that EU legislative texts prioritise referential patterns to navigate multilingual legislation. The phrase functions as a referential marker to establish broad categorical references, ensuring legal consistency across different legal traditions within the EU. This is crucial, as Biel (2015) highlights, because EU directives and regulations aim for uniform application across jurisdictions, necessitating precise yet adaptable terminology. The contrast between BoLC and other corpora, such as BLaRC (79.21 pmT) and CHELAR (100.12 pmT), underscores the heightened need for referential clarity in EU law, reinforcing Biel's distinction between national and supranational legal drafting styles.

The phrase *as such* exhibits notable stability across CHELAR (51.92 pmT) and BLaRC (51.41 pmT), suggesting its longstanding role in British Common Law for marking categorical distinctions. This stability implies that *as such* functions as a well-established linguistic marker, reinforcing precise legal categorisations without necessarily bearing direct legal weight. The phrase serves a primarily discursive function, helping legal texts delineate and qualify conceptual boundaries. This consistency aligns with Pontrandolfo's (2023) distinction between "legal phraseology" and "phraseology in legal language". While the former comprises formulaic expressions with direct legal implications, such as *beyond reasonable doubt* or *without prejudice*, the latter, where *as such* belongs, consists of linguistic structures that aid clarity and coherence in legal texts without altering substantive legal meanings. Its presence in British legal corpora reflects a preference for precise categorisation, an essential feature of Common Law tradition, which relies heavily on precedent and case-by-case reasoning. The slightly lower frequency of *as such* in BoLC (39.59 pmT) may suggest that EU legal discourse employs alternative mechanisms for clarification. Given that EU legal texts are often drafted in multiple languages and subsequently translated, the need for phraseological adaptability might lead to variations in preferred linguistic structures. Multilingual drafting constraints necessitate precision while avoiding ambiguous phrasing that may not translate uniformly across legal systems. Consequently, EU legal texts may favour more explicit lexical or syntactic means of expressing categorical distinctions, such as *in that sense* or *in this capacity*, which provide clarity without potential ambiguity in translation.

The prominence of *by virtue of* in BoLC (332.88 pmT) compared to CHELAR (183.56 pmT) and BLaRC (82.90 pmT) highlights an important theoretical implication regarding the evolution of legal phraseology across different legal traditions. As noted by Bhatia (2010), legal language frequently employs complex prepositions to indicate causation, justification or the source of legal authority. In this context, *by virtue of* functions as a formal mechanism for establishing a direct link between a legal provision and its underlying justification, making it particularly relevant in legal texts where precision and explicitness are paramount. The overwhelming presence of *by virtue of* in BoLC suggests that modern EU legal drafting places a heightened emphasis on explicitly codifying legal justifications and entitlements. This observation aligns with Biel's (2015) findings, which indicate that EU legal texts often exhibit a strong preference for unambiguous formulations to ensure clarity across multiple linguistic and legal systems. Given the multilingual nature of EU legal drafting, the use of standardised expressions like *by virtue of* helps maintain consistency and interpretive stability across different language versions, reducing the risk of ambiguity in legal obligations. By contrast, the significantly lower frequency of *by virtue of* in BLaRC (82.90 pmT) and CHELAR (183.56 pmT) may reflect historical drafting conventions within British Common Law, where causative relationships have traditionally been expressed through alternative formulations such as *pursuant to*, *under* or *in accordance with*. The preference for such variations aligns with broader historical trends in British legal drafting, particularly the movement toward plainer legal language. The Law Reform Commission of Victoria (2017) highlights a conscious shift away from unnecessarily complex legal terminology in favour of more accessible language, a trend that may account for the relative decline of *by virtue of* in British legal corpora. Furthermore, the contrast in frequency between CHELAR and BLaRC suggests that different branches of British legal discourse may exhibit varying degrees of reliance on formal causative expressions. While CHELAR retains a moderate use of *by virtue of*, BLaRC, which comprises case law and legal argumentation, appears to favour more flexible or context-specific expressions. This distinction may stem from the inherently dynamic nature of case law where judicial reasoning often relies on argumentative strategies that incorporate a wider range of linguistic structures.

In contrast, phrases such as *for and concerning* and *for and during* appear almost exclusively in CHELAR, reinforcing Rábade's (2007) assertion that older British Common Law texts frequently relied on intricate multi-word phrases to delineate complex legal relationships. These constructions, often characteristic of traditional legal drafting, served to establish nuanced connections between legal subjects, obligations and conditions, ensuring thoroughness and precision in legal interpretation. Their presence in CHELAR suggests that historical British legal texts favoured elaborate phraseology as a means of reducing ambiguity, a hallmark of the conventional reliance of legal English on redundancy and explicitness to pre-empt interpretative disputes. The near absence of these expressions in BLaRC and BoLC indicates a significant shift in legal drafting practices towards simpler, more transparent linguistic constructions. This transition aligns with broader linguistic trends observed by Dvořáková (2022), who argues that contemporary British legal writing increasingly prioritises clarity over syntactic complexity. The preference for more direct and streamlined expressions reflects an effort to make legal texts more accessible to both legal professionals and laypersons, moving away from the dense, archaic structures that historically characterised legal English. This evolution can also be contextualised within the wider plain language movement, which seeks to make legal discourse more comprehensible without sacrificing precision. As noted by the Law Reform Commission of Victoria (2017), modern legal drafting increasingly emphasises brevity and readability, advocating for the elimination of unnecessarily convoluted phraseology. The decline of *for and concerning* and *for and during* in contemporary legal corpora suggests that drafters now favour alternative constructions that convey the same meaning with greater efficiency, such as *regarding*, *concerning* or *during the period of*, which reduce redundancy while maintaining legal accuracy. Moreover, the absence of these phrases in BoLC suggests that EU legal drafting conventions may further reinforce this trend. Given the multilingual nature of EU law, where clarity and consistency across translations are paramount, legal drafters may deliberately avoid complex multi-word expressions that could introduce interpretative discrepancies across different language versions.

The phrase *in respect of* is notably prevalent in legal texts, particularly within the context of EU law, where it plays a crucial role in maintaining consistency across diverse legal systems. Its highest frequency in the BoLC corpus (936.62 pmT) underscores its function in ensuring harmonised terminology, aligning with Robertson and Mac Aodha's (2023) argument that harmonisation facilitates legal integration, particularly within the EU, where multilingualism necessitates precise and stable phrasing. The use of deferential phrases like *in respect of* contributes to achieving equivalence in meaning across different languages and legal traditions, reinforcing its value in legal drafting. The continued presence of this phrase in BLaRC (458.25 pmT) and CHELAR (222.50 pmT) further highlights its enduring significance in British legal language, suggesting that, despite linguistic evolution, certain expressions persist due to their functional necessity. This aligns with Toktobaev and Urmatova's (2024) observation that foundational legal phrases endure because of their established roles in legal discourse. Furthermore, the internationalisation of contract law reflects a broader movement towards adopting harmonised legal frameworks, often incorporating traditional phrases to ensure clarity and consistency across jurisdictions (Li 2024). The prevalence of *in respect of* exemplifies this trend, demonstrating how legal language balances precision with adaptability in an increasingly globalised legal landscape.

The persistence of antiquated expressions in legal terminology is exemplified by the analysis of the phrase *from time to time*. This phrase exhibits a relatively high frequency in both CHELAR at 59.33 pmT and BoLC at 57.02 pmT, in contrast to its lower occurrence in BLaRC at 26.01 pmT. This disparity suggests that both historical British Common Law and contemporary EU legal texts place significant value on periodicity markers, potentially as a component of procedural or precedent-based obligations, as noted by Giampieri in 2016. The reduced frequency in BLaRC may indicate a shift in modern British legal reporting towards more direct and alternative expressions for denoting periodicity. Adams (2024) notes that this expression remains in use in modern legal drafting to clarify that a right is not limited to a single occasion. Instead, it implies use on one or more occasions, effectively serving to ensure that a party is not restricted to exercising a right only once. In contexts involving discretion, *from time to time* is used to convey the meaning of "on one or more occasions", thereby providing clarity regarding the scope of a given right.

The phrase *in the event of* appears consistently across all three corpora, underscoring its fundamental function in contingency language, a key characteristic of legal drafting (Anderson 2006). Its frequent usage reflects the necessity for legal texts to anticipate and account for potential future occurrences, ensuring comprehensive coverage of possible scenarios. The slightly higher occurrence in BLaRC (29.69 pmT) suggests a heightened emphasis on articulating hypothetical legal conditions, reinforcing Solan's (2018) argument that legal texts must accommodate indeterminacy to maintain flexibility in application. This aligns with the broader notion that legal language must balance precision with the ability to address unforeseen circumstances. However, this reliance on contingency language also exemplifies a persistent tension in legal discourse: while such structures enhance adaptability, they may simultaneously introduce layers of complexity that challenge clarity. This paradox highlights an inherent difficulty in legal drafting, that is, ensuring that legal provisions are both comprehensive and comprehensible, a challenge that remains at the heart of legal linguistic scholarship.

The phrase *irrespective of* emerges as the most prevalent in the BLaRC corpus, registering 22.22 pmT, in contrast to 10.31 pmT in BoLC and a markedly lower 1.85 pmT in CHELAR. This disparity indicates a modern British predilection for incorporating explicit disclaimers and a commitment to neutral legal language, a trend that accords with contemporary linguistic preferences for precision and directness (Ďuricová 2023). This heightened frequency in BLaRC not only reinforces the notion that modern legal drafting favours unambiguous formulations but also suggests that explicit disclaimers are deemed essential in ensuring that legal documents can withstand varied interpretations and unforeseen contingencies. The deliberate use of *irrespective of* functions as a linguistic tool designed to circumscribe the application of clauses, thereby reducing interpretative vagueness and enhancing the overall clarity of the text. In contrast, the minimal occurrence in CHELAR may be indicative of an older linguistic tradition where such disclaimers were less central to legal drafting. This variation underscores an evolution in legal language: while earlier styles may have accepted a degree of ambiguity or assumed contextual understanding, contemporary approaches prioritise explicitness to mitigate the risks of misinterpretation. Thus, the observed frequency differences not only reflect shifting stylistic preferences over time but also highlight the inherent tension between maintaining legal precision and managing the complexities of legal discourse.

The phrase *without prejudice* appears most frequently in BLaRC (47.63 pmT), is moderately present in BoLC (36.40 pmT) and is comparatively rare in CHELAR (7.42 pmT). This distribution supports Pontrandolfo's (2023) analysis of how legal phraseology evolves in response to changing legal and communicative needs. While *without prejudice* does not introduce direct legal effects, it serves as a crucial linguistic device to limit legal liability, reinforcing its role in safeguarding legal positions without compromising substantive rights. The notably higher frequency in modern British legal reporting, particularly in BLaRC, suggests an increasing emphasis on explicit legal disclaimers, aligning with broader trends towards precision and accessibility in legal drafting (Didikin 2020). This reflects a legal culture that prioritises clarity and the mitigation of interpretative ambiguity, ensuring that legal statements are carefully framed to prevent unintended consequences. In contrast, the significantly lower occurrence in CHELAR may indicate that earlier legal drafting conventions relied less on explicit disclaimers, potentially assuming a greater degree of implicit legal understanding between parties. This shift highlights how legal language adapts to contemporary demands for greater explicitness and transparency. However, while such disclaimers enhance certainty, they also contribute to the complexity of legal texts, illustrating the ongoing challenge of balancing precision with readability in legal discourse.

5.2 Deixis

The analysis of deictic elements across the three legal corpora seems to indicate significant disparities in the frequency of *legalese* expressions, which may suggest a significant evolution in the style and complexity of legal language. These findings could potentially reflect both the historical contexts and specific legal requirements inherent within each corpus. CHELAR, which encompasses texts from 1535 to 1999, exhibits a pronounced reliance on formal, often archaic deictic terms. In contrast, the lower frequencies observed in BLaRC and BoLC may hint at a gradual shift towards a more streamlined and accessible style in contemporary British and EU legal documents. This evolution could be interpreted as an adaptation to changing societal expectations regarding legal clarity and accessibility (Table 5.2).

The phrase *above-mentioned* is notably prevalent in the Corpus of Historical English Legal Acts and Reports (CHELAR), appearing at a frequency of 35.23 occurrences per million tokens (pmT). This is in stark contrast to its significantly lower frequency in the British Law Report Corpus (BLaRC) (3.09 pmT) and the Body of Legal Contracts (BoLC) (3.76 pmT). Such a disparity aligns with Bhatia's (2010) observation that deictic markers, such as *above-mentioned*, play a fundamental role in maintaining internal coherence and ensuring continuity within legal discourse. These markers have historically been used to create explicit cross-references within complex legal documents, reducing ambiguity and

Table 5.2 Corpus analysis of deictic elements

	CHELAR		BLaRC		BoLC	
Legalese elements	No.	Freq. pmT	No.	Freq. pmT	No.	Freq. pmT
Above mentioned, above-mentioned	19	**35.23**	31	3.09	206	3.76
Aforementioned	4	**7.42**	20	1.99	63	1.15
Aforesaid	1005	**1,863.42**	55	5.48	1,015	18.53
Hereinafter	22	**40.79**	87	8.67	640	11.68
Hereof	11	**20.40**	49	4.88	449	8.20
Heretofore	12	**22.25**	1	0.10	6	0.11
Hereunto	2	**3.71**	1	0.10	28	0.51
The said	3581	**6,639.70**	424	42.25	4,463	81.46
Therein	198	**367.12**	129	12.85	1,097	20.02
Thereinafter	5	**9.27**	0	0.00	6	0.11
Thereinbefore	3	**5.56**	0	0.00	0	0.00
Thereof	548	**1,016.07**	275	27.40	3,560	64.98
Thereunder, thereupon	115	**213.23**	73	7.27	629	11.48
Therewith	15	**27.81**	14	1.39	187	3.41
Wherefore	26	**48.21**	0	0.00	0	0.00
Whereof	120	**222.50**	8	0.80	138	2.52

reinforcing textual structure. However, the noticeable decline of this term in modern legal texts suggests a broader linguistic shift within legal drafting. The increasing preference for clearer indexing systems and improved document structuring has reduced the reliance on archaic anaphoric referencing, signalling a move towards more transparent and user-friendly legal language. This trend reflects the evolving priorities in legal drafting, where accessibility, clarity and efficiency are increasingly favoured over the retention of traditional formalities that, while historically significant, may introduce unnecessary complexity.

Similarly, the phrase *aforementioned* exhibits a comparable pattern of usage, with a frequency of 7.42 occurrences per million tokens (pmT) in CHELAR compared to significantly lower frequencies in BLaRC (1.99 pmT) and BoLC (1.15 pmT). This trend reinforces Coulthard and Johnson's (2007) assertion that historical legal texts frequently relied on personal and social deixis to ensure clarity and maintain unambiguous reference within complex legal discourse. The markedly lower frequency of *aforementioned* in modern legal texts reflects a broader linguistic movement towards simplification and increased readability. As Adams (2024) critiques, the persistence of such antiquated legal expressions can sometimes serve to obscure meaning rather than enhance precision. The observed decline in the use of such terms signals a deliberate shift towards plainer language in legal drafting, aligning with contemporary efforts to enhance accessibility while preserving the necessary level of precision and legal certainty. This evolution underscores the growing recognition that legal texts must be both comprehensible to a wider audience and functionally effective within legal practice.

A particularly striking example of this linguistic shift is the term *aforesaid*, which appears at an exceptionally high frequency in CHELAR with 1,863.42 occurrences per million tokens (pmT). In contrast, its presence in modern legal corpora is significantly diminished, with only 5.48 pmT in BLaRC and 18.53 pmT in BoLC. This stark decline corroborates Tiersma's (1999) argument that spatial deictic terms, often employed anaphorically, were once a fundamental feature of historical legal drafting but have now been largely supplanted by more direct and transparent alternatives. Duckworth and Spyrou (1995: 80) further contend that the continued use of such expressions "sacrifices clarity for gravity", reinforcing the view that modern legal drafting prioritises accessibility over rigid adherence to traditional legal formalities. This linguistic evolution reflects a broader movement within legal discourse towards enhanced clarity and efficiency, ensuring that legal texts remain precise while becoming more comprehensible to both legal professionals and the wider public. By reducing reliance on archaic formulations, contemporary legal drafting aligns with the increasing demand for legal language that is both functional and accessible without compromising its authoritative nature.

The presence of the term *hereinafter* in CHELAR (40.79 occurrences per million tokens, pmT) compared to its significantly lower frequency in BLaRC (8.67 pmT) and BoLC (11.68 pmT) highlights the enduring yet increasingly restricted role of formal deixis in contemporary legal drafting. Giampieri (2024) emphasises that temporal deixis, such as *hereinafter*, has traditionally been crucial in structuring legal obligations over time, ensuring precision in cross-referencing and the chronological sequencing of legal provisions. However, the noticeable decline in its usage suggests a broader shift towards more explicit, reader-friendly phrasing that enhances accessibility without sacrificing legal certainty. This trend reflects the ongoing evolution of legal language, where clarity and precision are progressively prioritised over rigid adherence to archaic formulations. By replacing such formalistic expressions with more straightforward alternatives, modern legal drafting seeks to facilitate comprehension for both legal professionals and laypersons, aligning with contemporary efforts to make legal documents more transparent and navigable.

Further reinforcing this linguistic shift, the term *hereof* appears in CHELAR at a frequency of 20.40 occurrences per million tokens (pmT), yet it is markedly less common in more recent legal corpora, with only 4.88 pmT in BLaRC and 8.20 pmT in BoLC. Abate (1998) notes that such terms are characteristic of traditional legal English due to their capacity to encapsulate complex references in a concise manner, thereby enhancing textual cohesion within legal documents. However, the significant decline in their usage in modern legal texts suggests that drafters increasingly favour more explicit and transparent phrasing, opting for language that is readily understandable to a wider audience. This shift towards greater clarity and accessibility aligns with broader efforts to modernise legal drafting, ensuring that legal documents remain precise while minimising potential ambiguity. By moving away from archaic and highly formalised expressions, contemporary legal language is evolving to facilitate ease of comprehension without compromising its technical accuracy or legal integrity.

The findings for *heretofore* (CHELAR 22.25 pmT, BLaRC 0.10 pmT, BoLC 0.11 pmT) further exemplify the archaic nature of certain deictic expressions within legal English. As Pavlíčková (2008) observes, terms such as *heretofore* once played a crucial role in temporal deixis, providing a precise means of referring to prior events or conditions within legal discourse. However, their near disappearance in modern legal drafting suggests a clear preference for more straightforward and transparent alternatives that enhance readability and reduce ambiguity. A comparable pattern emerges with *hereunto* (CHELAR 3.71 pmT, BLaRC 0.10 pmT, BoLC 0.51 pmT), further reinforcing the notion that contemporary legal English has moved away from formalised spatial deixis in favour of improved clarity and accessibility. This decline in the use of highly traditional legal expressions underscores the broader linguistic shift within legal drafting, where simplicity and precision are increasingly prioritised. By phasing out these archaic terms, modern legal language seeks to balance the need for legal accuracy with the growing demand for comprehensible and user-friendly legal texts, ensuring that legal documents remain both functional and accessible to a wider readership.

A particularly striking finding is the exceptionally high frequency of the phrase *the said* in historical legal texts, with 6,639.70 occurrences pmT in CHELAR, compared to significantly lower frequencies in modern legal corpora (BLaRC 42.25 pmT, BoLC 81.46 pmT). The overwhelming reliance on this expression in older legal documents lends strong support to the argument put forth by both Tiersma (1999) and Giampieri (2016), who highlight that such formulaic constructions were once indispensable for ensuring precise referential specificity within legal discourse. By explicitly linking a given noun to a previously mentioned entity, *the said* functioned as a key mechanism for maintaining clarity and consistency in complex legal texts. However, its dramatic decline in contemporary legal drafting signals a broader linguistic shift towards greater efficiency and readability. Modern legal drafters increasingly favour more streamlined phrasing that reduces redundancy while preserving clarity, aligning with the wider movement towards accessible legal language. This evolution underscores the legal profession's growing recognition that precision need not come at the expense of readability, as legal texts become more comprehensible to both professionals and non-specialist audiences alike.

In terms of spatial deixis, the term *therein* exhibits a significant decline in frequency, appearing 367.12 times pmT in CHELAR, compared to markedly lower occurrences in more recent legal corpora (BLaRC 12.85 pmT, BoLC 20.02 pmT). As both Abate (1998) and Williams (2023) observe, legal terms prefixed with *there-*, such as *therein*, *thereof* and *thereunder*, once played a crucial role in providing precise cross-referencing mechanisms within legal texts, reducing ambiguity in complex legal provisions. However, their intricate and somewhat archaic nature has led to a decline in their use, as modern legal drafting increasingly prioritises linguistic clarity and ease of comprehension. This reduction in frequency reflects a broader movement towards simplifying legal language, ensuring that legal documents remain both precise and accessible. By replacing these formalised terms with more explicit alternatives, contemporary legal discourse aligns with the ongoing effort to enhance readability and facilitate a clearer understanding of legal texts for both professionals and the wider public.

Further reinforcing this linguistic shift, terms such as *thereinafter* and *whereof* exhibit a dramatic decline in usage, highlighting the broader movement away from archaic legal constructions. *Thereinafter* appears with a frequency of 9.27 occurrences pmT in CHELAR, yet it is entirely absent from BLaRC (0.00 pmT) and occurs only marginally in BoLC (0.11 pmT). Similarly, *whereof*, which was once a staple of legal English, has seen a substantial reduction, from 222.50 pmT in CHELAR to just 0.80 pmT in BLaRC and 2.52 pmT in BoLC. This decline aligns with Duckworth and Spyrou's (1995) argument that such expressions, though historically significant for precision and formalism, have been largely supplanted by clearer and more transparent constructions in modern legal drafting. The diminishing use of these terms underscores the evolving nature of legal language, where accessibility and readability are increasingly prioritised over rigid adherence to traditional phraseology. By replacing complex and potentially opaque formulations with more explicit alternatives, contemporary legal drafting continues to move towards greater clarity, ensuring that legal texts remain both functional and comprehensible to a wider audience.

Overall, the practical analysis corroborates theoretical insights regarding the role of deixis in legal language. The high frequency of formal deictic expressions in historical texts aligns with Bhatia's (2010) assertion that legal English has traditionally relied on referential markers to maintain textual cohesion. However, the marked reduction in their usage within contemporary corpora suggests a deliberate shift towards accessibility and clarity, mirroring broader linguistic trends in legal drafting. While some deictic elements remain essential in legal discourse for maintaining precision and coherence, modern legal texts increasingly favour simplified structures to enhance readability without sacrificing accuracy. This trend reflects the ongoing evolution of legal language, balancing the necessity of precise reference with the need for comprehensibility in contemporary legal practice.

5.3 Vagueness

The analysis of vagueness markers across the three corpora reveals discernible trends that may suggest a movement towards greater specificity in modern British and EU legal language when compared to historical British Common Law texts. However, while these shifts appear consistent, it is possible that such changes are influenced by a range of factors, including the evolving functions of legal documents, the differing jurisdictions represented and broader linguistic shifts within legal discourse (Table 5.3).

The term *howsoever* appears most frequently in CHELAR, with a recorded frequency of 11.12 occurrences pmT. In contrast, its presence is significantly diminished in more recent legal corpora, with only 0.50 pmT in BLaRC and a marginal 1.53 pmT in BoLC. This disparity suggests that historical British law reports may have relied more heavily on this term to introduce broad, all-encompassing provisions, thereby affording a degree of interpretative flexibility within legal texts. It could be argued that this linguistic flexibility was particularly valued in earlier legal contexts, where legal drafters sought to ensure inclusivity and adaptability in legislative and contractual language. As Dickerson (1986) observes, a certain level of vagueness in legal discourse can, in some instances, be advantageous, allowing laws to remain applicable to evolving circumstances and unforeseen legal issues. This view is echoed by Endicott (2000), who highlights that legal vagueness permits judicial discretion, ensuring laws can adapt to specific cases and shifting societal contexts. Similarly, Jónsson (2009) argues that vague legal language encourages interpretative flexibility, preventing the need for frequent

Table 5.3 Corpus analysis of vagueness elements

	CHELAR		BLaRC		BoLC	
Vagueness	No.	Freq. pmT	No.	Freq. pmT	No	Freq. pmT
Howsoever	6	**11.12**	5	0.50	84	1.53
Whatsoever	65	**120.52**	200	19.93	686	12.52
Whomsoever, whosoever	4	**7.42**	13	1.30	43	0.78
Wheresoever	7	**12.98**	3	0.30	9	0.16
Soever	6	**11.12**	0	0.00	2	0.04

legislative amendments. However, the sharp decline in *howsoever* in modern legal texts suggests a shift towards greater precision, with contemporary drafters prioritising clarity over broad, open-ended phrasing. While this trend enhances legal certainty, it may also reduce the adaptability once afforded by such expressions.

Similarly, the term *whatsoever* follows a comparable pattern, with a frequency of 120.52 occurrences pmT in CHELAR, far exceeding its occurrence in BLaRC at 19.93 pmT and BoLC at 12.52 pmT. This substantial presence in historical British Common Law texts suggests a strong preference for comprehensive language, where *whatsoever* functions to encompass all possible instances or interpretations of a particular concept. The reduced frequency in modern British and EU legal corpora may indicate a shift towards concision, reflecting a drafting strategy that seeks to avoid overly broad expressions. As Bajčić (2018) explains, legal language must balance abstraction with real-world application, and the decline in broad terms like *whatsoever* could signal an effort to enhance specificity in contemporary legal discourse. This aligns with Endicott's (2000) argument that while vagueness allows for judicial discretion, modern legal drafting often favours precision to ensure clarity. Likewise, Jónsson (2009) highlights that legal texts are increasingly structured to limit interpretative ambiguity, reinforcing the trend towards more precise language. Nevertheless, it remains plausible that *whatsoever* is retained in specific contexts where exhaustive coverage is deemed essential, particularly in contractual and statutory provisions that require an all-encompassing scope. This evolution underscores the ongoing refinement of legal language, balancing the need for certainty with the necessity of flexibility in interpretation.

The terms *whomsoever* and *whosoever* exhibit similar tendencies, appearing at 7.42 occurrences pmT in CHELAR, but at much lower frequencies in BLaRC (1.30 pmT) and BoLC (0.78 pmT). These findings suggest that historical British legal language relied on such terms to encompass any potential person within the scope of a legal statement, thereby ensuring open-ended inclusivity. The lower frequency observed in more recent legal texts may indicate a shift away from broad, undefined references in favour of more concrete terms that specify subjects more directly. As Solan (2012) notes, the tension between approximation and precision in legal language presents interpretative challenges, and the declining use of such terms likely reflects efforts to enhance clarity and predictability in legal drafting. This trend aligns with Bajčić's (2018) argument that legal drafters increasingly prioritise specificity over abstraction to improve legal certainty. Similarly, Jónsson (2009) suggests that modern legal texts aim to reduce ambiguity by avoiding terms that allow for overly broad interpretations. Nevertheless, *whomsoever* and *whosoever* may still find some use in areas of law where inclusive language remains necessary, such as in human rights legislation or contractual provisions requiring broad applicability. This evolution highlights the ongoing refinement of legal discourse, balancing the need for inclusivity with the imperative for precision in legal interpretation.

Wheresoever also follows this pattern, with a frequency of 12.98 occurrences pmT in CHELAR, compared to only 0.30 pmT in BLaRC and 0.16 pmT in BoLC. The high frequency observed in historical British Common Law texts suggests a preference for broad spatial references that encompass all possible locations, thereby ensuring comprehensive applicability within legal statements. The decline of *wheresoever* in modern legal texts may indicate a shift towards more precise spatial references, with contemporary legal drafting prioritising unambiguous and clearly defined terms. As Canale (2017) observes, while judges frequently interpret vague statutory language, modern trends indicate a concerted effort to curb indeterminacy, which may explain the reduced use of broad spatial terms. This aligns with Bajčić's (2018) argument that legal language increasingly favours specificity to enhance interpretative clarity, as well as Jónsson's (2009) view that ambiguity is being systematically reduced in modern legislative drafting. However, the specific legal contexts represented in CHELAR and BLaRC may also contribute to this variation, as different genres or types of legal documents require varying degrees of specificity. While *wheresoever* may no longer be a mainstay of legal drafting, it could still appear in contexts where exhaustive spatial coverage remains necessary, such as jurisdictional clauses or territorial applications of legal provisions. This shift ultimately reflects the broader evolution of legal language towards greater clarity and precision.

The term *soever* appears exclusively in CHELAR at 11.12 occurrences pmT and is almost entirely absent in both BLaRC (0.00 pmT) and BoLC

(0.04 pmT). This exclusive or near-exclusive reliance on the term in historical British legal texts suggests a stylistic preference for open-ended language, potentially allowing for broad interpretations that facilitated adaptable legal provisions. Its near-total absence from modern British and EU legal documents aligns with a broader trend towards precision, as contemporary legal drafting seeks to minimise vague constructions to enhance clarity and reduce interpretative freedom. As Endicott (2005) highlights, vagueness plays a crucial role in legal norms by allowing flexibility, yet modern legal texts increasingly prioritise specificity to ensure greater consistency in legal application. This transition mirrors Canale's (2017) argument that while judicial interpretation can accommodate indeterminate language, recent legislative drafting trends indicate a movement towards reducing ambiguity in favour of legal certainty. Similarly, Bajčić (2018) notes that contemporary legal discourse often balances abstraction with precision, suggesting that the decline of *soever* may reflect a strategic effort to avoid overly broad expressions. Nevertheless, it remains plausible that certain legal traditions or specialised legal genres continue to retain *soever* in specific contexts where exhaustive or unrestricted application is necessary, such as in trust law or contractual provisions seeking to preclude limitations. This shift underscores the ongoing evolution of legal language, where clarity and precision increasingly take precedence over traditional formalities.

Overall, the steady decline in the frequency of these vagueness markers from CHELAR to BLaRC and BoLC seems to reflect an evolving preference within modern legal language for specificity and precision. CHELAR reveals a historical reliance on open-ended, flexible language as a means of capturing all potential scenarios and interpretations within legal provisions. In contrast, the lower frequencies noted in BLaRC and BoLC could indicate that contemporary British and EU legal language increasingly favours unambiguous expressions, thus suggesting an intentional reduction in interpretative flexibility. This trend may reflect changing legal standards that prioritise predictability, consistency and transparency.

5.4 Complex or Archaic Verbs

The examination of complex or archaic verbs across the three corpora highlights notable changes that could indicate evolving linguistic practices in legal drafting. These shifts may be influenced by broader trends in legal language, which often retain traditional forms to maintain formality and precision. However, it is also plausible that some variations arise from the unique legal traditions, timeframes and genre differences present within each corpus (Table 5.4).

The modal verb *shall* exhibits considerable variation across the corpora, with a notably higher frequency in BoLC at 3,630.02 occurrences pmT, compared to 1,767.00 pmT in CHELAR and just 490.03 pmT in BLaRC. This substantial increase in BoLC shows that European Union legal drafters continue to adopt this modal in directives and judgments. As Tiersma (1999) and Williams (2023) observe, *shall* is one of the most debated terms in legal English due to its dual function in expressing both futurity and obligation, which can introduce ambiguity. However, as highlighted by Endicott (2005), legal language often retains prescriptive structures to ensure precision and minimise interpretative uncertainty, which may explain *shall*'s continued prominence in BoLC. At the same time, the overall frequency of *shall* does not necessarily reveal whether legal professionals, particularly judges, align with criticisms regarding its prescriptive use. Williams (2023: 103) notes that court judgments primarily focus on detailing case facts rather than engaging in linguistic deliberation. Furthermore, judges commonly employ *shall* with

Table 5.4 Corpus analysis of complex or archaic verbs

	CHELAR		BLaRC		BoLC	
Complex verbs	No.	Freq. pmT	No.	Freq. pmT	No	Freq. pmT
Shall	953	1,767.00	4,918	490.03	198,872	**3,630.02**
Deem	20	37.08	509	50.72	4,583	**83.65**
Endeavour	9	**16.69**	118	11.76	398	7.26
Estop	12	**22.25**	68	6.78	185	3.38
Fail to	36	66.75	2,633	**262.35**	8,443	154.11
Resolve	75	**139.06**	1,065	106.12	2,424	44.25
Vested in	61	**113.10**	123	12.26	1,301	23.75

first-person pronouns to indicate future action, a usage widely accepted in British English. The more contested use of *shall*, which plain language advocates argue should be replaced by *must* or *is to*, occurs in third-person contexts to express obligation. The lower frequency of *shall* in the BLaRC corpus reflects the language of judicial decisions, which is essentially descriptive by nature, focusing on the narration of past events rather than the formulation of new rules intended to regulate present or future circumstances. Nevertheless, *shall* tends to remain prevalent in certain legal contexts such as in contractual obligations or EU statutory provisions.

The verb *deem* appears most frequently in BoLC at 83.65 occurrences pmT, followed by BLaRC at 50.72 pmT and CHELAR at 37.08 pmT. This distribution suggests that *deem* remains a fixture in both modern British and EU legal texts, likely due to its function in formally assigning or asserting legal status. However, its widespread use is not without criticism, as its inherent ambiguity and authoritative tone can, in some instances, obscure rather than clarify legal meaning. As Duckworth and Spyrou (1995: 13) observe, *deem* functions as a more complex synonym for *consider to be*, yet it carries distinct implications that can create interpretative challenges. While often employed to establish definitive legal determinations, the verb has been criticised for its artificiality and the way it constructs legal fictions, stating that something *is* the case, regardless of whether it actually *is* so in reality. This can lead to potential inconsistencies, particularly in common law jurisdictions where judicial interpretation plays a crucial role. The notably high frequency of *deem* in BoLC may reflect the European Union's preference for rigidly defined legal frameworks, where clarity and standardisation take precedence over interpretative flexibility. However, this raises concerns about whether such rigid formulations allow for sufficient adaptability in complex legal disputes. Moreover, while *deem* appears less frequently in CHELAR, its presence in historical legal texts suggests that English legal drafting has long relied on formalised expressions that prioritise legal certainty over linguistic transparency.

The verb *endeavour* exhibits a clear decline across the corpora, with its highest frequency in CHELAR at 16.69 occurrences pmT, followed by 11.76 pmT in BLaRC and just 7.26 pmT in BoLC. This downward trend suggests a diminishing role for *endeavour* in modern legal drafting, likely due to its perceived vagueness and lack of enforceability. As Bhatia (2010) notes, *endeavour* often serves as a convoluted substitute for *try*, unnecessarily complicating legal language while failing to establish a firm obligation. Historically, the term may have been favoured for its ability to impose a duty to make reasonable efforts without guaranteeing a specific outcome, allowing flexibility in contractual or statutory obligations. Nevertheless, this flexibility also creates legal uncertainty, as it leaves room for subjective interpretation regarding the extent of effort required. In high-stakes legal contexts, such ambiguity can lead to disputes over whether a party has sufficiently "endeavoured" to fulfil an obligation. The notable reduction of *endeavour* in BoLC aligns with modern trends in legal drafting, which prioritise explicit and enforceable obligations over vague commitments. EU directives and contractual agreements increasingly favour direct alternatives such as *must* or *shall ensure*, which leave little room for ambiguity. This shift reflects a broader movement in legal language towards greater precision, ensuring that obligations are clearly defined and legally binding. Despite this decline, *endeavour* has not disappeared entirely, and its residual use may persist in contexts where flexibility is still desirable. However, its decreasing prevalence suggests that contemporary legal drafting is moving away from imprecise expressions, reinforcing the ongoing shift towards clarity, enforceability and reduced interpretative ambiguity in legal texts.

The verb *estop*, a term deeply rooted in common law doctrines, appears most frequently in CHELAR at 22.25 occurrences pmT, while its frequency is significantly lower in BLaRC at 6.78 pmT and BoLC at just 3.38 pmT. This marked decline suggests a diminishing role for *estop* in modern legal drafting, reflecting broader linguistic and doctrinal shifts within British and EU legal frameworks. As Bhatia (2010) observes, *estop* is an archaic legal verb meaning *prevent*, traditionally used in the context of estoppel doctrines to bar a party from asserting a claim or contradicting a previous position. Its declining frequency signals a move away from rigid common law terminology in favour of clearer, more universally comprehensible phrasing. The lower occurrence in BoLC is particularly telling, as it aligns with the EU's legal traditions, which do not centre around common law principles and instead emphasise codified statutes and regulations. This disparity seems to suggest that *estop* and related terminology may be losing relevance outside jurisdictions that adhere strictly to common law traditions. The reduced frequency of *estop* in BLaRC further supports the argument that British legal language is evolving towards greater accessibility and modernisation. While common law principles remain fundamental to the British legal system, contemporary legal drafting increasingly favours terminology that is more widely understood, even among those without formal legal training. The shift away from *estop* may also indicate a preference for explicit statutory provisions that achieve the same legal effect without reliance on doctrinal shorthand.

Conversely, the phrase *fail to* has seen a notable increase in usage, rising from 66.75 occurrences pmT in CHELAR to 262.35 pmT in BLaRC and 154.11 pmT in BoLC. This surge suggests that modern British legal texts increasingly favour *fail to* when explicitly describing omissions or instances of non-compliance, possibly due to its stronger legal connotation in imposing liability for inaction. Bhatia (2010) critiques *fail to* as an unnecessarily complex alternative to *does not*, advocating simpler phraseology to enhance clarity. However, the rising frequency of *fail to* in BLaRC suggests that legal drafters may prefer its more formal and assertive tone, particularly in contexts where legal obligations are framed in terms of compliance and breach. Unlike the more neutral *does not*, *fail to* carries an implicit expectation of duty, reinforcing the notion that a required action was not performed. This distinction likely explains its continued prevalence despite calls for simplification. The comparatively lower frequency of *fail to* in BoLC seems to suggest that EU legal drafting conventions may favour alternative formulations, potentially due to multilingual translation practices and jurisdictional variations across member states. Given the EU's emphasis on legal harmonisation and precision in drafting, different linguistic traditions may favour constructions that avoid the potential ambiguity or interpretative flexibility associated with *fail to*. This concern aligns with Mattissen's (2019) observations on the challenges of coordination and ambiguity in EU legal acts, where linguistic differences can lead to divergences in interpretation. As a result, EU legal drafters often prioritise explicit and unambiguous language to ensure uniform application, which may account for the preference for alternative constructions over *fail to* in EU legal contexts.

The verb *resolve* exhibits a declining frequency across the corpora, decreasing from 139.06 occurrences pmT in CHELAR to 106.12 pmT in BLaRC and further down to 44.25 pmT in BoLC. This trend suggests a shift away from *resolve* in legal drafting, possibly due to its inherent ambiguity. As Giampieri (2022: 30) explains, *resolve* can mean both *decide* and *reaffirm*, which may lead to interpretative uncertainty. Historically, *resolve* was widely used in British legal documents, particularly in legislative and judicial contexts where formal determinations were articulated. However, its diminishing presence indicates a growing preference for more precise alternatives that explicitly define the nature of a legal decision or commitment. The notably lower frequency in BoLC suggests that EU legal frameworks may favour different terminology for decision-making processes, potentially reflecting a divergence from traditional British Common Law vocabulary.

Finally, the phrase *vested in* exhibits a sharp decline across the corpora, appearing most frequently in CHELAR at 113.10 occurrences pmT, before dropping substantially in BoLC to 23.75 pmT and 12.26 pmT in BLaRC. This decrease seems to suggest a significant shift in legal drafting preferences, particularly in British law, where traditional formulations are being replaced with more contemporary and explicit expressions of ownership and rights allocation. As Longinotti (2009) explains, *vested in* signifies legally granted rights or entitlements, often implying permanence or irrevocability. However, its declining usage indicates that modern legal discourse may favour alternative constructions that specify the nature and conditions of rights more precisely. The marked reduction in BLaRC suggests that British legal texts are moving away from older, formalistic phraseology in favour of clearer, more direct language that reduces interpretative ambiguity. This shift aligns with broader trends in legal modernisation, where archaic terminology is increasingly replaced with expressions that enhance clarity and accessibility. The intermediate frequency of *vested in* in BoLC suggests that while the phrase remains relevant in EU legal drafting, alternative formulations may be gaining preference. This could reflect differences in legal traditions between British Common Law and EU frameworks, where multilingual drafting considerations and harmonisation efforts often lead to the adoption of more universally comprehensible terminology. Given the EU's focus on legal certainty, the reduced reliance on *vested in* may indicate a preference for terms that eliminate potential ambiguities associated with proprietary rights and authority.

In summary, CHELAR reflects the prevalence of complex and archaic verbs within traditional British Common Law, whereas both BLaRC and BoLC indicate a gradual but deliberate shift towards linguistic modernisation. The decline of terms such as *endeavour*, *estop* and *vested in* suggests an ongoing effort to enhance clarity and accessibility in legal English, minimising reliance on antiquated phraseology that may obscure meaning. However, the continued prominence of *shall* and *deem*, particularly in BoLC, demonstrates that certain archaic legal forms persist, likely due to their entrenched role in conveying authority and prescriptive legal obligations. This evolving balance between tradition and modernisation underscores the complexity of legal drafting, where precision, interpretability and legal certainty must be carefully calibrated to meet contemporary needs (Table 5.5).

The modal verb *will* appears with a frequency of 991.97 pmT in CHELAR, increasing to 1,145.67 pmT in BLaRC before declining to 639.20 pmT in BoLC. While this pattern may suggest a greater role for *will* in modern British legal texts, particularly within BLaRC, its function differs fundamentally from that of *shall*. Unlike *shall*, which typically conveys obligation, *will* is generally used to indicate futurity and, in most cases, excludes a mandatory meaning. The distinction between these modals is complex and has been widely debated in academic discussions on legal English.

Krapivkina (2017) highlights that *shall* significantly complicates legal discourse due to its ambiguous interpretations. The study outlines three key perspectives on its usage: restricting *shall* to a single, unambiguous meaning, eliminating it entirely from legal drafting, or preserving its

Table 5.5 Corpus analysis of "will" and "must" as alternatives to "shall"

	CHELAR		BLaRC		BoLC	
Alternatives to "shall"	No.	Freq. pmT	No.	Freq. pmT	No	Freq. pmT
Will	535	991.97	11,498	**1,145.67**	35,019	639.20
Must	383	710.14	9,899	**986.34**	41,814	763.23

various functions despite the potential for confusion. To improve clarity and accessibility, particularly for non-experts, Krapivkina suggests replacing *shall* with alternative modal verbs such as *must* or *may*, which provide more precise expressions of obligation and permission.

The rise in *will* from CHELAR to BLaRC may reflect shifting stylistic preferences in judicial language rather than a direct replacement of *shall* for expressing obligation. As Williams (2023) notes, court judgments operate under a distinct set of linguistic conventions compared to legislative texts or directives. Judgments frequently employ *will* in first-person constructions, often as part of judicial reasoning rather than as a prescriptive device. The subsequent decline in BoLC further reinforces the idea that modal usage varies significantly across legal genres, with EU legal documents potentially favouring alternative expressions better suited to transnational legal discourse.

Analogously, the modal verb *must* shows a similar pattern, appearing at 710.14 pmT in CHELAR, increasing to 986.34 pmT in BLaRC and to 763.23 pmT in BoLC. This suggests that *must* has also become a significant alternative to *shall*, particularly within modern British legal discourse. The relatively high frequency of *must* across all three corpora may indicate its function in conveying obligation or necessity, qualities that are often paramount in legal contexts. The consistent presence of *must* could reflect a broader trend towards clarity and assertiveness in legal language, as it tends to convey mandatory requirements more explicitly than *shall*. Nevertheless, the fluctuations observed between CHELAR and BLaRC, followed by a slight decrease in BoLC, may suggest that while *must* remains relevant, its application varies depending on the specific context or jurisdiction.

Scholars have widely examined the decline of *shall* in legal English, identifying several alternative constructions that have taken its place. While *will* is not typically regarded as a substitute due to its different semantic function, *must*, *be to*, and the simple present have emerged as the main alternatives in legislative drafting. These shifts reflect broader efforts to enhance clarity and reduce ambiguity in legal texts. Williams (2013, 2023) notes that the transition away from *shall* in UK legislation became particularly noticeable in the early 2000s, though evidence suggests that this process had already begun in the preceding decade. In its place, *must* has gained traction due to its unequivocal expression of obligation, making it a preferred choice where legal prescriptions need to be clearly enforceable. Similarly, the *be to* construction has been increasingly adopted, particularly in contexts where obligations must be conveyed in a formal but less rigid manner. Despite their growing use in legal drafting, Williams (2023) observes that both *must* and *be to* have seen a decline in general British English since the mid-twentieth century. This suggests that their prominence in legal contexts is driven by the need for precision and enforceability rather than by broader linguistic trends. Garzone (2013) further supports this view, highlighting that while *shall* has become far less common, its replacements serve distinct functions depending on the type of legal text and the degree of obligation required. Ultimately, while *must* and *be to* have largely supplanted *shall* in legislative drafting, certain contexts may still retain traditional expressions due to historical precedent, stylistic conventions or the necessity of maintaining consistency within established legal frameworks.

5.5 Archaic Nouns

The analysis of archaic nouns across the three corpora reveals significant trends that shed light on the evolving nature of legal language. As evidenced by the data in Table 5.6, there is a discernible decline in the use of certain archaic expressions in modern legal contexts. This shift likely reflects broader efforts to modernise legal drafting, prioritising clarity and accessibility over traditional but potentially obscure terminology.

Table 5.6 Corpus analysis of archaic nouns

	CHELAR		BLaRC		BoLC	
Archaic nouns	No.	Freq. pmT	No.	Freq. pmT	No	Freq. pmT
Chattel	37	**68.60**	33	3.29	292	5.33
Deed	448	**830.66**	480	47.83	1,924	35.12
Escrow	2	**3.71**	16	1.59	19	0.35
Malice	12	**22.25**	111	11.06	295	5.38
(This) Instrument	65	**120.52**	325	32.38	6,300	114.99
(These) Presents	17	**31.52**	7	0.70	9	0.16

The term *chattel* refers to movable personal property, encompassing tangible items that are not fixed to land, such as furniture and livestock. In legal contexts, *chattel* has traditionally been used to distinguish personal property from real property, which includes land and buildings. As Cresswell (2021: 472) notes, *chattel*, often encountered in the phrase *goods and chattels*, means "a personal possession". The term originates from Old French *chatel*, derived from medieval Latin *capitale*, ultimately from Latin *capitalis* (of the head), linked to *caput* (head). This etymology reflects its historical association with property ownership, particularly in legal classifications of assets. Corpus data suggest that *chattel* has significantly declined in usage over time. In CHELAR, it appears with a frequency of 68.60 per million tokens (pmT). However, its presence diminishes sharply in more contemporary legal corpora, declining to 3.29 pmT in BLaRC and registering a slightly higher frequency of 5.33 pmT in BoLC. The substantial drop from CHELAR to BLaRC indicates that *chattel*, once a staple of British legal discourse, has largely been replaced by more modern terminology. This shift likely reflects broader efforts to make legal language more transparent and accessible to contemporary audiences. The preference for alternative terms aligns with Bhatia's (2010) argument that *chattel* could often be substituted with *goods* without any loss of legal precision. This linguistic simplification is part of a broader movement in legal drafting aimed at enhancing clarity by replacing archaic terms with more widely understood equivalents. Tiersma (1999) similarly notes this tendency in legal language, where historical terminology persists despite the availability of more accessible alternatives. The continued, albeit limited, presence of *chattel* in BoLC suggests that while its use has diminished overall, certain legal contexts, potentially those influenced by EU legal frameworks, still retain the term due to its traditional significance. The decline of *chattel* exemplifies a wider linguistic transformation in legal discourse. As legal texts increasingly favour clarity and accessibility, terms that were once foundational are gradually being replaced with more contemporary equivalents. The decreasing prominence of *chattel* in modern corpora reinforces the ongoing trend towards legal modernisation, ensuring that legal terminology remains comprehensible and functional in contemporary contexts.

The noun *deed* refers to a formal legal document that conveys ownership or rights concerning property. Historically, *deed* has been fundamental in legal transactions, particularly those involving real estate and the transfer of significant personal property. Its prominence is reflected in its high frequency of 830.66 pmT in CHELAR, underscoring its central role in legal discourse. However, its frequency declines significantly in more contemporary corpora, dropping to 47.83 pmT in BLaRC and further to 35.12 pmT in BoLC. This downward trend suggests a shift in legal drafting practices, where *deed*, despite its continued legal relevance, is being used less frequently in modern texts. A key factor in this decline may be the increasing preference for alternative expressions that align more closely with contemporary legal drafting conventions. As Bhatia (2010) observes, *deed* could often be substituted with *document* without sacrificing legal precision. This shift reflects a broader movement towards clearer and more accessible legal language, reducing reliance on historically entrenched terminology when simpler alternatives are available. The replacement of *deed* with *document* aligns with efforts to modernise legal discourse, making it more comprehensible to both legal professionals and the general public. This trend also relates to Garner's (2002) critique of the "noun plague", which is a tendency towards excessive nominalisation in legal writing. Traditional legal texts often favour abstract nouns, such as *deed*, over more straightforward alternatives, contributing to linguistic opacity. The observed decline in its frequency may therefore signal an effort to curb unnecessary nominalisation, favouring more transparent phrasing that enhances readability and precision. While *deed* remains an essential concept in legal contexts, particularly in property law, its diminishing usage in modern corpora reflects broader shifts in legal drafting practices. The preference for *document* over *deed* illustrates a movement towards linguistic clarity, reinforcing the ongoing transformation of legal language to accommodate contemporary communicative norms.

The term *escrow* refers to a financial arrangement in which a neutral third party temporarily holds funds or documents until predetermined conditions are fulfilled, thereby safeguarding the interests of all parties involved in a transaction. Traditionally significant in property transfers, contract execution and commercial transactions, *escrow* functions as a protective mechanism to ensure compliance with agreed terms before the exchange of assets. Although still relevant in modern financial and legal contexts, the term appears to be gradually falling out of common legal usage, possibly in favour of more accessible terminology. Corpus data support this shift. In CHELAR, *escrow* appears with a frequency of 3.71 pmT, but this decreases to 1.59 pmT in BLaRC and further declines to just 0.35 pmT in BoLC. This downward trend suggests a broader linguistic evolution in legal discourse, where complex or archaic terms are being phased out in favour of clearer and more intuitive alternatives. Duckworth and Spyrou (1995) acknowledge the historical importance of *escrow*, particularly in contract law, but its diminishing use aligns with wider efforts to simplify legal language for greater accessibility. This trend is also noted by Coulthard and Johnson (2007), who highlight ongoing legal reforms aimed at reducing lexical complexity to improve comprehensibility for non-specialists. The decline of *escrow* in legal discourse may also reflect shifts in financial and technological practices. With the rise of digital transactions, automated payment processing and electronic contracts, the mechanisms once explicitly described as *escrow* are now often embedded within broader legal and financial frameworks. Instead of explicitly referencing *escrow*, modern contracts may describe the function in more practical terms, such as "conditional fund holding" or "third-party account management", thereby avoiding reliance on historical terminology.

The noun *malice* refers to the intention or desire to cause harm or injury to another party, particularly within legal contexts concerning torts or criminal law. It has traditionally been integral to discussions about intent and culpability, particularly in cases where the presence or absence of malicious intent determines guilt or liability. However, while *malice* continues to hold significance in certain legal frameworks, its use appears to be declining in contemporary legal discourse, as indicated by corpus frequency data. The term registers a frequency of 22.25 pmT in CHELAR but declines to 11.06 pmT in BLaRC and further to 5.38 pmT in BoLC. This trend suggests that while *malice* remains relevant in specific legal contexts, its prominence is waning, potentially reflecting a broader linguistic shift in legal terminology. Etymologically, *malice* derives from the Latin *malus* ("bad") and is linked to words such as *malign*, *malaise* and *malevolent*. According to Cresswell (2021: 857), it has been a legal term since the fifteenth century, particularly in phrases such as *malice aforethought* (premeditated intent), which distinguishes murder from manslaughter. The historical weight of the term may contribute to its continued, albeit declining, presence in legal discourse. A critical analysis of this decline reveals multiple possible explanations. The drop from CHELAR to BLaRC may indicate an increasing preference for terminology that better encapsulates modern legal interpretations of intent and culpability. Contemporary legal systems tend to favour more precise or nuanced language, distinguishing between different forms of intent, such as *recklessness*, *wilful intent* and *negligence*, rather than relying on a broader and somewhat ambiguous term like *malice*. This aligns with trends in legal drafting and judicial reasoning, which often aim for clarity and specificity to prevent misinterpretation. Moreover, the historical roots of *malice* may contribute to its diminishing use. Duckworth and Spyrou (1995) highlight that the term originates from the Latin *malitia*, meaning "spite". While *malice* has long carried connotations of wrongful intent, modern legal discourse increasingly prioritises terms that unambiguously convey the legal threshold required for culpability. This perspective is supported by Tiersma (1999: 131), who observes that legal language often retains archaic terms despite the availability of clearer and more accessible synonyms. In this case, the persistence of *malice* may reflect the conservative nature of legal language, where historical continuity is sometimes valued over linguistic modernisation.

The phrase *(this) instrument* refers to a formal legal document or agreement, often used interchangeably with *contract* or *deed*. Its presence in legal texts suggests a preference for formal terminology in drafting. Corpus analysis reveals a notable fluctuation in its usage as it appears with a high frequency of 120.52 per million tokens (pmT) in CHELAR, declines to 32.38 pmT in BLaRC and then rises again to 114.99 pmT in BoLC. This pattern suggests a shift in drafting conventions, that is, while *instrument* was widely used in historical legal texts, its frequency declined in some modern British legal documents before resurging in other jurisdictions, possibly due to its continued relevance in EU-influenced legal frameworks. The resurgence of *(this) instrument* in BoLC highlights the persistence of formal legal terminology, even in contexts where more accessible alternatives, such as *document*, might suffice. Bhatia (2010) observes that *instrument* is often retained despite the availability of simpler equivalents, reinforcing the tendency of the legal profession to preserve established terminology. Coulthard and Johnson (2007) further attribute this linguistic conservatism to the prioritisation of legal precision over stylistic diversity, ensuring that documents maintain a degree of specificity that alternative terms may not always convey. A similar pattern is evident in the phrase *(these) presents*, historically used in legal documents to acknowledge gifts or agreements. The frequency of this expression has declined dramatically: from 31.52 pmT in CHELAR to just 0.70 pmT in BLaRC, and further to only 0.16 pmT in BoLC. This steep reduction suggests that the phrase is increasingly regarded as archaic and redundant, aligning with broader trends towards clarity and accessibility in legal drafting. As Tiersma (1999) explains, *these presents* can be replaced with *the present writing* without sacrificing legal precision. This shift exemplifies the modernisation of legal language where obsolete formulations are gradually phased out in favour of clearer alternatives, while still maintaining the authoritative tone traditionally associated with legal discourse.

Overall, the corpus data on archaic legal nouns provide insight into the broader evolution of legal language. The declining frequencies of terms such as *chattel*, *escrow* and *(these) presents* illustrate a shift towards contemporary alternatives that prioritise accessibility and reader comprehension. However, the sustained relevance of *deed* and *(this) instrument* suggests that certain archaic expressions continue to hold significance, particularly in contexts where precision and tradition remain paramount. As Tiersma (1999) and Coulthard and Johnson (2007) have argued, the persistence of such terms can be attributed to their established legal meanings, their role in preserving authoritative tone and the legal profession's resistance to linguistic change. Nonetheless, legal language continues to evolve, with a growing emphasis on simplification, provided that essential legal precision is maintained. Kelley (2018) discusses this balance in relation to nominalisation, highlighting how legal terminology adapts over time while retaining the functional core that ensures clarity and enforceability in legal contexts.

5.6 Law Latin

The data from Table 5.7 show the frequencies of different Law Latin phrases across the three corpora, showing how their usage has changed over time. This change may have been influenced by a range of factors, including shifts in legal practice, the preference for clearer language and regional differences in legal traditions. However, it is important to consider that these trends are not uniform and the use of these Latin expressions can still hold particular relevance in specific contexts or legal systems.

The phrase *a fortiori*, meaning "with stronger reason", historically played a role in legal argumentation by using the strength of one argument to support another. Its frequency in CHELAR stands at 18.54 per million tokens (pmT), indicating that it was relatively common in historical British legal texts. However, its usage declines sharply in more recent legal corpora, dropping to 5.78 pmT in BLaRC and further to just 1.64 pmT in BoLC. This substantial reduction suggests a broader shift away from Latin legal expressions in favour of clearer, more direct language in modern legal discourse. The decline in *a fortiori* aligns with Williams's (2023) argument that Latin expressions persist in legal discourse primarily due to historical convention rather than practical

Table 5.7 Corpus analysis of Law Latin

	CHELAR		BLaRC		BoLC	
Law Latin	No.	Freq. pmT	No.	Freq. pmT	No	Freq. pmT
A fortiori	10	**18.54**	58	5.78	90	1.64
Bona fide	9	**16.69**	80	7.97	364	6.64
De facto	3	5.56	225	**22.42**	214	3.91
De jure, de iure	3	5.56	59	**5.88**	41	0.75
Et seq	3	5.56	58	**5.78**	35	0.64
Ex parte	18	**33.37**	281	28.00	1,463	26.70
In re	29	53.77	597	**59.49**	94	1.72
Inter alia	22	40.79	431	**42.95**	1,235	22.54
Inter partes	3	**5.56**	23	2.29	131	2.39
Ipso facto	3	**5.56**	32	3.19	32	0.58
Prima facie	14	25.96	319	**31.79**	905	16.52
Pro bono	1	**1.85**	17	1.69	24	0.44
Viva voce	2	**3.71**	0	0.00	7	0.13

necessity. While such phrases may carry an air of authority and precision, their diminishing usage suggests that contemporary legal drafting increasingly prioritises accessibility over tradition. As legal language evolves, there is a growing preference for plain English alternatives that ensure clarity for both legal professionals and the general public. This trend also reflects broader movements in legal drafting aimed at enhancing comprehensibility, as discussed by Tiersma (1999). The decreasing frequency of *a fortiori* exemplifies the gradual phasing out of Latin terminology in favour of more transparent legal reasoning. Although such expressions may still appear in specialised legal arguments, their reduced presence in modern corpora indicates that legal language is adapting to contemporary communicative norms, making complex reasoning more accessible to a wider audience.

Similarly, *bona fide*, meaning "in good faith", demonstrates a gradual decline from 16.69 pmT in CHELAR to 7.97 pmT in BLaRC, and further to 6.64 pmT in BoLC. While *bona fide* remains a common term in legal discussions, particularly in contractual and other legal obligations, its decreasing frequency across the corpora suggests a broader linguistic shift towards replacing Latin expressions with more accessible English equivalents. However, this trend must be evaluated in light of the continued importance of *bona fide* in legal contexts, as it embodies the legal principle of good faith, a crucial doctrine in contract and commercial law (Bhatia 2010). The concept of good faith is deeply embedded in legal systems, particularly in common law and civil law traditions, where it serves as a fundamental criterion in assessing the fairness and enforceability of agreements. Therefore, while its usage may be diminishing in general legal discourse, its presence in contemporary legal discussions supports Mattila's (2013: 161) assertion that Latin continues to play a symbolic role in maintaining professional identity within the legal field. Furthermore, the endurance of *bona fide* suggests that certain Latin terms retain their doctrinal significance despite broader trends towards modernisation.

Conversely, *de facto*, meaning "in practice" or "in fact", exhibits an interesting fluctuation. It appears with a frequency of 5.56 pmT in CHELAR, significantly rises to 22.42 pmT in BLaRC, before falling back to 3.91 pmT in BoLC. This fluctuation could indicate the increased relevance of *de facto* in legal contexts where distinctions between legal principles and practical realities are frequently discussed. The peak in BLaRC suggests that, during that period, legal discourse placed greater emphasis on distinguishing between formal legal status (*de jure*) and practical application (*de facto*), a distinction often crucial in areas such as constitutional law, governance and human rights jurisprudence. Williams (2023) highlights that Latin has endured due to its precision in legal argumentation, which may explain the peak in its usage within BLaRC. However, the decline of *de facto* in BoLC suggests a preference for plain English alternatives in modern legal drafting, in line with broader EU initiatives to simplify legal language.

The term *de jure*, meaning "by law", and its variant *de iure* appear with a frequency of 5.56 pmT in CHELAR, slightly increasing to 5.88 pmT in BLaRC before sharply declining to 0.75 pmT in BoLC. The decline in BoLC suggests a move away from formal Latin terminology, reflecting Saha's (2010) observation that legal Latin, while still present, is losing ground to English equivalents in contemporary legal frameworks. This decline could be indicative of a broader shift in legal drafting, where clarity and accessibility are prioritised over adherence to traditional legal language. Nevertheless, its historical importance, particularly in constitutional law, aligns with the argument that Latin persists in legal contexts where the distinction between *de jure* (what is legally mandated) and *de facto* (what occurs in practice) remains crucial (Laster 2001; Giampieri 2016). While the reduced frequency of *de jure* suggests an increasing reliance on English alternatives, its continued presence in legal discourse highlights its enduring conceptual significance. The distinction between *de jure* and *de facto* remains particularly relevant in cases involving governance, human rights and political legitimacy, where legal mandates and practical realities often diverge. The sharp decline in BoLC might reflect efforts to modernise legal language, yet the persistence of *de jure* in earlier corpora underscores its value in precise legal argumentation. As such, while its overall usage may be waning, its role in legal analysis remains essential, reinforcing the view that Latin terms continue to function as markers of legal precision and doctrinal continuity within specialised fields.

The phrase *et seq.*, meaning "and the following", maintains relative stability at 5.56 pmT in CHELAR and 5.78 pmT in BLaRC but drops sharply to 0.64 pmT in BoLC. This decline suggests that while *et seq.* was historically prevalent in British legal texts, its use has diminished in modern legal writing, likely due to a preference for more explicit references (Bhatia 2010). This shift aligns with broader movements to replace Latin abbreviations with clearer language, making legal documents more comprehensible to non-specialists (Duckworth and Spyrou 1995). However, the decline of *et seq.* may also indicate an evolving preference for direct citations over shorthand notation, reflecting an effort to reduce ambiguity in legal texts. The shift away from Latin abbreviations can be attributed to modern legal drafting guidelines that advocate for unambiguous and reader-friendly language, particularly in jurisdictions where legal literacy varies widely. While the term remains recognisable among legal professionals, its decreasing frequency suggests that precision and accessibility are increasingly prioritised over tradition. Moreover, this trend reflects broader linguistic reforms aimed at improving legal transparency and ensuring that legal texts are equally interpretable by both professionals and the general public.

The term *ex parte*, meaning "from one side only", demonstrates consistently high frequencies across all three corpora, with 33.37 pmT in CHELAR, 28.00 pmT in BLaRC and 26.70 pmT in BoLC. This stability indicates that *ex parte* remains a crucial legal term, particularly in judicial proceedings involving unilateral motions. Tiersma (1999) notes that while some Latin phrases have become archaic, others persist due to their precise legal connotations. The sustained usage of *ex parte* reflects its necessity in procedural law, particularly in emergency legal applications where unilateral action is required. The term is indispensable in legal discourse, as it describes a procedural mechanism that allows a party to seek judicial intervention without notifying the opposing party, a crucial aspect of certain protective orders, injunctions and urgent applications. Despite broader shifts towards plain English in legal drafting, the persistence of *ex parte* underscores its functional indispensability. Unlike other Latin terms that have declined due to accessibility concerns, *ex parte* remains entrenched in legal discourse, illustrating that clarity and tradition can coexist when the meaning of a term is both precise and indispensable to judicial processes. Its continued use highlights that while legal language is evolving, certain Latin expressions retain their authority due to their unique role in procedural accuracy and efficiency.

The phrase *in re*, meaning "in the matter of", maintains high frequencies in CHELAR (53.77 pmT) and BLaRC (59.49 pmT) but drops significantly to 1.72 pmT in BoLC. The high frequency in historical legal texts underlines its longstanding use in case law, particularly in probate and administrative law, where matters involving estates, guardianship and public administration often require an impersonal designation. The sharp decrease in BoLC supports the argument that modern EU legal drafting prioritises direct and explicit language over traditional Latin expressions (Garner 2004; Bhatia 2010). This decline also reflects the general movement towards greater transparency in legal writing, where ambiguous or archaic terminology is increasingly replaced with unambiguous English phrases. Additionally, the reduction in *in re* suggests a shift in citation practices, as contemporary case law often adopts more standardised case-naming conventions that do not rely on Latin markers. The decline may also be indicative of a broader tendency within legal discourse to move away from impersonal procedural formulations in favour of subject-specific case titles that enhance clarity for both legal professionals and the general public.

The expression *inter alia*, meaning "among other things", remains fairly consistent across all three corpora, with 40.79 pmT in CHELAR, 42.95 pmT in BLaRC and 22.54 pmT in BoLC. This suggests that *inter alia* continues to serve as a valuable linguistic tool, particularly in legal drafting where enumerations are necessary but exhaustive lists are impractical. Its ability to succinctly introduce non-exhaustive lists has likely contributed to its resilience in legal discourse. The decline in BoLC could indicate a preference for plainer language in EU legal texts, aligning with efforts to improve readability and accessibility. Nevertheless, its continued presence suggests that certain Latin phrases remain indispensable due to their brevity and clarity (Giampieri 2022). The endurance of *inter alia* illustrates how legal language retains terms that serve a specific functional purpose, particularly where they provide efficiency without sacrificing precision. Furthermore, its continued relevance may stem from the necessity of precise yet flexible language in legislative drafting, where legal provisions often require non-exhaustive enumerations to accommodate broad applications without the constraints of an overly rigid list format. The decline in BoLC, however, suggests that alternative expressions such as "including but not limited to" may be gradually replacing *inter alia* in certain contexts, particularly where efforts to enhance legal accessibility are most pronounced.

By contrast, *inter partes*, meaning "between the parties", follows a declining trend, decreasing from 5.56 pmT in CHELAR to 2.29 pmT in BLaRC and 2.39 pmT in BoLC. This decline aligns with the broader movement towards simplifying legal terminology, as discussed by Tiersma (1999). While historically significant, its decreasing usage suggests that modern legal discourse favours English equivalents for accessibility and clarity. The reduction in *inter partes* may be particularly significant in the context of procedural law, where legal reforms aim to make court rulings more transparent to non-specialists. The preference for plain English alternatives reflects a shift towards making legal concepts more comprehensible to litigants, policymakers and the public. However, despite this decline, *inter partes* remains in use in specific areas of law, particularly intellectual property and dispute resolution, where its meaning is both precise and well-established. Its continued presence in these domains highlights that some Latin terms persist due to their ability to encapsulate complex legal relationships in a concise manner. The persistence of *inter partes* in intellectual property law, for example, suggests that while general legal drafting trends favour plain language, specialised fields with established terminological frameworks continue to uphold Latin phrases where they enhance legal certainty and precision.

The expression *ipso facto*, meaning "by the fact itself", follows a similar trend, declining from 5.56 pmT in CHELAR to 3.19 pmT in BLaRC and further to 0.58 pmT in BoLC. The decline suggests that, despite its logical precision, *ipso facto* has been largely replaced by simpler English expressions in legal argumentation (Giampieri 2016: 430). This shift reflects broader trends in legal drafting that prioritise accessibility and directness over traditional Latin formulations. The decreasing frequency of *ipso facto* may also indicate a preference for explicitly linking cause and effect in legal reasoning, rather than relying on Latin phrases that, while precise, may be unfamiliar to non-specialists. Moreover, its diminished use in BoLC aligns with the European Union's emphasis on linguistic clarity, further contributing to the marginalisation of Latin expressions in modern legal documentation.

The term *prima facie*, meaning "at first glance", remains relatively stable, with frequencies of 25.96 pmT in CHELAR, 31.79 pmT in BLaRC and 16.52 pmT in BoLC. Its continued use highlights its significance in evidentiary and procedural law, where initial assessments of evidence are crucial. The stability of *prima facie* supports Williams's (2023) argument that while legal Latin is declining overall, key terms persist due to their essential function in legal reasoning. Unlike other Latin expressions that have been phased out in favour of plain English, *prima facie* retains its place in legal discourse due to its concise encapsulation of preliminary legal judgments. This term remains particularly important in judicial reasoning, where courts must determine whether sufficient evidence exists before proceeding with a case. The decline in BoLC, however, suggests a slight shift towards alternatives such as "on its face" or "evident at first sight", particularly in more recent EU-influenced legal texts that aim to enhance clarity for broader audiences (The Joint Practical Guide 2023).

The phrase *pro bono*, meaning "for the public good", remains relatively low in frequency, declining from 1.85 pmT in CHELAR to 1.69 pmT in BLaRC and further to 0.44 pmT in BoLC. This decline suggests that while the concept of *pro bono* remains important in legal practice, the term itself is used less frequently in legal texts, possibly replaced by more descriptive alternatives (Duckworth and Spyrou 1995). The decreasing use of *pro bono* in legal documentation may reflect a broader trend towards elaborating on the nature of legal aid services rather than relying on a succinct Latin phrase. Additionally, the low frequency across all corpora suggests that discussions of voluntary legal services are more common in professional and policy-oriented discourse rather than in legal statutes and case law. Despite its decline in formal legal texts, *pro bono* remains a widely recognised term in the legal profession, particularly in ethical guidelines and public-interest advocacy, indicating that its relevance persists outside the strict confines of legal drafting.

Finally, *viva voce*, meaning "by live voice" or "oral testimony", exhibits a sharp decline from 3.71 pmT in CHELAR to 0.00 pmT in BLaRC, with a minimal recovery to 0.13 pmT in BoLC. This decline underscores the trend towards replacing Latin phrases with direct English equivalents such as "oral evidence" (Garner 2004). The near disappearance of *viva voce* from modern legal texts is indicative of a broader linguistic shift towards clarity and accessibility, particularly in jurisdictions influenced by the European Union's commitment to transparent legal communication. The preference for "oral testimony" or "spoken evidence" over *viva voce* highlights the efforts of the legal profession to eliminate unnecessary complexity in legal terminology. While *viva voce* retains some relevance in academic and procedural contexts, its reduced frequency suggests that its utility is no longer sufficient to counterbalance the demand for comprehensible legal language.

In conclusion, while the use of Latin in legal English is in decline, certain terms persist due to their historical significance and precision. The shift towards plain language in legal drafting reflects the attempt of the legal profession to enhance accessibility while preserving essential legal terminology. This balance between tradition and modernisation highlights the ongoing evolution of legal language, where clarity, precision and authority are increasingly intertwined. The persistence of select Latin terms demonstrates that while legal language is becoming more inclusive, the need for accuracy in legal discourse ensures that some expressions remain indispensable despite broader simplification efforts.

The analysis of alternatives to Latinism expressions across CHELAR, BLaRC and BoLC reveals significant trends in the evolution of legal language, with a marked shift from Latin phrases to more straightforward English expressions. The data from Table 5.8 show the varying frequencies of these alternative terms, highlighting the growing preference for

Table 5.8 Corpus analysis of some alternatives to Latinisms

	CHELAR		BLaRC		BoLC	
Alternatives to Latinism	No.	Freq. pmT	No.	Freq. pmT	No	Freq. pmT
Among(st) other(s) (things)	56	**103.83**	280	27.90	710	12.96
And the following	0	0.00	88	**8.77**	174	3.18
At a first glance	0	0.00	0	0.00	0	0.00
At first glance	0	0.00	3	0.3	6	0.6
Between the parties	35	64.90	806	**80.31**	1,823	33.28
For free	0	0.00	16	**1.59**	60	1.10
Good faith	2	3.71	152	15.15	962	**17.56**

clarity and accessibility in legal discourse, especially as legal practices evolve across different jurisdictions.

The phrase *among(st) other(s) (things)*, which serves as a direct substitute for the Latin expression *inter alia*, appears with a high frequency of 103.83 pmT in CHELAR, indicating its common use in historical British legal texts. However, its frequency significantly decreases to 27.90 pmT in BLaRC and further drops to 12.96 pmT in BoLC. This decline across the corpora suggests a shift towards less formal and more direct expressions in legal language. The reduction in usage across the corpora likely reflects the growing preference for simpler, more accessible language, particularly in modern legal contexts. While *amongst other things* was once a staple in legal writing, its decreasing frequency points to a broader trend of moving away from Latin-based terminology in favour of clear, plain language. Goldstein and Lieberman (2016) argue that the use of *inter alia*, or its English equivalent, *among other things*, is often unnecessary and should generally be avoided in legal writing. They encourage a more concise and direct approach, suggesting that eliminating such phrases enhances clarity and reduces redundancy.

The phrase *and the following* has gained some traction in modern legal discourse as a substitute for *et seq.*, ostensibly reflecting a preference for precise and explicit language. It appears in BLaRC with a frequency of 8.77 pmT and at 3.18 pmT in BoLC, yet it is entirely absent in CHELAR. This distribution suggests that its usage is more common in contemporary legal texts than in historical ones, where the Latin *et seq.* was traditionally favoured. However, its relatively low frequency indicates that it is far from being a definitive replacement. Garner (2023) critiques *et seq.* for its vagueness and imprecision, arguing that it leaves readers uncertain about the exact range of referenced sections. He contends that legal writing should prioritise clarity by explicitly citing the full span of sections (e.g., §§ 64–67) rather than relying on ambiguous shorthand. While this argument is persuasive, it raises the question of whether *and the following* is a meaningful improvement or simply another imprecise alternative. Although it is in English rather than Latin, *and the following* still lacks specificity and forces readers to infer the extent of the referenced material. In this respect, it may offer little advantage over *et seq.* and could be seen as a superficial rather than substantive shift towards plain language. Furthermore, modern citation standards, such as those outlined in *The Bluebook* and ALWD, discourage the use of *et seq.* precisely to eliminate ambiguity, reinforcing the broader movement towards explicit referencing (ibid.). If clarity is the ultimate goal, then replacing *et seq.* with *and the following* may be an insufficient solution. A more rigorous approach would involve fully specifying the relevant sections, thereby ensuring precision rather than merely exchanging one vague phrase for another.

The terms *at first glance* and *at a first glance*, which could serve as English alternatives to the Latin phrase *prima facie*, exhibit minimal presence across the three corpora analysed. Specifically, *at first glance* appears with frequencies of 0.00 pmT in CHELAR, 0.3 pmT in BLaRC and 0.6 pmT in BoLC, while *at a first glance* is entirely absent from all three corpora, each recording a frequency of 0.00 pmT. These data suggest that neither variation has gained significant traction in legal writing. The near absence of these English alternatives points to the continued dominance of *prima facie* in legal contexts, despite the broader movement towards plain language. As previously noted, *prima facie* retains its place in legal discourse due to its concise encapsulation of preliminary legal judgments (Williams 2023). Unlike other Latin expressions that have been phased out in favour of plain English, *prima facie* persists because of its precise function in legal reasoning. This preference is likely due to its established usage, which offers a clear and efficient means of conveying that, at first examination, there is sufficient evidence to proceed with a case. The low frequencies of these English alternatives also highlight a broader tendency in legal writing to rely on traditional Latin terms, which are deeply embedded in the legal lexicon and often perceived as more authoritative. While there may be a gradual shift towards terms like *on its face* or *evident at first sight*, especially in EU-influenced legal texts that aim for greater clarity (The Joint Practical Guide 2023), *prima facie* remains a standard in judicial reasoning.

The phrase *between the parties*, serving as a substitute for the Latin term *inter partes*, demonstrates notable fluctuations in its frequency of usage across different legal corpora. In the CHELAR corpus, it appears with a frequency of 64.90 pmT, underscoring its historical significance as a direct English equivalent of *inter partes*, which pertains to matters arising between the parties involved in legal proceedings. This frequency reflects its role as an accessible and practical alternative to Latin terminology, aligning with broader trends in English legal language that favour clarity and comprehensibility. In the BLaRC corpus, the frequency increases to 80.31 pmT, indicating that *between the parties* has gained greater prominence in contemporary legal discourse. This rise may be attributed to modern efforts to simplify legal language and make it more accessible to non-specialist audiences, particularly within jurisdictions like the United Kingdom where plain English initiatives have influenced legal drafting practices. The growing prevalence of this phrase suggests a shift towards linguistic modernisation and away from traditional reliance on Latinisms. However, in the BoLC corpus, the frequency drops significantly to 33.28 pmT, potentially signalling a reversion to more formal or traditional expressions within certain EU legal contexts. This decline could reflect the enduring preference for Latin terms, such as *inter partes*, in specific legal traditions that value their precision and historical continuity. The European Union's multilingual legal framework often favours terminology that can be uniformly understood across member states and, as also noted by Ristikivi (2005), Latin expressions may serve this purpose better than their vernacular equivalents.

The phrase *for free*, as an alternative to *pro bono*, appears with a frequency of 1.59 pmT in BLaRC and 1.10 pmT in BoLC, but is absent in CHELAR. This suggests that while *for free* has emerged as a more casual alternative to *pro bono* in modern legal discourse, its use is still limited. The higher frequency in the modern corpora may reflect the growing tendency to use simpler and more familiar language in legal contexts, especially in relation to free services. However, the absence of this phrase in CHELAR points to the traditional preference for the more formal *pro bono* in historical legal texts, particularly in relation to voluntary legal services provided for the public good. Despite its presence in modern corpora, *for free* has not fully supplanted the more established *pro bono* in legal usage, especially in formal or official documents.

The term *good faith*, a direct alternative to the Latin *bona fide*, shows a steady increase in usage, with a frequency of 3.71 pmT in CHELAR, 15.15 pmT in BLaRC and 17.56 pmT in BoLC. The rising frequency across the corpora indicates that *good faith* has become the preferred term in both British and EU legal contexts, likely due to its clarity and straightforward meaning. While *bona fide* remains a common term in legal discussions, particularly in contract law, *good faith* has gained ground as the more accessible English equivalent. Its increasing frequency in BLaRC and BoLC reflects the ongoing shift towards clearer and more transparent language in modern legal texts, where the focus is on ensuring that concepts like honesty and sincerity in legal dealings are easily understood.

In conclusion, the analysis of alternatives to Latinisms across the three corpora reveals a clear trend towards the use of more accessible, English-based expressions in legal writing. While Latin terms such as *inter alia* and *prima facie* continue to hold significant value in legal discourse, the increasing frequency of alternatives like *amongst other things*, *between the parties*, *for free* and *good faith* reflects a broader movement towards simplicity and clarity in legal language. The use of these alternatives varies across different corpora, reflecting both the historical and modern preferences for legal expression, as well as the influence of regional legal traditions. While Latin phrases are unlikely to disappear entirely, their use seems to be declining in favour of English alternatives, which are perceived as more transparent and accessible to contemporary legal audiences.

5.7 Law French

The analysis of Law French terms across the three corpora provides insightful trends into the evolution of legal language, especially the transition from traditional Law French terms to more modern English alternatives. The data presented in Table 5.9 demonstrate varying frequencies of Law French terms, reflecting both their historical importance and their diminishing use in contemporary legal contexts.

The presence of the term *attorney/solicitor general* in CHELAR (31.52 pmT) and its increase in BLaRC (34.18 pmT) underscore its sustained relevance in British legal discourse, reinforcing its established role within the hierarchical structure of legal offices in the United Kingdom. By contrast, its absence from BoLC suggests a decline in its prominence within EU legal contexts, which may indicate a broader shift away from traditional Anglo-Norman legal terminology in supranational legal

Table 5.9 Corpus analysis of Law French

	CHELAR		BLaRC		BoLC	
Law French	No.	Freq. pmT	No.	Freq. pmT	No	Freq. pmT
Attorney / solicitor general	17	31.52	343	**34.18**	0	0.00
Abut	2	3.71	8	0.80	49	0.89
Appurtenance	185	**343.02**	2	0.20	22	0.40
Arrear	6	**11.12**	11	1.10	112	2.04
Arrearage	16	**29.67**	0	0.00	0	0.00
Burgess	21	**38.94**	11	1.10	0	0.00
Cestui que trust	6	**11.12**	1	0.10	9	0.16
Commence	49	**90.85**	829	82.60	4,839	88.33
Commencement	20	37.08	315	31.39	8,523	**155.57**
Covenant	229	**424.60**	415	41.35	2,303	42.04
Demise	173	**320.77**	97	9.67	522	9.53
Embezzle	3	**5.56**	1	0.10	4	0.07
Embezzlement	1	**1.85**	6	0.60	0	0.00
Feoffment	94	**174.29**	0	0.00	6	0.11
Presentment	30	**55.62**	6	0.60	1	0.02

frameworks. This discrepancy aligns with the observations of Tiersma (1999) and Williams (2023), both of whom argue that while the legacy of Law French persists in legal nomenclature, it has evolved in response to jurisdictional and linguistic developments. However, the extent to which this transformation reflects deliberate linguistic reform versus the organic divergence of legal traditions remains open to debate. The diminished presence of *attorney/solicitor general* in EU legal texts could be symptomatic of a broader preference for streamlined, pan-European legal terminology that prioritises neutrality and cross-border intelligibility. Given that the EU's legal framework is inherently multilingual, terms with strong historical or jurisdictional associations, particularly those rooted in English common law, may be gradually supplanted in favour of more universally comprehensible alternatives (Robertson and Mac Aodha 2023). This shift is further compounded by modern legal reforms that emphasise accessibility and clarity, reducing reliance on archaic or jurisdiction-specific legal lexicons. Yet, one could argue that this trend risks eroding some of the historical and doctrinal nuances embedded in traditional legal terminology, potentially limiting the interpretative depth available to legal practitioners operating within multiple jurisdictions.

The observed variation, therefore, highlights not only the adaptability of legal language but also the tensions between linguistic tradition and legal modernisation. While the term remains entrenched in British legal discourse, its marginalisation in EU contexts may reflect broader ideological and practical shifts in legal drafting and interpretation. This divergence ultimately raises questions about the extent to which legal terminology should preserve historical continuity versus adapting to evolving linguistic and jurisdictional landscapes.

The declining frequency of *abut* across CHELAR (3.71 pmT), BLaRC (0.80 pmT) and BoLC (0.89 pmT) suggests that, while the term remains relevant in property law, its usage is progressively diminishing. This trend aligns with Burnley's (1992) argument that many historically embedded Law French terms have been supplanted by simpler, more intuitive equivalents. The availability of alternatives such as *adjoin* or *border*, which convey similar legal meanings with greater accessibility, reinforces this linguistic shift. However, it is worth considering whether this transition represents a genuine enhancement of clarity or whether it risks losing certain legal distinctions. While *abut* carries a precise, technical connotation in property law, often implying direct contact without an intervening space, the broader terms replacing it may introduce interpretative ambiguities, potentially requiring additional legal clarification in specific contexts.

A similar pattern emerges with the dramatic decline of *appurtenance*, which appears at 343.02 pmT in CHELAR but plummets to 0.20 pmT in BLaRC and 0.40 pmT in BoLC. This steep reduction underscores the move away from archaic Law French terminology in favour of more explicit expressions such as *incidental rights*, a shift noted by Bhatia (2010) as part of a broader effort to enhance legal comprehensibility. The preference for modern, descriptive phrasing is largely driven by legal reform initiatives that prioritise accessibility, ensuring that legal texts are intelligible not only to specialists but also to a wider public. However, while terms like *incidental rights* may be more transparent, they also introduce a degree of subjectivity, as their scope and interpretation can vary depending on jurisdiction and legal context. By contrast, *appurtenance*, despite its archaic origins, has historically carried a fixed legal meaning, reducing potential disputes over interpretation.

These lexical shifts illustrate a fundamental tension within legal drafting: the balance between historical precision and contemporary clarity. While the decline of *abut* and *appurtenance* reflects a broader movement towards more accessible legal language, it also raises questions about whether certain technical nuances are being sacrificed in the process. The legal profession must therefore navigate this linguistic evolution carefully, ensuring that efforts to modernise terminology do not inadvertently compromise legal certainty and doctrinal stability.

Similarly, the term *arrear* declines from 11.12 pmT in CHELAR to 1.10 pmT in BLaRC, with a minor increase to 2.04 pmT in BoLC, while *arrearage* (29.67 pmT in CHELAR) disappears entirely from both BLaRC and BoLC. This pattern strongly suggests that *arrearage* has become obsolete in contemporary legal discourse, supplanted by more transparent alternatives such as *overdue payments*. This trend aligns with Tiersma's (1999) argument that legal terminology, historically characterised by redundancy due to the coexistence of Law French and Latin synonyms, has undergone systematic simplification. However, while the elimination of redundant terms may enhance clarity, it also raises questions about whether it leads to a loss of legal precision. The case of *arrearage* exemplifies this tension. Although *overdue payments* is undeniably more accessible to a lay audience, it lacks the specific legal connotations that *arrearage* once carried, particularly in contexts such as family law and financial obligations. *Arrearage* historically denoted accumulated unpaid amounts rather than just overdue sums, a distinction that could be significant in legal proceedings. The decline of such terminology, therefore, may simplify legal texts at the cost of reducing their technical exactitude, potentially requiring additional clarification in contracts and statutes. This linguistic shift reflects a broader movement towards efficiency and accessibility in legal writing. As legal systems increasingly prioritise plain language to enhance public comprehension and reduce misinterpretation, archaic or overly technical terms are phased out in favour of more direct expressions. However, while this movement is generally beneficial for transparency, it also necessitates careful scrutiny to ensure that simplification does not erode important legal distinctions. The replacement of *arrearage* with *overdue payments* thus illustrates not only the modernisation of legal terminology but also the ongoing challenge of balancing clarity with doctrinal precision.

The significant decline in the term *burgess* from 38.94 pmT in CHELAR to 1.10 pmT in BLaRC, and its complete absence from BoLC, reflects the broader modernisation of civic and parliamentary terminology. This shift aligns with Williams (2004), who highlights how archaic legal terms are increasingly being replaced with contemporary alternatives that better align with present-day governance structures. Historically, *burgess* denoted a freeman or representative of a borough, a designation that has become largely obsolete due to legislative reforms that have reshaped the composition and terminology of local and parliamentary representation. The diminishing presence of such terms suggests not only a linguistic evolution but also a deeper transformation in the legal and political frameworks that once necessitated them. However, this decline raises the question of whether the erasure of historically significant legal vocabulary might contribute to the loss of valuable doctrinal and institutional knowledge embedded within these terms.

A parallel trend is evident in the decline of *cestui que trust*, which drops from 11.12 pmT in CHELAR to 0.10 pmT in BLaRC and 0.16 pmT in BoLC. The theoretical perspectives of Tiersma (1999) and Duckworth and Spyrou (1995) support the notion that legal terms once central to property and trust law are increasingly being replaced by more accessible English equivalents, such as *beneficiary of the trust*. While this linguistic shift promotes clarity, it is not without its complexities. *Cestui que trust* carried precise legal implications derived from its historical use in equity law, whereas *beneficiary of the trust*, though more intuitive, may lack the same level of specificity in certain legal contexts. This evolution reflects a broader movement towards making legal texts more comprehensible to non-specialists, yet it also necessitates careful consideration of whether such substitutions preserve the necessary legal precision.

Ultimately, the decline of terms like *burgess* and *cestui que trust* underscores the ongoing tension between preserving legal tradition and adapting legal language to modern communicative needs. While these changes align with contemporary efforts to enhance legal accessibility, they also raise critical questions about whether the simplification of legal terminology might, in some cases, obscure the historical and doctrinal nuances essential to legal interpretation. This linguistic evolution, therefore, is not merely a matter of replacing archaic vocabulary but also of ensuring that clarity does not come at the expense of conceptual depth and legal accuracy.

It is worth noting, however, that not all Law French terms are in decline. The term *commence* appears with relative stability across CHELAR (90.85 pmT), BLaRC (82.60 pmT) and BoLC (88.33 pmT), indicating its continued relevance in legal texts despite broader linguistic shifts. Similarly, *commencement* follows a comparable pattern but increases significantly in BoLC (155.57 pmT), suggesting its sustained importance in formal EU legal documentation. This persistence highlights an important countertrend within legal language: while many archaic terms are being phased out in favour of simpler alternatives, others remain integral due to their precision and established usage. Leonardi and Giampieri (2024) argue that certain traditional legal terms endure precisely because of their technical accuracy and formal character, making them resistant to linguistic modernisation. The continued use of *commence* and *commencement* underscores the careful balance between tradition and modernisation in legal discourse. While efforts to simplify legal language have led to the decline of many Law French terms, those that serve indispensable legal functions remain largely unaffected. *Commencement*, for instance, is crucial in delineating the exact start of legal proceedings obligations, or legislative enactments, making it a term whose specificity cannot easily be substituted without risking ambiguity. Unlike archaic legal terms that have fallen into disuse due to redundancy or complexity, *commence* and *commencement* retain a clear, functional role that ensures their ongoing presence in legal writing. This trend suggests that legal modernisation does not equate to wholesale lexical replacement but rather a selective refinement of terminology. The persistence of these terms demonstrates that legal language evolves not merely through simplification but through the retention of historically significant vocabulary where precision and clarity are paramount. As such, while the broader movement towards accessibility continues to shape legal drafting, the endurance of terms like *commencement* reflects the necessity of maintaining certain linguistic conventions to uphold legal accuracy and procedural certainty.

Conversely, *covenant* experiences a dramatic decline from 424.60 pmT in CHELAR to 41.35 pmT in BLaRC and 42.04 pmT in BoLC, reflecting a significant shift in legal drafting practices. The stark reduction in its frequency suggests that while *covenant* was once a cornerstone of contract law, modern legal texts increasingly favour *agreement* or *contract*, terms that offer greater immediacy and accessibility. This shift aligns with Baker's (1998) observation that Law French-derived legal terminology has been progressively displaced by English equivalents, a trend driven by the broader movement to streamline legal language and enhance its clarity. However, while this transition promotes accessibility, it is not without implications. *Covenant* historically carried a precise legal meaning, particularly in property law and certain contractual contexts, where it referred to a binding promise enforceable by law, often with specific remedies attached. By contrast, *agreement* and *contract*, though more widely understood, encompass a broader range of legal relationships, potentially introducing ambiguities where *covenant* once provided doctrinal specificity. The decline of *covenant* thus raises questions about whether simplification always serves legal precision or whether, in some instances, it risks obscuring important legal distinctions.

The word *demise* experiences a significant decline from 320.77 pmT in CHELAR to 9.67 pmT in BLaRC and 9.53 pmT in BoLC, reinforcing Garner's (2004) argument that historically significant property law terms are being phased out in favour of more accessible alternatives such as *transfer of property*. Traditionally, *demise* carried a specific legal meaning, particularly in leasehold contexts where it referred to the conveyance of an estate for a term of years. Its decline suggests a broader preference for terminology that is immediately comprehensible to legal professionals and laypersons alike. However, this transition also raises concerns about whether replacing precise legal terms with more general phrases might obscure important legal distinctions. For instance, *transfer of property* is a broader term that encompasses various legal mechanisms, whereas *demise* historically referred specifically to leasehold transfers. The loss of such specificity could necessitate further clarification in legal drafting to avoid ambiguity.

A similar pattern is evident in the decline of *embezzle* (5.56 pmT in CHELAR, 0.10 pmT in BLaRC and 0.07 pmT in BoLC) and *embezzlement* (1.85 pmT in CHELAR, 0.60 pmT in BLaRC, absent from BoLC). This reduction reflects a broader simplification of legal language, aligning with modern drafting principles that favour plain English over archaic or technical terminology. The decreasing use of these terms suggests that alternative phrasings, such as *misappropriation of funds*, may be gaining prominence due to their greater clarity. However, *embezzlement* carries specific connotations within criminal law, referring to the fraudulent appropriation of property by a person in a position of trust. If the term is replaced by broader, less precise alternatives, this could have implications for legal interpretation and enforcement, potentially affecting how such offences are prosecuted.

The term *feoffment*, which appears at 174.29 pmT in CHELAR but is virtually absent in modern corpora, serves as a clear example of the obsolescence of Law French-derived terminology in property law. Historically, *feoffment* was a fundamental concept in medieval land tenure, referring to the transfer of a freehold estate through a formal ceremony involving livery of seisin. However, as Burnley (1992) notes, such terms have been rendered largely redundant by the shift towards more transparent and universally comprehensible legal language. This linguistic transition reflects broader efforts to modernise legal discourse, ensuring that legal principles are accessible to a wider audience, including non-specialists. The disappearance of *feoffment* is not merely a linguistic shift but also a reflection of substantive legal changes. The decline of feudal landholding structures and the increasing formalisation of property transactions through written deeds have rendered such terminology archaic. Modern legal texts now favour terms such as *land grant* or *property conveyance*, which provide a clearer and more intuitive description of land transfers without requiring historical legal knowledge. This shift aligns with contemporary drafting principles that prioritise precision and accessibility, as advocated by Tiersma (1999).

Presentment follows a similar trajectory to other historical legal terms, dropping from 55.62 pmT in CHELAR to 0.60 pmT in BLaRC and 0.02 pmT in BoLC. This dramatic decline reflects the broader trend in legal discourse towards simplifying terminology, especially within criminal law. Historically, *presentment* referred to the formal presentation of a criminal charge or accusation, often by a grand jury or other body, which has since been largely replaced by terms like *charge* or *accusation*. This shift, as Williams (2023) notes, represents the broader movement towards legal transparency, where the emphasis is placed on clarity and comprehensibility, ensuring that legal processes are more accessible to both legal professionals and the public. The reduction in the use of *presentment* and its replacement with *charge* aligns with modern efforts to eliminate antiquated legal phrases that may create confusion. In this case, *presentment*, though precise within historical contexts, is arguably more complex and less intuitively understood by a contemporary audience than *charge*, which directly communicates the legal action of formally accusing someone of a crime. Williams's analysis further supports this, highlighting how the simplification of legal language is driven by a desire to make legal proceedings more understandable, especially for those without legal expertise.

In conclusion, the evolving usage of Law French-derived terms in modern legal discourse highlights a broader trend towards simplification and accessibility in legal language. The shift towards plain English reflects efforts to make legal texts more comprehensible to both legal professionals and the public. Nevertheless, this simplification also raises important questions about the balance between clarity and precision. While eliminating archaic terms enhances transparency, it can sometimes obscure legal nuances and historical distinctions. Therefore, the ongoing evolution of legal language must carefully navigate the tension between modernisation and the preservation of legal specificity, ensuring that legal terms remain both accessible and functionally precise.

5.8 Formulaic Expressions

The analysis of formulaic expressions across the three corpora provides some interesting insights into how traditional legal phrases, once ubiquitous in legal texts, have evolved over time. These formulae, deeply ingrained in the language of historical legal documents, reflect a shift towards more modern and simplified legal drafting, particularly in British and EU contexts, while also highlighting the continued relevance of certain expressions in formal legal settings. A detailed examination of each

Table 5.10 Corpus analysis of formulae

	CHELAR		BLaRC		BoLC	
Formulae	No.	Freq. pmT	No.	Freq. pmT	No	Freq. pmT
In witness whereof	2	**3.71**	0	0.00	0	0.00
Know all men (by these presents)	2	**3.71**	0	0.00	0	0.00
Nothing in this / the	7	12.98	363	**36.17**	1,019	18.60
Now therefore	1	**1.85**	2	0.20	18	0.33
Of the first part… of the second part	14	**25.96**	1	0.10	15	0.27
Of the one part… of the other part	11	**20.40**	1	0.10	34	0.62
On the one hand… on the other hand	3	5.56	294	**29.29**	531	9.69

phrase reveals both significant declines in usage as well as the persistence of specific terms, suggesting that while legal language is modernising, some formulaic expressions remain embedded in legal discourse for their clarity and formality (Table 5.10).

The phrase *in witness whereof*, historically a standard closing expression in formal contracts and legal documents, appears in CHELAR with a frequency of 3.71 pmT but is entirely absent in both BLaRC and BoLC. However, this absence may not necessarily indicate a wholesale decline; rather, it reflects its restricted use within contractual contexts. Given that both BLaRC and BoLC encompass broader legal discourse rather than solely contract law, the lack of occurrences in these corpora is unsurprising. While there is a general trend towards more accessible legal drafting, as Tiersma (1999) argues, the complete disappearance of this phrase from modern legal language is not as clear-cut. Traditionally, the phrase affirmed the authenticity of a document, carrying with it the weight of ritualistic legal formulae once believed to possess symbolic and talismanic significance (Tiersma 1999). However, contemporary contract drafting still retains many formal conventions, and *in witness whereof* continues to be used in certain contexts, particularly in contracts and deeds. This ongoing presence aligns with Biel and Engberg's (2013) assertion that while legal language is evolving, it remains flexible in response to the demands for clarity and efficiency. Although modern legal drafting increasingly prioritises accessibility, formal expressions such as *in witness whereof* persist where tradition and legal certainty are valued. Rather than signifying a complete shift away from archaic language, the selective retention of such phrases reflects the nuanced evolution of legal discourse, balancing historical precedent with contemporary readability.

Similarly, the phrase *know all men (by these presents)*, once a standard opening in legal documents, appears in CHELAR with a frequency of 3.71 pmT but is absent in both BLaRC and BoLC. However, this omission is likely to reflect its specific use in contractual language rather than a complete disappearance. Given that BLaRC and BoLC cover a broader spectrum of legal writing, its absence in these corpora is expected. A remnant of medieval legal tradition, this phrase originally functioned as a formal declaration of the purpose of a document and involved parties, lending it authority and solemnity. While once considered essential to reinforce the legitimacy of a document, its presence in modern legal texts is now largely stylistic, as Kopaczyk (2009: 95) observes. Although contemporary drafting favours clarity, the phrase persists mainly in contracts where conventional legal formality remains important. In other words, its absence in general legal corpora may suggest a broader trend towards clarity and conciseness over rhetorical tradition. This shift aligns with Pontrandolfo's (2023) argument that legal texts are evolving to remove unnecessary formalities in favour of more direct and functional language that enhances comprehensibility. However, as noted above, in the context of contracts and similar legal instruments, such expressions still persist where formality and legal convention hold significance.

In contrast, the phrase *nothing in this/the* demonstrates a notable increase in frequency, appearing at 12.98 pmT in CHELAR, surging to 36.17 pmT in BLaRC, before declining to 18.60 pmT in BoLC. This upward trend, particularly in BLaRC, signals the continued relevance of this formula in legal texts, particularly within British law, where it serves a crucial functional role in clarifying exceptions and limitations within legal provisions (Bhatia 2010). Such a formulaic expression helps to delineate boundaries within legal clauses, ensuring that exceptions or restrictions are clearly articulated, thus reducing ambiguity and enhancing legal precision. The increased frequency in BLaRC indicates that this phrase remains a precise and familiar linguistic tool in modern legal drafting. This supports Gotti's (2012) observation that formulaic clusters, such as *nothing in this/the*, contribute to the uniformity and predictability of legal documents. By employing established expressions, legal drafters ensure that documents maintain a certain level of consistency, which is crucial in both drafting and interpretation. The formulaic nature of such phrases ensures that their meaning remains stable across various legal contexts, reinforcing legal certainty and clarity. Nevertheless, the slight decline in BoLC, specifically in EU legal texts, suggests a potential shift towards alternative formulations that prioritise linguistic economy without sacrificing legal certainty (Nystedt 2000). The move away from more formal, formulaic expressions in EU legal writing may indicate a growing preference for streamlined, concise language, reflecting broader trends in European legal drafting towards simplicity and clarity. This shift aligns with the EU's ongoing efforts to make legal texts more accessible and comprehensible to a wider, multilingual audience. Thus, while *nothing in this/the* remains a key feature in British legal discourse, its reduced presence in EU legal corpora suggests a rethinking of legal language aimed at further enhancing accessibility and efficiency in legal communication.

The formula *now therefore* exhibits a significant decline, with a frequency of 1.85 pmT in CHELAR, dropping to 0.20 pmT in BLaRC and 0.33 pmT in BoLC. Traditionally used to introduce resolutions or final agreements, this phrase epitomises the ceremonial aspect of legal language, often marking a formal shift in the content or intent of a document (Giampieri 2022). Historically, such expressions served a performative function, signifying a clear transition or conclusion within legal texts. However, the declining frequency of *now therefore* in general legal corpora may reflect broader trends in legal drafting where formal connectors are increasingly seen as unnecessary. This supports Pontrandolfo's (2023) argument that contemporary legal writing favours conciseness over archaic structures. Nevertheless, as with other traditional legal expressions, *now therefore* continues to appear in certain types of contractual documents where its formal function remains relevant. Modern legal writing tends to prioritise efficiency and clarity, moving away from overly ritualistic language towards more direct, functional expressions. Yet, the persistence of phrases like *now therefore* in specific legal subgenres highlights the balance between maintaining legal convention and adapting to evolving drafting standards. The variation in frequency across different corpora underscores the importance of considering subgenre distinctions when assessing linguistic change in legal discourse.

The phrase *of the first part… of the second part* appears at 25.96 pmT in CHELAR but plummets to 0.10 pmT in BLaRC and remains low at 0.27 pmT in BoLC. Once a common method for distinguishing contractual parties, this phrase has largely been replaced by more straightforward identifiers such as *Party A* and *Party B*. The steep decline in BLaRC signals a decisive shift in British legal drafting away from redundant, formulaic expressions, a trend that Pontrandolfo (2023) attributes to ongoing efforts to enhance readability and accessibility. By moving away from cumbersome phrases like *of the first part… of the second part*, British legal language embraces a more direct, user-friendly approach that simplifies the drafting process while preserving legal clarity. The slight persistence of this phrase in BoLC, while minimal, may reflect the continued reliance on formal structures in EU legal texts. In EU legal drafting, maintaining linguistic consistency across different jurisdictions is often crucial, and some traditional conventions may be retained to ensure uniformity and clarity (Nystedt 2000). This continued use, however, does not negate the broader trend towards simplification in EU legal language where modern alternatives like *Party A* and *Party B* are gradually gaining preference for their simplicity and efficiency.

Similarly, a parallel trend can be observed with the phrase *of the one part… of the other part*, which appears at 20.40 pmT in CHELAR, declines to 0.10 pmT in BLaRC and rises slightly to 0.62 pmT in BoLC. The substantial reduction in British legal texts strongly suggests a clear preference for contemporary identifiers, reinforcing the argument that modern legal drafting is focused on eliminating archaic conventions in favour of clarity and precision (Biel and Engberg 2013). The slight increase in BoLC indicates that EU legal frameworks may retain a degree of formality in contractual language, likely due to the need to accommodate the diverse linguistic traditions and formal structures inherent in EU legal instruments (Giurizzato 2008).

Conversely, the phrase *on the one hand… on the other hand* exhibits an interesting fluctuation, appearing at 5.56 pmT in CHELAR, surging to

29.29 pmT in BLaRC and declining to 9.69 pmT in BoLC. This structure remains highly relevant in British legal texts, particularly in contexts that require a balanced presentation of contrasting legal arguments. As Kopaczyk (2009) notes, such formulaic structures have a distinct rhetorical function, aiding in the organisation and presentation of opposing viewpoints. The surge in frequency within BLaRC suggests that this phrase plays a critical role in British legal discourse, particularly in persuasive legal writing, where the clear juxtaposition of contrasting arguments is essential for structuring legal reasoning. The decline in BoLC, however, signals a shift in EU legal texts towards more direct and simplified structures, possibly reflecting a broader trend towards linguistic simplification in transnational legal contexts (Tiersma 1999). In EU legal drafting, the emphasis may be placed on achieving clarity and efficiency across different linguistic and legal systems, favouring more straightforward constructions that do not rely on rhetorical flourish. The reduction of *on the one hand… on the other hand* in BoLC could thus be interpreted as part of this ongoing movement to make legal language more accessible and direct, in line with modern drafting principles that prioritise comprehensibility and precision. The persistence of *on the one hand… on the other hand* in British judicial texts, however, underscores its continued utility in the articulation of balanced legal arguments. This phrase serves a functional and rhetorical purpose, helping to organise legal reasoning in a clear and persuasive manner, especially when presenting opposing perspectives. The continued usage in British legal drafting indicates that, despite broader trends towards simplification, certain rhetorical tools remain vital in ensuring that complex legal arguments are presented effectively. Conversely, its decline in EU legal texts may indicate a preference for more concise language and simpler structures, reinforcing the idea that different legal contexts prioritise different aspects of language, such as clarity, persuasion and efficiency.

In conclusion, the apparent decline or absence of certain traditional legal expressions in modern corpora do not necessarily signify their complete disappearance from legal language. These phrases remain in use within specific legal subgenres, particularly in contracts, where they continue to play a functional and ceremonial role. While there is a broader trend towards more concise and accessible legal drafting, the ongoing use of these expressions in particular contexts demonstrates the continued relevance of formal conventions within certain areas of legal practice.

5.9 Sexist Language and Gender Bias

The historical context of women's roles within legal frameworks reveals a complex interplay of societal norms and legal restrictions that significantly influenced their status, agency and, obviously, lexical issues related to sexist terminology. This analysis highlights how the roles of female counterparts were often perceived as fundamentally different from those of men, shaped by prevailing patriarchal ideologies (Table 5.11).

Historically, English legal terminology has relied heavily on Latin-derived suffixes to indicate gender distinctions. The suffix *-tor* has

Table 5.11 Corpus analysis of sexist language

	CHELAR		BLaRC		BoLC	
Sexist language	No.	Freq. pmT	No.	Freq. pmT	No	Freq. pmT
Administrator, executor, testator, prosecutor	804	**1,490.73**	594	59.19	3,277	59.82
Administratrix, executrix, testatrix, prosecutrix	78	**144.62**	26	2.59	96	1.75
Heirs male	108	**200.25**	0	0.00	30	0.55
Heirs female	7	**12.98**	0	0.00	2	0.04
Her, hers, she	1890	**3,504.33**	31,604	3,149.05	57,206	1,044.18
Him, his, he	8165	**15,139.10**	91,305	9,097.70	282,995	5,165.51
If a man	40	**74.17**	7	0.70	17	0.31
If a woman	3	**5.56**	3	0.30	8	0.15
If a person, if someone/somebody	2	3.71	107	**10.66**	326	5.95
Men	32	**59.33**	480	47.83	1,155	21.08
Women	7	12.98	297	**29.59**	923	16.85
Men and women	0	0.00	38	**3.79**	153	2.79
Men or women	0	0.00	0	0.00	4	**0.07**
A man or a woman, a man and a woman	0	0.00	2	0.20	64	**1.17**

traditionally been used to denote male actors (e.g., *executor, administrator, testator, prosecutor*), while *-trix* was employed for their female counterparts (e.g., *executrix, administratrix, testatrix, prosecutrix*). However, data from the CHELAR corpus reveal a strong preference for *-tor* forms, with terms such as *executor* and *administrator* appearing at a frequency of 1,490.73 pmT, in stark contrast to their *-trix* equivalents, which are recorded at a mere 144.62 pmT. This substantial disparity suggests that the lower frequency of *-trix* forms reflects the historically diminished representation of women in roles traditionally occupied by men. As noted in previous discussions on gendered suffixes, male-oriented terms often served as generic descriptors, likely even when referring to female subjects, reinforcing the perception of men as the default standard in legal discourse (Marchand 1960). The persistence of *-tor* terms in CHELAR suggests that, despite their original gendered association, they have become entrenched as neutral descriptors over time, further marginalising the visibility of women in similar roles. While terms such as *administrator* and *executor* were historically linked to male figures, their widespread usage in legal contexts has contributed to their gradual reclassification as gender-neutral terms. This linguistic shift reflects broader efforts to promote gender inclusivity in legal language, aligning with the recognition that legal terminology can perpetuate discrimination if not carefully revised (EIGE 2019). In numerous contemporary jurisdictions, gender-specific *-trix* forms have largely fallen out of common usage, mirroring the broader decline of gendered legal terminology. This transformation is partly driven by legal reforms aimed at eliminating explicit gender distinctions, a trend evident in the adoption of terms such as *personal representative* in estate management (ibid.). The decreasing prevalence of *-trix* forms is further substantiated by corpus data from BLaRC and BoLC. Within BLaRC, *-trix* terms occur at a mere 2.59 pmT, while in BoLC, they appear even less frequently at 1.75 pmT. This decline demonstrates the diminishing relevance of these terms in modern legal discourse, as well as a growing commitment to linguistic inclusivity. The prominence of gender-neutral terminology is particularly evident in BoLC, which encompasses EU legal language, an area that frequently prioritises inclusivity and transnational applicability. Similarly, the reduced frequency of gender-specific terms in BLaRC, which focuses on contemporary British legal reports, reflects the UK's evolving approach to gender inclusivity in legal drafting, in line with the 2007 policy mandating gender-neutral legislative language (Bailey 2020). These findings reaffirm the broader movement towards eliminating linguistic biases in legal discourse, ensuring that legal language aligns with modern principles of equality and neutrality.

The development of gendered legal terminology in English inheritance law reflects not only the technical specificity of medieval jurisprudence but its deeper function as a tool of patriarchal social engineering. The legal language of succession, particularly in the form of terms such as *heirs male* and *heirs female*, codified a structure in which the transmission of property was fundamentally aligned with gendered hierarchies. Through the formal, highly formulaic deployment of these terms in deeds, settlements and statutes, medieval and early modern law embedded the subordination of women within the very grammar of property relations. The Statute *De Donis Conditionalibus* (1285), which enabled the creation of fee tails, institutionalised gendered succession by allowing landowners to direct inheritance "to the heirs of the body", with further specificity often added, most commonly *heirs male*. This allowed the aristocracy to restrict the descent of estates to male descendants, thereby preserving patrilineal continuity and preventing land from passing to daughters, who, through marriage, could transfer it to another lineage. Such legal instruments, notably entails and marriage settlements, systematically restricted succession to "heirs male of the body", thereby excluding daughters except in the absence of male issue. These provisions reflected not merely social custom but legally codified principles designed to preserve dynastic integrity through the male line (Baker 2019). One illustrative case from CHELAR (1853) reads: "*to the use of the heirs male of the body of the said Edward Shelley… and for default of such issue…*" This example exemplifies the legal precision used to construct multi-generational, exclusively male inheritance lines. The clause does not merely specify a preferred successor; it articulates a hierarchy of male heirs, each embedded within the previous generation. The recursive formulation reveals a structural commitment to patrilineal descent, with male succession treated as the legal and social default. Female succession is not only absent from this provision but deliberately excluded until all male lines are extinguished. The language thus encodes the patriarchal ideology that underpinned aristocratic landholding, that is, women's capacity to inherit was considered both a threat to dynastic continuity and an anomaly within legal logic. By contrast, references to *heirs female* are markedly rare and, when present, consistently subordinated to male alternatives. In a 1727 extract from CHELAR, the term arises only after seven degrees of male succession are exhausted: "*for want of such issue male... to the use of the heirs female of the body of the said earl...*". This example clearly shows how female inheritance is explicitly contingent upon the failure of an extended male line. Not only is it a secondary mechanism, it is also temporally and hierarchically deferred, mobilised only after multiple generations of male heirs have been ruled out. This marginal positioning affirms that the legal system treated female succession not as a right in parallel to that of males, but as a fallback provision within an otherwise patrilineal framework. Corpus data support this qualitative interpretation with quantitative evidence. In CHELAR, the term *heirs male* appears with a frequency of 200.25 pmT while *heirs female* appears only 12.98 pmT. This imbalance affirms the centrality of male primogeniture in historical legal discourse. Furthermore, the term *heirs male* disappears entirely from the BLaRC corpus and appears only 30 times in BoLC (0.55 pmT), while *heirs female* is virtually absent, appearing only twice (0.04 pmT). The chronological distribution reinforces this shift. The final recorded use of *heirs male* is in 1853 while *heirs female* disappears even earlier, in 1727. This decline coincides with major statutory reforms in the twentieth century that abolished fee tail creation (Law of Property Act 1925) and allowed disentailment, thereby rendering gendered succession clauses legally redundant. The disappearance of such terms in contemporary corpora, and particularly the marginal presence of *heirs male* in BoLC (0.55 pmT), signals their incompatibility with modern legal frameworks grounded in equality and non-discrimination, principles now enshrined in instruments such as Article 21(1) of the *Charter of Fundamental Rights of the European Union* (European Union 2010). The data do not merely confirm the formal decline of certain terms; they reveal the ideological transformation of English inheritance law. Where once legal instruments were meticulously crafted to preserve male dynasties, contemporary law emphasises equality and individual rights. The Inheritance (Provision for Family and Dependants) Act 1975, for instance, allows courts to redistribute estates based on need rather than lineage or sex. The symbolic rejection of male-preference primogeniture in the Succession to the Crown Act 2013 further underscores this shift. Nevertheless, residual traces of gendered succession persist. Hereditary titles, duchies, baronies, earldoms, often remain governed by their original letters patent, many of which restrict succession to "heirs male of the body lawfully begotten". These titles, although no longer tied to estate ownership, continue to reproduce archaic gender hierarchies, maintained through legal inertia and requiring individual legislative change to amend. This lingering use of medieval terminology reveals the durability of patriarchal legal forms and their resistance to broader social change.

Pronoun usage and references to gendered groups across the CHELAR, BLaRC and BoLC corpora provide a revealing portrait of how gendered language within British legal discourse has evolved, particularly in response to broader socio-political shifts and institutional reforms. In CHELAR, the language is marked by an overt masculine bias: male pronouns (*he, him, his*) appear at a frequency of 15,139.10 pmT, whereas female pronouns (*she, her, hers*) register only 3,504.33 pmT. This pronounced imbalance exemplifies a linguistic tradition in which male figures were positioned not simply as the majority, but as the unmarked default, effectively universalising the male subject in legal contexts. Such disproportionate usage is not incidental; it is symptomatic of a deeper ideological structure wherein legal authority, rationality and personhood were discursively aligned with masculinity.

This masculinised discourse is equally evident in the nominal references to gendered groups. In CHELAR, *men* are mentioned at a frequency of 59.33 pmT, vastly outnumbering references to *women*, which occur at just 12.98 pmT. Notably, phrases that attempt to recognise both genders, *men and women* (0.00 pmT), *men or women* (0.00 pmT) and *a man or a woman/a man and a woman* (0.00 pmT), are entirely absent from this corpus. This absence is striking, suggesting a legal discourse that not only privileges the male subject but systematically excludes female visibility altogether. The result is a discursive landscape in which male experience and legal agency are linguistically centralised, while women are either marginalised or omitted. This imbalance was further institutionalised through statutory mechanisms, most notably the 1850 Act, which stipulated that masculine terms in legal texts should be interpreted as including the feminine, a principle later reaffirmed by the Interpretation Act of 1978 (Bailey 2020). While framed as a practical measure, this approach reinforced the grammatical and symbolic dominance of masculine forms by suggesting that inclusivity could be achieved without explicitly naming women. In practice, it allowed male terms to stand in for all people, thereby erasing gender difference under a thin veil of supposed neutrality. Such linguistic strategies did not promote true inclusivity but entrenched a conceptual model in which the male legal subject functioned as the norm against which all others were measured.

By contrast, the BLaRC and BoLC corpora show evidence of significant linguistic transformation. References to *women* increase substantially, rising to 29.59 pmT in BLaRC and 16.85 pmT in BoLC, while mentions of *men* decline to 47.83 pmT and 21.08 pmT, respectively. Although an imbalance remains, particularly in BLaRC, the narrowing differential represents a tangible shift towards greater gender visibility and balance. Even more notable is the emergence of explicitly inclusive constructions. The phrase *men and women*, which is completely absent from CHELAR, appears at 3.79 pmT in BLaRC and 2.79 pmT in BoLC, suggesting a deliberate effort to name both genders rather than subsume one under the other. Similarly, formulations such as *a man or a woman/a man and a woman* increase from 0.00 pmT in CHELAR to 0.20 pmT in BLaRC and 1.17 pmT in BoLC. Although these frequencies remain relatively low, their presence is symbolically significant, marking a discursive recognition of the need for explicit gender inclusion.

Some inclusive phrases remain underused. For example, *men or women* does not appear at all in CHELAR or BLaRC and occurs only marginally in BoLC (0.07 pmT). This suggests that while binary-inclusive language is gaining traction, it remains unevenly integrated into legal drafting practices. Nevertheless, the overall trend across the corpora aligns with the UK government's 2007 directive mandating gender-neutral language in legislation (ibid.), which appears to have catalysed a gradual yet discernible shift in drafting conventions. These shifts are not confined to noun phrases. They also manifest in hypothetical constructions, which offer a particularly clear view of how legal texts construct imagined or generic legal subjects. In CHELAR, gendered expressions such as *if a man* dominate, with a frequency of 74.17 pmT, while *if a woman* is used sparingly (5.56 pmT). This pattern reinforces the same male-default logic observed in pronoun and group references: legal possibility and obligation are primarily imagined through a male lens. In contrast, the later corpora reveal a growing preference for gender-neutral hypothetical formulations. In BLaRC, *if a person* and *if someone/somebody* collectively occur at 10.66 pmT; in BoLC, this figure is 5.95 pmT. Though still relatively modest in absolute terms, these figures represent a clear departure from earlier gendered norms, indicating a strategic move towards neutral, inclusive legal personhood.

The increasing use of neutral and inclusive forms, both in references to individuals and to groups, signals a broader reconfiguration of the legal subject. No longer constructed solely as male by default, the legal person in contemporary texts is more likely to be represented in non-gendered or explicitly inclusive terms. This linguistic development has significant implications. As Mossman (1994) argues, the dominance of masculine language in legal discourse has historically shaped who is seen as a legitimate bearer of rights, duties and authority. By breaking down these gendered linguistic hierarchies, contemporary legal drafting participates in a wider cultural shift towards gender equity, recognising that language plays a central role in legitimising or marginalising particular identities within the law.

In sum, the comparative analysis of CHELAR, BLaRC and BoLC reveals a trajectory from gendered exclusion towards greater representational inclusivity. While the legacy of male-default language remains evident, particularly in the continued disproportion of references and the underrepresentation of certain inclusive phrases, the data reflect a clear and meaningful trend. Legal language, long a vehicle for institutionalising patriarchal norms, is being actively retooled to reflect contemporary commitments to gender equality. These changes, however incremental, mark a critical step in the broader project of constructing a legal discourse that is not only neutral in theory but inclusive in practice.

5.10 Concluding Remarks

This corpus-based analysis provides a comprehensive view of how legal language has evolved over time, specifically examining the use of archaic terminology, gender inclusivity, precision in language and formulaic expressions across three distinct legal corpora: CHELAR, BLaRC and BoLC. Each corpus reveals unique linguistic characteristics, shaped by historical, national or transnational legal practices. Overall, the findings show an ongoing transformation in legal language, increasingly guided by goals of clarity, accessibility and inclusivity which seem to be in line with broader societal expectations and demands.

A key finding in this analysis is the widespread simplification of legal language, especially in the gradual phasing out of archaic vocabulary and complex Latin terms that were prevalent in historical British legal texts. Terms such as *a fortiori* and *bona fide*, once commonly used within CHELAR, have seen a substantial decrease in frequency in more modern corpora like BLaRC and BoLC where they are often replaced by more straightforward English expressions. Similarly, formal phrases which are typical of *legalese*, such as *the said* and *therein,* have diminished in modern texts, thus indicating a shift towards less convoluted language. The reduction in complex Latinisms and formal *legalese* supports a trend towards the plain language movement within British and EU legal systems, reflecting a deliberate move to reduce redundancy and increase transparency for readers, including the lay public.

Another important linguistic shift observed in the analysis is the adoption of gender-neutral language, especially in professional and referential terms. Historical British legal texts were characterised by male-oriented language and often employed gender-specific terms, such as *executrix* or *he* for generic references. However, more recent British and EU corpora show a significant shift towards inclusive and gender-neutral terms, with phrases like *personal representative* and pronouns such as *they* replacing traditional male-associated terms. This adaptation mirrors the growing emphasis on equality and inclusivity in modern legal discourse where gender-neutral language ensures fairer representation and respect for diversity. The shift is both substantial and intentional, thus underscoring the alignment of the legal field with contemporary social values by avoiding language that could reinforce gender biases. The corpus data clearly demonstrate both the longstanding dominance and the gradual decline of gendered legal terms in English inheritance law. The marked prevalence of *heirs male* over the infrequent and subordinate *heirs female* reflects the legal marginalisation of women in the common law tradition, empirically supporting broader arguments concerning legal and social transformation. For centuries, this linguistic and legal framework upheld male control over lineage and property, as shown by the quantitative evidence of the historical predominance and subsequent decline of sexist masculine terminology. However, legislative reform and cultural change have largely eliminated these gendered terms from English law, which now retains them only in the narrow and largely symbolic realm of hereditary honours.

Moreover, the analysis highlights a discernible reduction in the use of vague or open-ended terminology, which is often ambiguous and can lead to interpretative challenges in legal texts. Terms indicating broad possibilities, such as *howsoever* and *whatsoever*, were frequently used in older British legal texts to cover a wide range of scenarios, providing flexibility in interpretation. Yet, these expressions have seen a significant decline in BLaRC and BoLC, replaced by more precise terms that limit ambiguity and thus minimise interpretative freedom. The reduced reliance on vague terminology reflects a modern preference for specificity, which is crucial in law to ensure predictable and consistent interpretations across jurisdictions. This trend aligns with the wider push for greater transparency and accountability in legal texts, driven by both the legal community and the public's expectation of a more straightforward and comprehensible legal language.

Furthermore, traditional formulaic expressions in legal texts have largely fallen out of favour. Historical phrases such as *in witness whereof*, typically found in contracts, and *know all men by these presents*, commonly used in powers of attorney, were once staples of British legal discourse. However, they survive chiefly in specific subgenres such as contractual documents and formal authorisations. Their gradual disappearance from modern legal texts, particularly in BLaRC and BoLC, seems to suggest a significant shift towards simpler and more accessible drafting conventions. Modern legal writing tends to replace such formulaic expressions with concise alternatives that retain legal meaning while reducing formality. Although certain formulaic elements remain in use within highly formalised contexts, such as contracts, their reduced prevalence underscores the modern shift towards legal language that is more relevant, efficient and easier to understand.

Additionally, jurisdictional and cultural differences between British and EU legal systems are reflected in variations across the corpora. For example, the prescriptive use of *shall*, prominent in EU-focused BoLC, contrasts with its more limited presence in British legal texts within BLaRC. In British court judgments, where much of the text narrates past events or facts, the use of *shall* is highly restricted. This suggests that while British legal texts have largely transitioned towards less rigid and more precise language, the EU's multilingual and diverse legal framework may still favour traditional terminology like *shall* to ensure consistency in drafting rules over time. Such variations demonstrate the adaptability of legal language in response to jurisdiction-specific requirements, thus underscoring the impact of regional and cultural influences on modern legal drafting practices. This adaptability signifies the effort of the legal profession to balance tradition with evolving linguistic preferences that meet contemporary needs within different legislative contexts.

Overall, the corpus-based analysis of these legal texts points to a progressive and intentional transformation in British and EU legal language, which now strives to meet the demands of clarity, inclusivity and accessibility. The findings illustrate how legal language has shifted away from its historically complex and formal origins towards a style that prioritises transparency, reflecting the legal community's efforts to make law more accessible to broader audiences. The gradual reduction of complex Latinisms, vague expressions, gendered language and traditional formulae aligns with broader legal reform movements advocating for the simplification and modernisation of legal language. As a result, legal language today is not only more comprehensible but also more socially aware, integrating respect for diversity and equity into its phrasing. This evolution in legal drafting reflects an ongoing re-balancing within the legal profession, aiming to ensure that legal documents are both precise and accessible while retaining the authority and formality appropriate to the law.

Bibliography

Abate, Salvatore C. 1998. *Il documento legale anglosassone*. Hoepli.

Adams, Kenneth. 2024. *A Manual of Style for Contract Drafting*. 5th ed. Chicago, IL: ABA Publishing.

Anderson, Scott. 2006. *Legal Indeterminacy in Context*. Ohio State University, Doctoral dissertation. OhioLINK Electronic Theses and Dissertations Center.

Bailey, Diggory. 2020. *Breaking Down Gender Stereotypes in Legal Writing*. Civil Service publication.

Bajčić, Martina. 2018. Coping with Vague EU Legal Concepts. In *Transnational, European, and National Labour Relations. Europeanization and Globalization*, ed. G. Sander, V. Tomljenović, and N. Bodiroga-Vukobrat, 97–107. Cham: Springer Link.

Baker, John H. 1998. The Three Languages of the Common Law. *McGill Law Journal* 43:5–24.

Baker, John H. 2019. *Introduction to English Legal History*. Oxford University Press.

Bhatia, Vijay K. 2010. *Textbook on Legal Language and Legal Writing*. New Delhi: Universal law publishing Co. Pvt. Ltd.

Biel, Łucja. 2015. Phraseological Profiles of Legislative Genres: Complex Prepositions as a Special Case of Legal Phrasemes in EU Law and National Law. *Fachsprache - International Journal of Specialized Communication 37* (3–4): 139–160.

Biel, Łucja, and Jan Engberg. 2013. Research Models and Methods in Legal Translation. *Linguistica Antverpensia, New Series - Themes in Translation Studies 12*:1–11.

Burnley, David. 1992. Lexis and Semantics. In *The Cambridge History of the English Language Volume II 1066–1476*, ed. Norman Blake, 409–499. Cambridge: Cambridge University Press.

Canale, Damiano. 2017. What Inferentialism Tells Us About Combinatory Vagueness in Law. In *Pragmatics and Law. Perspectives in Pragmatics, Philosophy and Psychology*, ed. F. Poggi and A. Capone, vol. 10, 43–66. Cham: Springer Link.

Coulthard, Malcolm, and Johnson, Alison. 2007. *An Introduction to Forensic Linguistics*. London/New York: Routledge.

Coulthard, Michael, and Alison Johnson. 2010. Introduction. In *The Routledge Handbook of Forensic Linguistics*, ed. Michael Coulthard and Alison Johnson, 1–16. London / New York: Routledge.

Cresswell, Julia. 2021. *The Oxford Dictionary of Word Origins*. Oxford: Oxford University Press.

Dickerson, Reed. 1986. *The Fundamentals of Legal Drafting*. 2nd ed. Boston: Little, Brown and Company.

Didikin, Anton. 2020. Speech Acts and Actions in Legal Language: Conceptual Analysis. *Proceedings of the Institute of State and Law of the RAS* 15 (1): 12–26.

Duckworth, Mark, and Arthur Spyrou, eds. 1995. *Law Words: 30 Essays on Legal Words and Phrases*. Sydney: Centre for Plain Legal Language.

Ďuricová, Alena. 2023. Kontextabhängigkeit von Rechtsbegriffen als Übersetzungsproblem. Acta Facultatis Philosophicae Universitatis Ostraviensis. *Studia Germanistica* 31:5–13. https://doi.org/10.15452/studiagermanistica.2022.31.0001.

Dvořáková, Eva. 2022. The Features of Legal Language in British Legislation: a Diachronic Perspective. *Fachsprache* 44 (3–4): 112–129. https://doi.org/10.24989/fs.v44i3-4.2022.

Endicott, Timothy. 2000. *Vagueness and law*. Oxford: Oxford University Press.

Endicott, Timothy. 2005. The Value of Vagueness. In *Vagueness in Normative Texts*, ed. Vijay K. Bhatia, Jan Engberg, Maurizio Gotti, and Dorothee Heller, 27–48. Bern: Peter Lang.

European Institute for Gender Equality (EIGE). 2019. *Toolkit on Gender-sensitive Communication*. Luxembourg: Publications Office of the European Union.

European Union. 2010. Charter of Fundamental Rights of the European Union. In *Official Journal of the European Union C83* (Vol. 53, p. 380). European Union.

Garner, Bryan A. 2002. *The Elements of Legal Style*. 2nd ed. Oxford: Oxford University Press.

Garner, Bryan A. 2004. *Black's Law Dictionary*. 8th ed. St Paul, MN: Thomson/West.

Garner, Bryan A. 2023. *The Redbook: A Manual on Legal Style*. 5th ed. West Academic Publishing.

Garzone, Giuliana. 2013. Variation in the Use of Modality in Legislative Texts: Focus on Shall. *Journal of Pragmatics* 57:68–81.

Giampieri, Patrizia. 2016. Is The European Legal English Legalese-Free? *Italian Journal of Public Law* 8 (2): 424–440.

Giampieri, Patrizia. 2022. How (Un)readable are the European and UNESCO Cultural Conventions in the Digital Era? *IJLLD* 10 (2): 22–42.

Giampieri, Patrizia. 2024. *Corpus-based Translation of Private Legal Documents.* Amsterdam: John Benjamins.

Giurizzato, Antonella. 2008. Dificultad de reformulación de las fórmulas fraseológicas y léxicas en la traducción legal del inglés al español. In *Terminología, Traducción y Comunicación especializada. Homenaje a Amelia de Irazazábal, Actas del Congreso Internacional 11–12 de octubre 2007*, ed. Carmen Navarro, 231–246. Verona: Edizioni Fiorini.

Goldstein, Tom, and Jethro K. Lieberman. 2016. *The Lawyer's Guide to Writing Well.* Berkeley / Los Angeles / London: University of California Press.

Gotti, Maurizio. 2012. Text and Genre. In *The Oxford Handbook of Language and Law*, ed. Peter Tiersma and Lawrence M. Solan, 52–66. Oxford University Press.

Jónsson, Ólafur Páll. 2009. Vagueness, Interpretation, and the Law. *Legal Theory* 15 (3): 193–214.

Kelley, Christopher R. 2018. An essay on legal writing in plain English. *Kyiv-Mohyla Law and Politics Journal* 4: 175–193.

Kopaczyk, Joanna. 2009. (Multi-word) Units of Meaning in 16th-century Legal Scots. In *Selected Proceedings of the 2008 Symposium on New Approaches in English Historical Lexis (HEL-LEX 2)*, ed. R. W. McConchie, 88–95. Somerville, MA: Cascadilla Proceedings Project.

Krapivkina, O. A. 2017. Semantics of the Verb Shall in Legal Discourse. *Jezikoslovlje* 18 (2): 305–317.

Laster, Kathy. 2001. *Law as Culture.* Annandale: The Federation Press.

Law Reform Commission of Victoria. 2017. *Plain English and The Law report.* https://www.lawreform.vic.gov.au/wp-content/uploads/2022/04/Plain-English-and-the-Law-republished_forweb.pdf

Leonardi, V., and Giampieri, P. 2024. Translating Employment Contracts: Insights from Corpus Linguistics. *Annali del Dipartimento di Metodi e Modelli per l'Economia, il Territorio e la Finanza*, 115–134. https://doi.org/10.13133/2611-6634/1672

Li, Yun. 2024. La internacionalización del derecho civil de contratos. *Revista Misión Jurídica* 17 (27): 163–181.

Longinotti, Daniela. 2009. Problemi specifici della traduzione giuridica: Traduzione di sentenze dal tedesco all'inglese. *Quaderni di Palazzo Serra* 17:1–38. http://www.lcm.unige.it/ricerca/pub/17/longinotti.pdf.

Marchand, Hans. 1960. *The Categories and Types of Present-Day English Word Formation: A Synchronic-Diachronic Approach.* Wiesbaden: Otto Harrassowitz.

Mattila, Heikki E. S. 2013. *Comparative Legal Linguistics: Language of Law, Latin and Modern Lingua Francas*. 2nd ed. Translated by Christopher Goddard. London: Routledge.

Mattissen, Johanna. 2019. *Coordination, Ambiguity and Divergence in Legal Acts of the European Union*. ZERL-Zeitschrift für Europäische Rechtslinguistik.

Mossman, Mary Jane. 1994. The Use of Non-Discriminatory Language in the Law. *Canadian Bar Review* 73 (3): 347–371.

Nystedt, Jane. 2000. L'italiano nei documenti della CEE: le sequenze di parole. In *Linguistica giuridica italiana e tedesca. Atti del Convegno di studi 'Linguistica giuridica italiana e tedesca: obiettivi, approcci, risultati'*, ed. Daniela Veronesi, 273–284. Padova: Unipress.

Pavlíčková, Eva. 2008. Ways of Addressing in Legal Discourse. *Discourse and Interaction* 1 (1): 87–98.

Pontrandolfo, Gianluca. 2023. The Importance of Being Patterned. Old and New Perspectives on Legal Phraseology. In *Handbook of Terminology*, ed. Łucjia Biel and Hendrik J. Kockaert, vol. 3, 124–151. Amsterdam: John Benjamins.

Rábade, Luis Iglesias. 2007. Some Lexical Collocational Patterns in Late Middle English Legal Texts. *Miscelánea: A Journal of English and American Studies* 35 (35): 31–56. https://dialnet.unirioja.es/servlet/articulo?codigo=2725045.

Ristikivi, Merike. 2005. Latin: the Common Legal Language of Europe. *Juridica International* 10:199–202.

Robertson, Colin D., and Máirtín Mac Aodha. 2023. Legal Terminology of the European Union. In *Handbook of Terminology*, ed. Łucja Biel and Hendrik J. Kockaert, vol. 3, 244–270. John Benjamins Publishing Company.

Saha, Tushar Kanti. 2010. *Textbook on Legal Methods, Legal Systems & Research*. New Delhi: Universal Law Publishing.

Solan, Lawrence M. 2012. Linguistic Issues in Statutory Interpretations. In *The Oxford Handbook of Language and Law*, ed. Peter Tiersma and Lawrence M. Solan, 87–99. Oxford: Oxford University Press.

Solan, Lawrence M. 2018. The Interpretation of Legal Language. *Annual Review of Linguistics* 4 (1): 337–355.

The Joint Practical Guide of the European Parliament, the Council and the Commission for Persons involved in the Drafting of European Union Legislation. 2023. Luxembourg: Office for Official Publications of the European Communities.

Tiersma, Peter. 1999. *Legal Language*. Chicago: University of Chicago Press.

Toktobaev, B., and A. Urmatova. 2024. Legal Terminology: The Meaning of Unification and the Relationship Between the Concept of Harmonization. *Bulletin of Science and Practice* 10 (10): 305–309. https://doi.org/10.33619/2414-2948/107/37.

Williams, Christopher. 2004. Legal Language and Plain Language: An Introduction. *ESP Across Culture* 1:111–124.

Williams, Christopher. 2013. Changes in the Verb Phrase in Legislative Language in English. In *The Verb Phrase in English: Investigating Recent Language Change with Corpora*, ed. Bas Aarts, Joanne Close, Geoffrey Leech, and Sean Wallis, 353–371. Cambridge: Cambridge University Press.

Williams, Christopher. 2023. *The Impact of Plain Language on Legal English in the United Kingdom*. London/New York: Routledge.

6

Artificial Intelligence and The Legal Field

6.1 Historical Background of AI

Artificial Intelligence has been conceptualised in numerous ways by scholars. Turing (1950), for instance, was among the first to propose the hypothesis that computers could exhibit intelligent behaviour. Similarly, McCarthy et al. (1955) speculated that machines might be capable of formalising and replicating human intelligence. Subsequently, McCarthy (1959) further recognised that:

> Interesting work is being done in programming computers to solve problems which require a high degree of intelligence in humans. However, certain elementary verbal reasoning processes so simple that they can be carried out by any non-feeble-minded human have yet to be simulated by machine programs (ibid.: online). 20

A significant turning point occurred with the advent of knowledge-based systems during the 1960s and early 1970s. These new paradigms introduced decision-making programmes that were applied across various fields to offer expert-level support (Buchanan and Shortliffe 1984). A notable example of this was MYCIN, a computer-based system designed

V. Leonardi, P. Giampieri, *Legal English through the Ages*,
https://doi.org/10.1007/978-3-032-02172-4_6

to assist physicians in diagnosing bacterial infections and selecting appropriate treatment regimens (Van Melle 1978). The 1960s were also pivotal for the establishment and institutionalisation of academic laboratories dedicated to artificial intelligence, such as the Massachusetts Institute of Technology (MIT) (Buchanan 2006). In 1965, the first expert forum on machine intelligence was held in Edinburgh, Scotland. This was followed by additional forums, conferences and expert gatherings, including the creation of the Association for Computing Machinery's Special Interest Group on Artificial Intelligence (ACM SIGART) and the International Joint Conference on Artificial Intelligence (IJCAI) in 1969. In 1980, the American Association for Artificial Intelligence (AAAI) was established with the aim of organising conferences for its members located in North America.

More recent definitions and applications of artificial intelligence have increasingly centred on human intelligence, focusing on concepts such as "case-based reasoning, analogy, induction, reasoning under uncertainty, and default reasoning" (Buchanan 2006: 60). Russell and Norvig (2010), for instance, assert that intelligent machines are capable of thinking both humanly and rationally. Similarly, Weaver (2013) describes AI as systems or programmes that can emulate aspects of human intelligence. Monostori (2019) further emphasises the human intelligence component within AI, highlighting its capacity to demonstrate faculties such as "reasoning, learning, goal-seeking, problem-solving, and adaptability" (Monostori 2019: 47). The European Regulation 2024/1689 (2024) defines AI in the following terms:

> 'AI system' means a machine-based system that is designed to operate with varying levels of autonomy and that may exhibit adaptiveness after deployment, and that, for explicit or implicit objectives, infers, from the input it receives, how to generate outputs such as predictions, content, recommendations, or decisions that can influence physical or virtual environments. (ibid.: 46)

6.2 Integrating AI in the Legal Field

AI has emerged as a fundamental component across various sectors, and its application in the legal field has attracted considerable interest in recent years (Brooks et al. 2020; Thomson Reuters 2023a, b). This section aims to provide a comprehensive overview of the use of AI in the legal domain by investigating its historical development, analysing its various uses and assessing the benefits and drawbacks identified by academics and researchers.

AI has gained significant prominence in the legal domain in the twenty-first century, driven by advancements in machine learning (ML) and natural language processing (NLP). These innovations have transformed various legal processes and workflows. Machine learning applications have gradually reduced human intervention in labour-intensive legal processes (Brooks et al. 2020: 139). ML algorithms exploit large datasets to automatically learn and predict, classify and detect anomalies (Domingue et al. 2016: 69). This capability has enabled the application of ML in tasks such as topic identification and document arrangement (Domingue et al. 2016: 67). As far as natural language processing (NLP) is concerned, the processes of discovery, contract analysis and predictive activities have facilitated the introduction of new practices within law firms or the modification of existing ones (Alarie et al. 2018; Brooks et al. 2020). For instance, NLP enables users to extract and comprehend concepts from specialised terminology and associate them with organised knowledge (Lyko et al. 2016: 53). In other words, the applications of AI within the legal field are varied and encompass a wide range of functions, including document review and contract analysis (Alarie et al. 2018; Yamane 2020; Sheeba 2023), as well as predictive legal analytics (Ashley 2017; Abbott 2020; Sheeba 2023; Thomson Reuters 2023b).

Scholars such as Susskind and Susskind (2022) and Susskind (2023) assert that AI has reshaped the legal landscape through its role in automating routine legal tasks, leading to increased efficiency and cost-effectiveness. Repetitive operations can be automated, thus reducing costs (Brooks et al. 2020; Sheeba 2023), making legal services more affordable and accessible (Sheeba 2023). Susskind and Susskind (2022) and Susskind (2023) foresee a progressive shift from human expertise to machine intelligence in many legal domains. They envision courts becoming online forums, the legal business being AI-based on a global scale, the emergence of disruptive start-ups and virtually led legal training. In this scenario, a new set of legal jobs will obviously emerge. In this respect, it is worth mentioning Alternative Service Providers (ALSPs) (Curle 2017; Brooks et al. 2020), which are non-law firms that provide an array of legal services ranging from litigation support to IP (intellectual property) management. These new business entities are gaining ground in the AI-driven legal landscape, offering much lower rates and more expedited services compared to traditional law firms (Brooks et al. 2020). AI can also foster legal literacy and competency. Ashley (2017) emphasises the role of AI in extracting meaningful insights from vast legal datasets, enabling lawyers to make more informed and targeted decisions. Innovative legal applications are emerging that will revolutionise the legal field by seamlessly integrating computational models of legal reasoning with legal texts. Such tools will empower lawyers to generate compelling arguments for or against specific legal controversies, forecast potential outcomes and provide detailed explanations that legal professionals can independently evaluate. These ground-breaking applications will streamline legal information retrieval and facilitate cognitive computing.

Cognitive computing is grounded in intelligent machine methodologies and systems that emulate the activities and cognitive processes of the human brain (Raghavan et al. 2016). Consequently, emerging applications of AI are poised to foster a synergistic relationship between humans and technology, wherein each entity complements the strengths and capabilities of the other. This collaborative dynamic is expected to enhance problem-solving and decision-making processes across various domains, ultimately leading to more effective outcomes. This sentiment is echoed by Abbott (2020), who examines how AI enhances legal research and decision-making processes through its capacity to process substantial volumes of legal information. Nevertheless, the potential of AI may be constrained by outdated legal frameworks. As the influence of intelligent machines extends beyond mere information provision to actively driving and determining administrative processes and policy choices, the question of liability necessitates thorough examination, particularly concerning client representation and legitimacy. In this context, Abbott's (2020) work elucidates the legal constraints and complexities associated with the rise of intelligent machines.

The integration of artificial intelligence into various sectors has reached such a level of prevalence that certain academic groups are beginning to explore the possibility of granting legal personhood to intelligent machines, thereby leading to the concept of Artificial Intelligence Entities (AIE) (Doomen 2023). Nevertheless, this notion remains overly complex to be implemented at present. The legal scientific community has expressed considerable scepticism regarding this issue. Alqodsi and Gura (2023), for instance, highlight significant concerns pertaining to liability for damages resulting from misuse of services, accountability for AI-induced discrimination and the challenges associated with presenting evidence in court for faults or injuries caused by AI, among others. A growing body of literature assesses the reliability of AI in translation training and practice (Constantin et al. 2024). Prieto Ramos (2024) conducted a survey involving institutional translators, which revealed that the perceived skills translators need nowadays are language and textual competences, strategic competences (including MT post-editing) and thematic competences (Prieto Ramos 2024: 167–168). For this reason, Quinci (2024) raises significant considerations regarding the training of students in Translation Studies and the professional development of translators in MT and post-editing activities. The integration of AI technologies into translation practices necessitates a re-evaluation of existing curricula to ensure that they adequately prepare students for the evolving demands of the profession.

6.2.1 Advantages of AI in the Legal Field

As previously discussed, one of the primary advantages of integrating AI into the legal profession is the potential for enhancing both efficiency and accuracy (Brooks et al. 2020; Gigi et al. 2023; Sheeba 2023; Wu et al. 2023). Sheeba (2023) asserts that AI enables legal professionals to broaden their skill sets by automating labour-intensive tasks, allowing them to concentrate on strategic insights and complex problem-solving. This view is corroborated by Wu et al. (2023), who argue that lawyers can significantly benefit from AI-assisted writing (AIAW), which improves efficiency in drafting legal documents and briefs through the use of intelligent software solutions. Furthermore, AI-generated content (AIGC) can assist in creating tailored social media posts, thereby increasing a law firm's visibility and business prospects (Wu et al. 2023).

In addition to these benefits, AI also offers significant advantages in specific legal applications. The drafting of smart contracts, for instance, is another area where AI can be particularly effective (Gigi et al. 2023). In the context of traditional real estate transactions, paperwork and manual processes are often time-consuming and susceptible to errors. Smart contracts automate repetitive tasks, thereby reducing the need for extensive paperwork and improving overall efficiency (ibid.). Autto et al. (2024) explore the transformative potential of generative AI in contract design and thinking. They argue that traditional contracts often prioritise failure, rendering them complex and ineffective and advocate for proactive contracting principles to enhance clarity and usability. The authors highlight the role of AI tools, such as ChatGPT, in generating contract content and structure, while emphasising the importance of ethical considerations and human oversight in this process.

Several scholars argue that the use of AI fosters accuracy within legal processes. Brooks et al. (2020) assert that AI can expedite repetitive tasks that require minimal professional judgement. By automating these functions, AI allows legal practitioners to focus on more complex, judgement-driven activities, thereby enhancing overall accuracy. Sheeba (2023) further contends that AI-driven algorithms are specifically designed to process vast amounts of data, such as "big data" (Laney 2001; Cavanillas et al. 2016), both rapidly and accurately. Consequently, the likelihood of human error in these contexts is significantly diminished.

AI is also regarded as an innovation driver. Hadfield (2016) notes that traditional legal systems rely heavily on bureaucratic mechanisms, legislatures and courts for law-making, rendering them slow and resource-intensive. This inefficiency prevents the legal framework from adequately addressing the needs of businesses, governments and individuals (see also Abbott 2020). In response, Hadfield advocates the integration of regulatory systems with new, technology-driven models and methodologies.

The author suggests that such frameworks can effectively manage innovations through tech-based solutions.

The field of law librarianship has similarly been transformed by the advent of AI. Kroski (2020) has conducted a pioneering study into the evolving practices of law librarians, predicting significant role changes. The research highlights the potential benefits of AI in key areas such as legal research and administrative tasks. Kroski (2020) emphasises that legal professionals are leveraging AI tools to streamline routine tasks, and law schools are rapidly adapting their curricula to accommodate the evolving demands of the legal profession.

Regarding fair and impartial justice, a recent report by the European Union Agency for the Operational Management of Large-Scale IT Systems in the Area of Freedom, Security, and Justice (eu-LISA) and the European Union Agency for Criminal Justice Cooperation (Eurojust) (henceforth "eu-LISA and Eurojust Report") (2022) underscores the pivotal role of AI in enhancing access to justice. The report asserts that fair and impartial justice can be facilitated through "anonymisation of court decisions, speech-to-text conversion and transcription, machine translation, chat-bots supporting access to justice, and robotic process automation" (eu-LISA and Eurojust Report 2022: 10). Furthermore, AI applied to legal translation has proven beneficial in investigations, reducing both the time and cost of sworn translations. In most cases, the report posits that "only post-editing will be necessary instead of translation" (eu-LISA and Eurojust Report 2022: 18). However, Escribe and Mitkov (2023) suggest that further advancements in machine translation (MT) algorithms are required. They argue that post-editing (PE) activities should be incorporated into the system to refine MT parameters and fully automate the PE process. In practice, the authors recommend designing PE systems as interactive models in which corpus consultation plays a fundamental role, as corpora continue to serve as "the cornerstone of the latest innovations in translation technology" (Escribe and Mitkov 2023: 57).

A report by Thomson Reuters (2023b: 11–13) outlines several other successful applications of AI in the legal sector. For instance, contract review and analysis can be automated to reduce time, costs and errors. Similarly, due diligence and compliance reviews can be performed by intelligent software. Legal research tasks, such as document analysis, review of legal briefs, citation suggestion and the identification of relevant arguments from past cases, can also be automated, along with e-discovery, which benefits from accurate analysis of pre-trial documents. Moreover, AI can generate statistical insights from past litigations and judgments, potentially influencing trial outcomes. Lastly, AI is capable of handling administrative tasks such as invoicing, further contributing to the efficiency of legal practice.

6.2.2 Disadvantages of AI in the Legal Field

While many researchers praise the potential of AI, others highlight significant drawbacks that must be promptly addressed. One major concern is the possibility of AI replacing human labour. The displacement of certain legal tasks by AI systems has sparked apprehension regarding job loss and the devaluation of human expertise (Buchanan 2006; Yamane 2020; Sheeba 2023). Hassani et al. (2020) note that AI is now capable of performing tasks traditionally executed by humans. However, the authors propose a solution through the use of Intelligence Augmentation (IA), which enhances human intelligence. By combining AI and IA, they argue, both technologies can coexist and be mutually beneficial to humanity.

Other scholars argue that intelligent machines will never fully replace humans in the legal profession (Oseid et al. 2019). While some fear that AI's growing sophistication threatens legal employment, others maintain that these concerns are unfounded. AI in the legal sector, they argue, highlights the unique qualities that distinguish effective lawyering, rather than replacing it. According to Oseid et al. (2019), lawyers possess skills beyond AI's capacity, such as empathetic listening, the ability to devise strategies to uncover hidden case elements and the application of expertise and judgement to resolve complex issues. These skills require an empathetic human touch that AI cannot replicate. This view is echoed by the Thomson Reuters survey (2023a: 10), where legal practitioners affirm that "the client relationship and understanding of a client's business (…) cannot be replicated" and that "legal work is more than just words". Remus and Levy (2017) support this, asserting that intelligent machines will never replace lawyers, as human expertise and personal interaction remain vital to the lawyer-client relationship. For instance, no software can tailor legal advice to a client's perceived risks and benefits, nor can any machine instil a sense of democratic participation in the law-making process (Remus and Levy 2017). Instead of supplanting their work, lawyers should use AI to augment it (Yamane 2020). Alarie et al. (2018) agree on that, suggesting that intelligent systems will assist legal professionals by enhancing their decision-making processes, leading to the emergence of "digital lawyers" (Susskind 2023). Calo (2015: 547) offers a unique perspective, positing that legal actors such as courts and juries will eventually need to determine whether anthropomorphic technology should be treated as socially meaningful.

In this evolving landscape, ethical concerns about biases in AI algorithms have become a central focus of academic debate (Sheeba 2023; Wu et al. 2023). Sheeba (2023) emphasises the need to consider privacy, confidentiality and bias when deploying AI systems. Crawford and Calo (2016) highlight the risk of bias in AI, which can lead to discriminatory outcomes (see also Leslie et al. 2021). They argue that the opacity of AI's decision-making processes worsens these problems, making it essential to address ethical considerations in AI's application to legal systems. As an example, they cite AI tools designed to prevent crime, which may inadvertently reinforce discrimination by targeting specific groups rather than reducing crime. Leslie et al. (2021) provide further examples, noting that stereotyping biases can become entrenched in AI design and training data. Calabresi (2021: 806) suggests implementing bias tests to eliminate racial discrimination and other prejudices. The European Union's AI Act (2024/1689) has introduced strict regulations, classifying AI systems used to apply the law to concrete cases as highly risky.

In the United States, the American Bar Association (ABA) has adopted professional conduct rules aimed at mitigating bias, which prohibit the use of AI to replace substantive legal work (Model Rules of Professional Conduct 2020) (Medianik 2018; Yamane 2020; Calabresi 2021). Yamane (2020) argues that AI programs should not offer legal advice without human involvement, suggesting that lawyers must always verify and supplement AI-generated data. This approach ensures that "human lawyers should not completely rely on AI programs" (Yamane 2020: 889).

Regarding privacy and confidentiality, AI algorithms must be designed with strong safeguards to protect sensitive client information. For example, large-scale AI models trained on publicly sourced data must avoid copyright infringement and comply with legal protocols (Wu et al. 2023). The eu-LISA and Eurojust Report (2022: 27) advocates a risk-based approach that weighs the costs and benefits of AI while preserving fundamental rights, including data protection. This approach aims to ensure the safe application of AI in practice.

In academia, the use of AI has also sparked ethical concerns. Emsley (2023) argues that AI tools such as ChatGPT should not be used by scholars, as they generate false references and misleading information, potentially leading to research misconduct. However, other researchers are exploring ways to develop machine-generated literature reviews that could rival or even surpass human writing (Visconti 2021; Zhang et al. 2022).

Calo's (2015: 549) ultimate questions focus on the new challenges posed by AI, which include "embodying data, harnessing unpredictability, and disentangling person from instrument". In this emerging AI landscape, he foresees the need for a new legal discipline, cyberlaw, to address the systematic changes required to maintain a balance of values in the face of technological advancements. Calo (2015: 553) argues that recalibrating laws is essential to preserving human values amidst these technological changes, and he advocates proactive legal frameworks to mitigate the potential harms associated with AI in the legal sector. He touches on important aspects such as strict liability in criminal law, foreseeability in tort law and necessary reforms in administrative law.

The literature on AI in the legal field offers a nuanced understanding of its applications, benefits and challenges. While some scholars emphasise the potential for increased efficiency and accuracy, concerns about ethics, confidentiality, bias and discrimination caution against an uncritical embrace of AI. Thus, the legal challenges associated with AI underscore the need for a careful and comprehensive approach to its integration into legal practice and the legal system as a whole.

6.2.3 AI-driven Tools for the Legal Domain

A growing array of AI-powered tools is available to legal firms, each offering specific functionalities that streamline and enhance various legal tasks. These tools are being adopted to automate tasks such as document analysis, contract review, legal research and case predictions (Mullen 2018; Gigi et al. 2023). Below is a summary of the key AI-driven legal solutions currently in use:

- **AttorneyIO**: A service that allows lawyers to input legal documents and receive output based on comparisons to existing cases.
- **CARA AI**: This tool processes uploaded legal documents, such as briefs and complaints, and customises the output according to user requests.
- **ChatGPT**: Although not initially designed for legal use, ChatGPT's application in legal firms has expanded significantly. It aids in generating contract drafts and assisting legal analyses, offering advice based on legal doctrines, case law and precedents (Thomson Reuters 2023a).
- **Diligen**: An AI-powered contract review software that detects key terms, provisions and generates contract summaries using machine learning (ML).
- **EVA**: A brief analyser that checks case history and identifies similar cases for legal research.
- **Everlaw**: A cloud-based e-discovery platform capable of document translation and processing large sets of legal files.
- **Evisort**: A natural language processing (NLP) tool that automates contract creation and data search.
- **Hyperlex**: A contract creation and analysis platform that supports users through the negotiation phase.
- **iManage**: An automatic classification platform that extracts critical information such as terms and clauses from legal documents.
- **Judicata**: An NLP-based tool that identifies relevant case law to aid legal research and case analysis.
- **Kira**: A contract review platform that retrieves required documents and identifies contract clauses.

- **Law Geek**: Assists in contract review, suggesting modifications and identifying missing clauses.
- **Lex Machina**: Provides insights into judges' and parties' case records, including predictions on motions' outcomes.
- **LexisNexis**: A comprehensive platform offering data analytics, legal research and a database of case law.
- **Luminance**: AI-driven document review and contract analysis software.
- **ROSS**: A document analyser that flags relevant cases for inclusion in legal briefs.
- **SmithAI**: A client engagement platform with virtual receptionist services, live chat and campaign services.
- **Westlaw Edge**: A suite of legal research tools that integrates AI-driven analytics, providing insights into judges, courts, attorneys and law firms.

As far as AI-powered solutions for legal firms are concerned, ChatGPT deserves significant attention due to its ability to enhance various aspects of legal practice. Developed by OpenAI in 2022, **ChatGPT** (Generative Pre-trained Transformer) is an AI chatbot that has seen rapid adoption by legal firms, despite not being originally tailored for the legal domain. Law firms use ChatGPT for generating contract drafts, providing legal analyses and even offering advice based on legal doctrines, precedents and case law (Thomson Reuters 2023a, b; Gigi et al. 2023).

A survey conducted among law firms in the UK, USA and Canada revealed that 82% of respondents believed ChatGPT and similar generative AI tools could be applied to legal work (Thomson Reuters 2023a: 7–8). ChatGPT's rapid growth further highlights its impact: it reached 1 million users within five days in 2022 compared to 2.5 months for Instagram in 2010, 10 months for Facebook in 2004 and 3.5 years for Netflix in 1999 (Thomson Reuters 2023b: 3).

While ChatGPT offers efficient solutions for language-based queries, document drafting and case analysis, it is not without its flaws. Notably, concerns about privacy and confidentiality persist (Thomson Reuters 2023a). Additionally, ChatGPT sometimes produces "hallucinations"—fabricated information that appears credible but is inaccurate (Thomson

Reuters 2023b: 5). This issue, often seen in AI-generated content, can lead to erroneous legal conclusions if unchecked (Emsley 2023; Guerreiro et al. 2023).

The challenge posed by "hallucinations" is not a novel issue within the academic field (see, for example, Emsley 2023, and the research paper by Guerreiro et al. 2023 focusing on "hallucinations" produced by NMT, neural machine translation solutions).

Consequently, the following section will investigate to what extent ChatGPT (3.5) can deliver meaningful responses to inquiries concerning legal language, particularly complex *legalese* features in a historical law report.

6.3 Applying AI to Detect *Legalese* and Make Legal Texts more Intelligible

The sample text is reported in Table 6.1. *Legalese* elements are written in bold to facilitate comprehensibility.

It is evident that the sample text is replete with *legalese* elements, which are marked in bold. In addition to the terms marked in bold, the text is

Table 6.1 Sample text sourced from the CHELAR

Clause 12 provided that "If **the purchaser shall make default** in the payment of any of the other instalments mentioned in clause 2 **hereof or any part thereof** on the due dates as provided in **the said** clause the Land Company may **(but subject to and without affecting in any wise the sale and the conveyance or the right thereto under clause 6 hereof)** by notice in writing sent by registered letter and addressed to the purchaser specifying which of the remedies **hereinafter** mentioned **the Land Company** intends to exercise, rescind this agreement and may either **enter into possession** of any **lands stores livestock and other equipment remaining unsold whereupon** all moneys already paid by the purchaser **shall be absolutely forfeited** to the Land Company and this contract shall **subject as aforesaid thereupon** become absolutely **null and void** or may **subject as aforesaid** resell **the same** at the purchaser's risk either by public auction or private contract (either together or in lots) subject to such **stipulations** as it may think fit and in such case any deficiency in price after giving credit for all sums paid by the purchaser or **his** nominees as part payment of the sum of 321,000l".

excessively lengthy, exceeding 200 words, and features no punctuation, with only a single comma present between "exercise" and "rescind". This lack of punctuation further hinders clarity, thus complicating comprehension. To enhance understanding, the *legalese* elements have been categorised and detailed in Table 6.2, which is organised into three columns: the first lists the *legalese* terms in the order they appear in the sample text; the second provides an explanation for their classification as *legalese*; and the third presents simplified, literature-based alternatives where relevant. These plain-language substitutes are sourced from academic literature (Tiersma 1999; Bhatia 2010; Williams 2023), offering well-researched options to improve comprehension and decrease complexity.

As shown in Table 6.2, there is a significant prevalence of *legalese* elements that require further attention. For instance, the term "shall" appears frequently throughout the text and may be more suitably replaced by "will" or "must" to enhance clarity. A similar observation can be made regarding the frequent use of deixis (e.g., "hereof", "the said", "hereinafter", "thereupon"), nominalisation (e.g., "make the payment", "enter into possession") and Latinisms (e.g., "null", "stipulation").

Furthermore, it is worth highlighting the term "rescind", which represents a particularly complex legal expression meaning "annul" or "cancel". According to Black's Law Dictionary (8th Edition), the term "rescind" is defined as "to abrogate or cancel (a contract) unilaterally or by agreement" (Garner 2004: 4075). This interpretation has been corroborated and explored in several judicial decisions, including *Tharpe v. Tracy* (1949) and *The Colonial Penn Insurance Company v. Guzorek* (1997).

Based on the analysis presented in Table 6.2, the sample text has been rewritten in plain language by a human, as illustrated in Table 6.3. The revised text has been meticulously crafted to ensure linguistic clarity and accessibility. Alternative formulations are provided within square brackets, with anonymised designations "XX" and "YY" employed to refer to the relevant parties. This approach not only facilitates comprehension but also ensures that the essential legal concepts are preserved while making them more approachable for a broader audience.

As observed in Table 6.3, the text is divided into distinct sentences with explicit subjects. The term "shall" has been replaced with "will" or "must" to enhance both clarity and directness. Moreover, the text

Table 6.2 *Legalese* elements in the sample text

Legalese element	Explanation	Plain equivalent
The purchaser	De-personalisation of the parties	Use the proper nouns of the parties
The Land Company	De-personalisation of the parties	Use the proper nouns of the parties
Shall	Archaic modal verb referring to either a future action or an obligation	Will, Must
Make default in the payment of	Nominalisation	Will not pay
Hereof	Deictic adverb meaning "of this document"	Omit or write "of this document"
Or any part thereof	Vagueness marker and deictic adverbial phrase meaning "or any part of the same document"	Omit
The said	Deictic phrase	Omit or mention "clause 2" again
(but subject to and without affecting in any wise the sale and the conveyance or the right thereto under clause 6 hereof)	Syntactic discontinuity	Break down the whole sentence and re-write it in smaller units
May (...) by notice in writing sent by registered letter and addressed to the purchaser specifying which of the remedies hereinafter mentioned the Land Company intends to exercise	Syntactic discontinuity	Break down the whole sentence and re-write it in smaller units
Hereinafter	Deictic adverb	In this document; Specified as follows
Enter into possession	Nominalisation	Possess; become the possessor

(*continued*)

Table 6.2 (continued)

Legalese element	Explanation	Plain equivalent
Lands stores livestock and other equipment remaining unsold	List of elements with no commas	Insert commas between the elements
Whereupon	Archaic deictic element	After which/that
Shall be absolutely forfeited	Passive construction with a Law French verb	Use the active voice specifying the agent and changing "forfeit" into "lose the right to... in favour of..."
Subject as aforesaid	Complex prepositional phrase with a deictic adverbial element	On the condition previously mentioned / stated
Thereupon	Temporal deictic element	After that; Subsequently
Null and void	Near-synonyms; Latinism	Void
The same	Unclear object	State the object, i.e., "lands stores livestock and other equipment remaining unsold"
Stipulation	Law Latin	Agreement
His	Sexist language	His or her; Their

Table 6.3 Human-written plain version of the sample text

Clause 12 mentioned [stated] that "If XX will not pay any of the other instalments mentioned in clause 2 of this document on the due dates as established [indicated; set] in clause 2, YY may cancel this agreement [make this agreement void] by giving a written notice to send to XX by registered post. In the written notice, YY must specify the remedies that it wants to exercise. According to clause 6, in exercising its right, YY must not affect the sale and the transfer of rights. Alternatively, YY may become the possessor of lands, stores, live stock and other equipment that is not sold. After that, XX will lose in favour of YY the right to all the sums already paid and this [the present] contract will be null. Alternatively, YY may resell the lands, stores, live stock and other equipment (either jointly or in parts) in a public auction or private contract at XX's risk. YY may agree to do so as it thinks proper. In this case, YY will consider any difference in price as a partial payment of the sum of £ 321,000".

deliberately avoids nominalisation and passive constructions, which frequently obfuscate meaning. The exclusion of Latinisms and syntactic discontinuities further contributes to the text's coherence, while the judicious application of commas significantly enhances readability and comprehension. This revised structure thus offers a more accessible and reader-friendly rendition of the original text.

It is also worth examining the responses produced by ChatGPT. This investigation may yield valuable insights into the capabilities of artificial intelligence in producing coherent and contextually appropriate text, thereby enriching our understanding of its potential applications. The implications of these findings could be significant, particularly concerning the evolving dynamics of automated writing assistance and its integration across a diverse array of academic, scientific and professional fields.

This scrutiny not only deepens our comprehension of AI's current functionalities but also stimulates critical discussions regarding ethical considerations and the reliability of AI-generated content in various contexts. As the landscape of artificial intelligence continues to evolve, it is essential to contemplate how these technologies can be employed responsibly, ensuring that they complement rather than undermine academic integrity and professional standards. This reflection is crucial as we navigate the challenges and opportunities presented by AI in contemporary discourse.

6.3.1 ChatGPT Prompts and Responses

The sample text was input into the ChatGPT interface, and the chatbot was prompted to identify *legalese* elements. The first prompt (P1) issued to the model was as follows:

P1: Identify the *legalese* elements in the following clause: "[sample text]".

The responses generated in reaction to this initial prompt were not particularly compelling, as illustrated in Table 6.4. This suggests that the model may require further refinement or more specific guidance to effectively recognise and articulate the nuances of legal language. Such

Table 6.4 ChatGPT answering the first prompt (P1)

The clause provided contains several *legalese* elements, which are characteristic features of legal language used in contracts. Here are some notable elements: 4. **Conditional Statement:** The clause begins with a conditional statement, using the phrase "If the purchaser shall make default". 5. **Reference to Other Clauses:** It refers to specific clauses within the agreement, such as "clause 2" and "clause 6". 6. **Enumerated Conditions:** The clause enumerates conditions that may trigger certain actions by using phrases like "on the due dates", "by notice in writing" and "specifying which of the remedies hereinafter mentioned". 7. **Legal Terminology:** The language includes legal terminology, such as "rescind this agreement", "enter into possession", "absolutely forfeited", "null and void", "resell the same" and "deficiency in price". 8. **Formal Notification:** It requires a formal notice in writing sent by registered letter to the purchaser. 9. **Enumerated Remedies:** The clause outlines specific remedies available to the Land Company, including rescinding the agreement, entering into possession and reselling the property. 10. **Specification of Risks:** It specifies that if the Land Company decides to resell the property, it will be done "at the purchaser's risk". 11. **Financial Calculations:** The clause includes financial calculations and considerations, such as "all moneys already paid by the purchaser", the total sum of "321,000l" and the calculation of any deficiency in price. 12. **Stipulations:** It mentions that the resale may be subject to "such stipulations as it may think fit". These elements collectively contribute to the legal precision and clarity required in contractual language.

observations highlight the challenges inherent in training artificial intelligence to understand complex legal terminology and concepts, which often necessitate a high degree of precision and contextual awareness. Further exploration of this issue could provide insights into improving AI's capabilities in legal text analysis, thereby enhancing its utility in legal contexts.

As illustrated in Table 6.4, ChatGPT does not provide a strict enumeration of *legalese* elements; rather, it engages in a discussion of specific components within the clause, assigning them legal nomenclature. For instance, the chatbot identifies "conditional statement" in item 1) of Table 6.4 and "formal notification" in item 5), stating that "[t]he clause begins with a conditional statement, using the phrase 'If the purchaser shall make default'" and "[i]t requires a formal notice in writing sent by registered letter to the purchaser". This approach provides a straightforward title and a clarification for the complex clause phrases "If the purchaser shall make default in the payment of any of the other instalments" and "by notice in writing sent by registered letter and addressed to the purchaser", respectively.

In other words, ChatGPT attempts to identify the contents of clauses by categorising them into specific legal classifications and conceptual frameworks. Nevertheless, this approach does not align with the requirements set forth in the initial prompt. Other examples include (2) "reference to other clauses", (3) "enumerated conditions" and (6) "enumerated remedies", among others. The chatbot seems to focus on elucidating the contents of the document without adequately addressing any form of *legalese*. The sole reference to "legal terminology" (and potentially *legalese*) is found in item (4), where the AI interface mentions "null and void". Beyond this singular reference, there is a conspicuous absence of mentions regarding legal jargon. Consequently, it appears that the meaning and implications of the term *legalese* may have been misinterpreted or insufficiently explored within this context. This observation raises important questions about the effectiveness of AI tools like ChatGPT in accurately identifying and articulating complex legal language, which is essential for their application in legal practice. Further investigation into this issue could enhance understanding of AI's capabilities and limitations in processing legal texts, ultimately informing its integration into legal workflows.

For the reasons mentioned above, the initial prompt is reformulated to enhance clarity. Therefore, the word *legalese* is simplified and its meaning explicitly defined. As *legalese* is often referred to as an "archaic", "old-fashioned" and an "intricate" aspect of legal language (Tiersma 1999: 93, 95, 214; Bhatia 2010: 22; Williams 2023), the reformulation of P1 ("P1-1") is as follows:

P1-1: Find archaic, intricate and old-fashioned language elements in the following clause "[*sample text*]".

The responses generated in reaction to this revised prompt are remarkably more compelling and are documented in Table 6.5. This improvement suggests that by explicitly defining the characteristics of *legalese*, the AI model is better equipped to identify and articulate the specific elements of language that may be considered outdated or unnecessarily complex. Such refinements not only enhance the effectiveness of AI in analysing legal texts but also contribute to a broader understanding of how language evolves within legal contexts. Further exploration of these findings could provide valuable insights into the implications of using clearer, more accessible language in legal documentation, thereby promoting greater comprehension among diverse audiences.

As illustrated in Table 6.5, ChatGPT successfully identifies several elements of *legalese* (e.g., "whereof", "null and void", "his", etc.). In certain instances, the chatbot highlights particularly obscure terms, noting that they exemplify an old-fashioned style and, consequently, are not aligned with contemporary usage. For example, the term "whereupon" is aptly recognised, with the chatbot indicating that it pertains to "a subsequent event or consequence". Similarly, the expression "his nominees" is acknowledged, with the observation that "the use of 'nominees' instead of a simpler term contributes to the formal and legalistic language".

Other interesting identifications include terms such as "shall", "hereof", "absolutely forfeited", "aforesaid", and "null and void". In these cases, plausible alternatives are suggested: "will", "of this", "entirely lost", "something mentioned earlier in the text" and "entirely invalid". However, it is worth noting that there is no reference made to syntactic discontinuities, passive constructions, sexist language, absence of punctuation marks, sentence length, nominalisation or deixis. Despite these omissions, the overall performance of the task can be considered satisfactory. It is likely that the system would benefit from more precise instructions in order to enhance the effectiveness of its responses.

The subsequent area of investigation, without extensively examining this hypothesis, concerns ChatGPT's response to the second prompt (P2), which requests a transformation of the intricate and obscure aspects of the sample text into a more accessible and intelligible final text. Based on the insights obtained from P1-1, expectations for P2 are high. The formulation of P2 is as follows:

Table 6.5 ChatGPT answering the reformulated initial prompt (P1-1)

The given clause contains several archaic, intricate and old-fashioned language elements. Here are some examples:

1. **"shall make default":** The use of "shall" for indicating future action is somewhat archaic. In modern language, we often use "will" instead.
2. **instalments":** The spelling "instalments" is an older form, and the modern spelling is "installments."
3. **"hereof":** This term, meaning "of this", is a more formal and less commonly used way of referring to something in legal language.
4. **"may (but subject to and without affecting in any wise)":** The phrase "subject to and without affecting in any wise" is quite formal and legalistic, contributing to the old-fashioned tone.
5. **"by notice in writing sent by registered letter":** The requirement for a notice in writing sent by registered letter is a formal and traditional method, often found in legal documents.
6. **"enter into possession":** This phrase, meaning to take possession, is a more formal way of expressing the idea.
7. **"remaining unsold":** The use of "remaining unsold" instead of a simpler phrase like "not yet sold" adds a layer of formality.
8. **"whereupon":** This term is somewhat archaic and is used to indicate a subsequent event or consequence.
9. **"absolutely forfeited":** The use of "absolutely forfeited" is a legalistic and formal way of stating that the moneys will be entirely lost.
10. **"subject as aforesaid":** This phrase is a legalistic way of referring back to something mentioned earlier in the text.
11. **"null and void":** This is a legal term indicating that the contract becomes entirely invalid.
12. **"resell the same at the purchaser's risk":** The phrase "at the purchaser's risk" is a formal and traditional way of stating that the buyer bears the risk in the resale process.
13. **"either by public auction or private contract":** The use of "either" and the structure of the sentence contribute to a formal and old-fashioned style.
14. **"(either together or in lots)":** The inclusion of this phrase in parentheses is a legalistic way of providing options in the resale process.
15. **"subject to such stipulations as it may think fit":** This is a formal way of stating that the resale is subject to conditions determined by the Land Company.
16. **"any deficiency in price after giving credit for all sums paid":** The phrase "deficiency in price" is a formal way of expressing any shortfall in the resale amount.
17. **"his nominees":** The use of "nominees" instead of a simpler term contributes to the formal and legalistic language.
18. **"part payment of the sum of 321,000l'":** The use of the symbol "l" for pounds is an older convention, and modern writing typically uses the abbreviation "£".

Overall, these elements collectively create a complex and formal legal language characteristic of older legal documents

P2: Change the intricate and old-fashioned legal language elements of the following clause into plain language: "[*sample text*]".

The answers produced in response to the second prompt do not meet expectations, as illustrated in Table 6.6. This result indicates that, despite the valuable insights obtained from the first prompt, ChatGPT may have encountered difficulties in effectively converting the identified complex and nuanced elements into a more comprehensible final text. This inconsistency prompts significant investigation into the model's ability to simplify legal terminology while preserving its fundamental meaning and subtleties. A deeper examination of these responses could yield important insights into the limitations of artificial intelligence in handling intricate legal documents and underscore potential areas for enhancement in subsequent versions of the model.

As clearly shown in Table 6.6, the final text functions as an interpretation or reformulation of the sample text. It is clear that this version is markedly different from the text provided in Table 6.3, which provides a plain language version of the sample text.

To some extent, however, the final text in Table 6.6 may be considered a simplified version, albeit in a more concise form, as it omits all of the *legalese* elements identified in Table 6.2. This suggests that while the chatbot has made progress towards clarity, the resulting text may not entirely fulfil the accessibility standards typically associated with plain language.

Regrettably, the chatbot's output remains unchanged even when the phrase "change (…) into" is reformulated as "replace (…) with" in a revised second prompt (labelled as P2-1). This suggests a limitation in the model's ability to modify its responses based on variations in phrasing, highlighting a potential area for improvement in its responsiveness and flexibility when addressing user instructions. Further investigation into these limitations could provide insights into enhancing AI performance in generating accessible legal texts.

P2-1: Replace the intricate and old-fashioned legal language elements of the following clause with plain language: "[*sample text*]".

Table 6.6 ChatGPT answering the second prompt (P2)

Clause 12 states that if the buyer fails to pay any of the other installment payments mentioned in clause 2 on the specified due dates, the Land Company has the right to take action. The Land Company can, through a written notice sent by registered mail to the buyer, specify which remedies it intends to use. In such a situation, the Land Company can either cancel the agreement, taking possession of any unsold lands, stores, livestock and equipment. If this happens, all the money the buyer has already paid will be forfeited to the Land Company, and the contract will become null and void.
Alternatively, the Land Company can, under the mentioned conditions, resell the property at the buyer's risk. This resale can occur through public auction or private contract, either as a whole or in parts. The Land Company can set stipulations for the resale. If there is a shortfall in the resale price after giving credit for all sums paid by the buyer, the buyer will be responsible for the difference.

6.3.2 Considerations

The purpose of this section was to evaluate the extent to which ChatGPT is capable of performing tasks within the legal domain, particularly in relation to the analysis of legal language. As mentioned earlier, the initial prompt that included the term "*legalese*" was likely beyond the scope of the chatbot's current capabilities. Specifically, ChatGPT struggled to identify distinct features of *legalese* and failed to produce consistent outcomes. However, when the initial prompt was reformulated or clarified—for example, by specifying "archaic, intricate, and old-fashioned language" rather than using the term "*legalese*"—the results showed a marked improvement. In this refined context, ChatGPT offered a more insightful analysis of the *legalese* elements within the extract from the legal document, occasionally suggesting plain language alternatives for several terms. By contrast, the same level of success was not achieved with the second prompt. In this case, the chatbot was instructed to rewrite the text in plain language, but instead, it produced a summary of the sample text rather than generating a new, self-contained legal document.

This analysis supports concerns raised in the existing literature regarding the tendency of AI models to generate "hallucinations" or nonsensical outputs. Users should be cautious in accepting AI-generated content at face value. In other words, it is essential that they verify the information against credible sources (Medianik 2018). Furthermore, users must have a foundational understanding of the subject matter in order to adjust and interpret AI outputs as necessary.

The limitations of this exploratory analysis arise from the fact that ChatGPT is not specifically designed as a legal domain-focused AI solution. Therefore, some degree of error was anticipated, as it is inherent in the system's design. Nevertheless, ChatGPT was chosen for this analysis due to the reasons outlined earlier: it is an AI-driven tool that is widely used by law firms and legal practitioners. Additional limitations of this investigation include the prompts themselves, which may not have been formulated with sufficient clarity or precision. However, the authors deliberately sought to design prompts that closely reflect real-world scenarios, where users tend to issue straightforward requests rather than elaborate, detailed queries. Future research could investigate whether similar or divergent results are obtained from AI platforms specifically tailored to the legal domain. Alternatively, further studies could examine whether variations in responses occur when prompts are refined or made more precise.

The following section will assess the extent to which machine translation (MT) and AI-driven solutions are capable of providing accurate and reliable translations, as well as back-translations, of an extract from a twentieth-century law report.

6.4 AI-driven Translation and Back-Translation

This section aims to evaluate the application of artificial intelligence (AI) and machine translation (MT) in the translation and back-translation of law reports from the CHELAR corpus. To achieve this objective, an extract comprising 106 words, written within the time frame of 1900 to 1949, is translated automatically from English into Italian using the DeepL and Google Translate MT platforms. The resulting target texts are subsequently post-edited, and a post-edited version is then back-translated into English using AI tools such as ChatGPT and ChatSonic.

Table 6.7 displays the original text alongside the automated translations into Italian generated by DeepL and Google Translate. Instances of mistranslation are marked in grey, while uncommon or non-standard legal terminology is emphasised in bold. This methodology not only enables a comparative evaluation of the translations but also highlights the complexities inherent in legal language, which can present difficulties for automated systems. The results of this analysis will enhance the understanding of the efficacy of AI and machine translation tools in managing legal texts, particularly regarding their accuracy and reliability. Given the historical context of the source material, this analysis may also reveal how advancements in translation technology have influenced the interpretation and accessibility of legal documents over time. Further exploration of these issues could provide valuable insights into the potential for AI-driven solutions to enhance legal translation practices in contemporary settings.

Firstly, it is crucial to acknowledge that the term "rescind", as underlined in Table 6.7, is now considered rather outdated, with the term "terminate" being the more contemporary and appropriate alternative in most legal contexts. This shift in terminology has been particularly emphasised in case law, such as in *Johnson v Agnew* (1980), a landmark case that dealt with the assessment of damages in the event of a breach of contract concerning the sale of land. In this case, the distinction between a contract "termination" and a contract "rescission" was definitively clarified, underscoring the significant legal implications of using each term.

The concept of contract "termination" operates prospectively. In practical terms, this means that, once a contract is terminated, the parties are released from their obligations for future performance. However, any obligations that have accrued prior to the termination remain enforceable and intact. Therefore, the parties are held accountable for any actions or payments due up to the point of termination, but no further performance is expected going forward. In contrast, contract "rescission" operates retrospectively. When a contract is rescinded, it is treated as though it had never been made in the first place. This means that the agreement is completely undone, erasing all rights and obligations that would have otherwise arisen from the contract. In effect, rescission restores the parties to the position they were in before the contract was ever agreed upon.

Table 6.7 Translation of an extract of CHELAR by DeepL and Google Translate

Source text (CHELAR 1900–1949)	Translation by DeepL	Translation by Google Translate
If the purchaser shall make default in the payment of any of the other instalments mentioned in clause 2 hereof or any part thereof on the due dates as provided in the said clause the Land Company may (but subject to and without affecting in any wise the sale and the conveyance or the right thereto under clause 6 hereof) by notice in writing sent by registered letter and addressed to the purchaser specifying which of the remedies hereinafter mentioned the Land Company intends to exercise, rescind this agreement and may either enter into possession of any lands stores live stock and other equipment remaining unsold.	*Se l'acquirente si rende inadempiente nel pagamento di una qualsiasi delle altre rate di cui alla clausola 2 del presente contratto o di una parte di esse alle date di scadenza previste dalla suddetta clausola, la Land Company può (ma con riserva e senza pregiudicare in alcun modo la vendita e la cessione o il diritto di cui alla clausola 6 del presente contratto), mediante* ***avviso*** *scritto inviato con lettera raccomandata e indirizzato all'acquirente, specificando quale dei rimedi di seguito menzionati la Land Company intende* ***esercitare****, rescindere il presente contratto e può entrare in possesso di tutti i terreni, le scorte vive e le altre attrezzature rimaste invendute.*	*Se l'acquirente è inadempiente nel pagamento di una qualsiasi delle altre rate menzionate nella clausola 2 o di parte di esse alle scadenze previste in detta clausola, la Società fondiaria può (ma soggetto a e* ***senza influenzare*** *in alcun modo la vendita e la cessione o il diritto* ***sulla*** *stessa di cui al* ***punto*** *6) mediante comunicazione scritta inviata tramite lettera raccomandata e indirizzata all'acquirente specificando quale dei rimedi di seguito menzionati la Società fondiaria intende* ***esercitare****, recedere dal presente contratto e potrà entrare in possesso di qualsiasi* ***terre*** *immagazzinano bestiame e altre attrezzature rimaste invendute.*

This retroactive approach can have significant consequences, particularly in cases where extensive contractual obligations or financial transactions have already been completed under the terms of the contract.

Before this crucial distinction was formally established in *Johnson v Agnew*, the terms "rescission" and "termination" were often used interchangeably, leading to significant confusion and inconsistency in both legal practice and judicial decisions. The lack of a clear differentiation between these two concepts often complicated the resolution of contract disputes, particularly in cases where damages and obligations were in question. The clarification provided by this case has since contributed to greater precision in legal drafting and interpretation, thereby minimising misunderstandings in contractual disputes.

This evolution in the use of terminology highlights the importance of linguistic precision in legal discourse. Lawyers, judges and legal scholars must remain vigilant in their use of language to ensure that the legal concepts being applied are accurately represented. The distinction between these terms is not merely semantic but carries substantive legal consequences that can affect the rights and obligations of the parties involved.

6.4.1 Analysis of the Automated Translations

As previously noted, the two automated target texts exhibit both mistranslations and instances of non-standard language. Mistranslations will be addressed first. It is evident that DeepL leaves "Land Company" in English in the Italian version, while Google Translate renders it as "*Società fondiaria*". Given that the extract does not provide any specific details (e.g., a company name) regarding the Land Company, it is reasonable to conclude that the term "*Società fondiaria*" is more appropriate than retaining the English name in the target text. Moreover, DeepL inaccurately interprets "subject to" as "con riserva" (meaning "with reservation"), whereas Google Translate translates it literally as "*soggetto a*" which is correct within the given context.

Furthermore, DeepL omits the translation of "thereto" in the phrase "the right thereto", which refers to "the sale". DeepL also incorrectly translates "rescind" as "*rescindere*", which is erroneous (Giampieri 2024).

As mentioned, the concept of "rescission" is rooted in common law and allows a party to set aside a contract in cases of mistakes or misrepresentations, among others. Conversely, Italian law permits "*rescissione*" when a party enters into a contract under peril or necessity, suffering a loss above half or greater value of the property exchanged or traded (Giampieri 2024: 93–94). Consequently, the term "*rescindere*" represents an inaccurate translation. Google Translate translates "rescind" as "*recedere*" (back-translation: "withdraw" or "terminate"), which is also incorrect. In instances of contract breach or default, a party may "*risolvere*" (back-translation: "terminate" or "cancel") a contract, as stipulated in Articles 1467 and 1785 of the Italian Civil Code. The term "*recedere*" should be reserved for situations where a party withdraws from a contract by providing written notice. Consequently, regarding the clause under consideration, the correct verb to use is "*risolvere*".

In relation to the phrase "stores live stock", both MT tools produce errors that could be characterised as "hallucinations". Specifically, DeepL fails to render the term "stores" altogether and mistranslates "live stock" as "*scorte vive*", which in back-translation means "living inventories". Conversely, while Google Translate correctly renders "live stock" as "*bestiame*", it misinterprets "stores" (in the sense of "*depositi*" or "*magazzini*", i.e., warehouses) by treating it as a finite verb and renders it as "*immagazzinano*" (back-translation: "they store"). As mentioned earlier, these target terms resemble hallucinations rather than simple mistranslations. The lack of a comma between "stores" and "live stock" likely contributed to the misinterpretation by both MT tools.

This analysis highlights the complexities involved in translating legal terminology and underscores the need for careful scrutiny when using automated translation tools in legal contexts. The intricate nature of legal language, especially where syntactical ambiguity exists, requires a level of precision that current MT systems may struggle to provide without human oversight.

As far as non-standard language is concerned, DeepL translates "without affecting" as "*senza pregiudicare*" (back-translation: "without prejudice / prejudging"), whereas Google Translate suggests "*senza influenzare*" (back-translation: "without affecting / influencing"). A review of the

Italian Gazzetta Ufficiale (Official Journal)[1] indicates that "*senza influenzare*" is less frequently used in formal contexts. Similarly, Google Translate suggests a wrong preposition in "*diritto sulla vendita*" (back-translation: "right on the sale"), which should be "*diritto alla vendita*" (back-translation: "right to the sale"). There are, in fact, no instances of the former in the *Gazzetta Ufficiale*. Moreover, Google Translate mislabels "punto 6" (back-translation: "point 6)" when it should correctly be "*clausola* 6" (back-translation: "clause 6)", as previously mentioned.

Both MT platforms also suggest the verb "*esercitare*", translating "exercise" as a collocate of "*rimedi*" ("remedies"). However, a search for "*rimedi che intende*" (back-translation: "remedies that [s/he] wants," with the omission of the subject) in the Italian governmental domain (i.e. gov.it) reveals that the verbs "*adottare*" and "*attivare*" (back-translations: "adopt" and "activate") are more appropriate. The term "*esercitare*" is not commonly used in this context; remedies are generally not "exercised", but rather provided by law or made available to individuals.

Google Translate ultimately proposes "*qualsiasi terre*" as the equivalent for "any lands". However, both the Italian Civil Code and the *Gazzetta Ufficiale* consistently use the term "*terreni*", as suggested by DeepL, rather than "terre", which is proposed by Google Translate. Moreover, "*qualsiasi terre*" is syntactically incorrect as the noun following "*qualsiasi*" should be singular (e.g., "*qualsiasi terreno*", meaning "any land").

On the whole, it can be observed that DeepL produced a greater number of mistranslations in the strictest sense whereas Google Translate exhibited several syntactical issues and instances of non-standard language at the collocational level. In light of these considerations, the target texts can now be post-edited. For the sake of consistency, the target text proposed by Google Translate serves as the foundation for the post-edited version presented in Table 6.8. The terms that have been modified are underlined.

This approach allows for a systematic refinement of the translations, addressing both mistranslations and non-standard language usage. The post-editing process will not only rectify errors but also align the text

[1] The Italian Gazzetta Ufficiale is consulted as it is a vast *repertoire* of old and new statutory documents, which most likely focus on the subject-matter addressed in this section.

Table 6.8 Post-edited target text

Source text	Post-edited target text
If the purchaser shall make default in the payment of any of the other instalments mentioned in clause 2 hereof or any part thereof on the due dates as provided in the said clause the Land Company may (but subject to and without affecting in any wise the sale and the conveyance or the right thereto under clause 6 hereof) by notice in writing sent by registered letter and addressed to the purchaser specifying which of the remedies hereinafter mentioned the Land Company intends to exercise, rescind this agreement and may either enter into possession of any lands stores live stock and other equipment remaining unsold.	*Se l'acquirente è inadempiente nel pagamento di una qualsiasi delle altre rate menzionate nella clausola 2 o di parte di esse alle scadenze previste in detta clausola, la Società fondiaria può (ma soggetto a e senza pregiudicare in alcun modo la vendita e la cessione o il diritto alla stessa di cui alla clausola 6) mediante comunicazione scritta inviata tramite lettera raccomandata e indirizzata all'acquirente specificando quale dei rimedi di seguito menzionati la Società fondiaria intende adottare, risolvere il presente contratto e potrà entrare in possesso di qualsiasi terreno magazzino bestiame e altre attrezzature rimaste invendute.*

more closely with standard legal terminology and phrasing, thereby improving its overall comprehensibility and usability. The necessity for post-editing highlights a critical aspect of using automated translation tools: while they can provide rapid translations, their outputs often require careful review and modification to ensure precision and adherence to legal standards. This underscores the importance of human oversight in the translation process, particularly in specialised fields such as law where terminology and context are paramount. Future investigations could further explore the effectiveness of various post-editing strategies in improving the quality of translations generated by AI and MT tools, ultimately contributing to more reliable outcomes in legal translation practices.

6.4.2 Analysis of the Automated Back-translations

This section focuses on an analysis of the automated back-translations into English of the post-edited target text. To facilitate this analysis, the ChatGPT and ChatSonic chatbots are employed. For the purposes of the examination, the following prompt is entered into each search field of the aforementioned AI systems:

Prompt: Translate the following text into English: "[text to translate]".

The back-translations are subsequently compared to the source text in order to identify any shortcomings. Therefore, both the source text and the AI-generated back-translations are presented in Table 6.9. Mistranslations are highlighted in grey whereas instances of non-standard language or syntactical issues are indicated in bold. This approach allows for a systematic evaluation of the effectiveness of these AI tools in

Table 6.9 Source text and automated back-translations by AI tools

Source Text	**Back-translation by ChatGPT**	**Back-translation by ChatSonic**
If the purchaser shall make default in the payment of any of the other instalments mentioned in clause 2 hereof or any part thereof on the due dates as provided in the said clause the Land Company may (but subject to and without affecting in any wise the sale and the conveyance or the right thereto under clause 6 hereof) by notice in writing sent by registered letter and addressed to the purchaser specifying which of the remedies hereinafter mentioned the Land Company intends to exercise, rescind this agreement and may either enter into possession of any lands stores live stock and other equipment remaining unsold.	If the purchaser defaults **on** the payment of any of the other installments mentioned in clause 2, or part thereof, by the **deadlines** stipulated in said clause, the land company may (but subject to and without in any way **prejudicing** the sale and transfer or the right **to the same as per** clause 6) by means of written communication sent via registered letter addressed to the purchaser specifying which of the following remedies the land company intends to **adopt**, terminate this contract and may take possession of any unsold land, warehouse, livestock, and other equipment.	If the buyer defaults in the payment of any of the other installments mentioned in clause 2 or part thereof on the due dates specified in said clause, the Land Company may (but subject to and without prejudice in any way to the sale and transfer or right thereto referred to in clause 6) by written notice sent by registered letter addressed to the buyer specifying which of the remedies mentioned below the Land Company intends to **adopt**, terminate this contract and may take possession of any unsold land, warehouse, livestock, and other equipment.

translating legal texts, which often contain complex terminology and subtle meanings. By closely examining the discrepancies between the original text and its back-translation, valuable insights can be gained into the strengths and limitations of automated translation systems when dealing with specialised language. The findings from this analysis will contribute to a broader understanding of how AI-driven translation tools can be refined to improve accuracy and reliability in legal contexts, where precise language is paramount. Furthermore, this investigation underscores the importance of post-editing by qualified professionals to ensure that automated translations meet the necessary standards for clarity and correctness.

In other words, this analysis aims not only to assess the quality of AI-generated translations but also to highlight areas for potential improvement, thereby enhancing further comprehension of the role of technology in legal language translation.

First and foremost, it is noteworthy that only one mistranslation appears in both back-translated texts, specifically the phrase "unsold land". This formulation is incorrect as the corresponding source text conveys a slightly different concept. The original phrase encompasses multiple elements, including lands, stores, livestock and equipment, as evidenced in the expression "any lands, stores, live stock and other equipment remaining unsold". In contrast, the back-translations imply that only "land" is the unsold item.

In terms of non-standard language, a recurring lexical issue regards the verb "adopt" as it collocates with "remedies". By entering the phrase "the remedies that" into the search field of the LawInsider contract database, it is possible to retrieve verb phrases such as "be available", "may have", "may pursue", "may seek" and "might flow from". For instance, sample phrases include "the remedies that may be available" and "the remedies that the landlord may have". Therefore, the use of "adopt" does not appear to be common within this context.

Further shortcomings are observed in the output from ChatGPT whereas ChatSonic demonstrates a higher degree of accuracy. A syntactical error noted is the inappropriate use of the preposition "on" in the phrase "defaults on the payments". The remaining concerns primarily involve non-standard or infrequent collocations. For example, "deadlines" would be better expressed as "due dates" when referring to payments; "without prejudicing the" should be replaced by "without prejudice to"; "right to the same" is preferable to "right thereto" and "as per clause" instead of "referred to in clause".

The findings suggest that the AI-generated back-translations are generally accurate, with ChatSonic demonstrating particular precision. It might be tempting to assume that these back-translations are reliable simply because they are produced by advanced AI systems, which typically outperform traditional machine translation (MT) tools due to their extensive training on large datasets. However, to further substantiate these results, the post-edited Italian target text will now be back-translated using Reverso, a trustworthy MT platform.

Table 6.10 provides a comparison of the source text and the back-translation by Reverso of the post-edited Italian text. This comparative analysis seeks to offer a thorough evaluation of the effectiveness of different translation methodologies, with particular attention to their accuracy in handling legal language.

Table 6.10 Source text and automated back-translation by Reverso

Source text	Back-translation by Reverso
If the purchaser shall make default in the payment of any of the other instalments mentioned in clause 2 hereof or any part thereof on the due dates as provided in the said clause the Land Company may (but subject to and without affecting in any wise the sale and the conveyance or the right thereto under clause 6 hereof) by notice in writing sent by registered letter and addressed to the purchaser specifying which of the remedies hereinafter mentioned the Land Company intends to exercise, rescind this agreement and may either enter into possession of any lands stores live stock and other equipment remaining unsold.	If the purchaser fails to pay any of the other instalments referred to in clause 2 or any part thereof within the **time limits** set out in that clause, the Land Company may (but subject to and without prejudice in any way to the sale and assignment or the right to the sale referred to in clause 6) by written notice sent by registered letter to the purchaser specifying which of the following remedies the Land Company intends to **adopt**, terminate this contract and may come into possession of any livestock warehouse land and other equipment that has been unsold.

The analysis indicates that the output produced by the MT system is largely acceptable. Nevertheless, there are certain occurrences of non-standard collocations, such as the phrase "time limits" being used in place of the more suitable term "due dates", along with the previously mentioned use of "adopt". In relation to the term "assignment" as it pertains to "land", it is worth noting how the phrase "assignment of land" appears more frequently than "conveyance of land" in both the *LawInsider* contract database and the UK governmental domain. This observation reflects a linguistic preference that may shape legal discourse and influence the drafting of legal documents. Consequently, it can be argued that AI-driven translation solutions now exhibit a level of accuracy comparable to that of traditional MT platforms, as demonstrated by recent studies (see Zhang et al. 2022). This finding highlights the growing sophistication of AI in translation, particularly in specialised fields such as legal language. Future research could investigate the broader implications of these advancements, particularly in terms of legal practitioners' increasing reliance on automated tools for translation tasks and the potential impact on the quality and efficiency of legal services.

6.4.3 Considerations

The aim of this section was to explore the accuracy and reliability of MT- and AI-driven (back-) translations. To achieve this, an extract from a law report dated between 1900 and 1949 was examined. The initial analysis focused on automatic translations into Italian, performed by the MT tools DeepL and Google Translate. These automated target texts exhibited various shortcomings at both lexical and syntactical levels, alongside instances of non-standard language and infrequent terms and collocations. Additionally, some "hallucinations"—nonsensical outputs—were identified.

A subsequent analysis involved back-translating a post-edited version of the target text into English using two AI solutions: ChatGPT and ChatSonic. The back-translations were compared to the original source text to identify any discrepancies or errors. In contrast to the first analysis, the second revealed only a few infrequent renderings, particularly in the output from ChatGPT. Mistranslations were limited to a single term whereas nonsensical outputs were not detected. To further validate these findings and address any claims regarding the superiority of AI tools over MT solutions, the same back-translation was conducted using a trustworthy MT platform, namely Reverso. The output from Reverso was also remarkably accurate, with only minor inaccuracies at the collocational level.

In light of the investigations carried out in this section, it can be concluded that the automatic translations of the law report extract are not entirely accurate and exhibit several shortcomings. Consequently, human supervision and intervention remain essential in this process. At present, both AI and MT systems have not yet outperformed human reasoning, knowledge and output capabilities. Conversely and surprisingly, automated back-translations seemed to perform better than their initial translations. It may be speculated that AI and machine translation systems have acquired language patterns from the original text provided. Nevertheless, this claim requires further examination.

The limitations of this analysis lie in the length of the text examined, which was probably too short to allow any generalisation of the findings. Nonetheless, the data analysed and results obtained indicate that AI still has a long way to go before it can compete with human intelligence, especially within the legal domain.

The following section will assess the extent to which chatbots are capable of transforming a gender-biased text into a gender-neutral document. To do so, a few extracts from twentieth-century law reports will be analysed.

6.5 AI and Gender Neutrality

The use of gender-neutral language in legal texts is an increasingly relevant topic as the legal profession seeks to modernise its language to reflect inclusivity and impartiality. This section investigates whether generative AI can assist in this endeavour by transforming gender-specific terms into gender-neutral language, while preserving the original meaning, sentence structure and interpretative integrity of legal texts.

This study evaluates three specific generative AI models, namely ChatGPT, Copilot and Gemini in order to assess their ability to neutralise gendered expressions without undermining the legal intent or altering the syntactic structure of the texts. Each model demonstrates advanced capabilities in natural language processing and has been tested for its ability to manage complex historical language, legal terminology and the subtle vocabulary often found in legal documents. The primary goal was to determine whether AI-driven tools could serve as reliable assistants to draft and revise gender-neutral legal texts, thus potentially saving legal professionals time and effort in updating or modernising documents.

Achieving effective gender neutrality requires a comprehensive and systematic approach. It is essential to identify all gendered references throughout the text and ensure that they are changed consistently. This process involves not only replacing specific words but also considering the broader context in which they are used. If neutrality is applied inconsistently, the resulting texts may appear fragmented or unclear, which can be particularly problematic in legal contexts. In law, every term must be harmonised to maintain coherence and clarity, as ambiguity can lead to misinterpretation or disputes over meaning. For instance, if some references are modified to be gender-neutral while others remain unchanged, this could create confusion about the rights and obligations defined in the text. Moreover, inconsistency in applying gender-neutral language might undermine the goal of inclusivity, as it could inadvertently highlight gender distinctions rather than eliminate them. Therefore, a meticulous approach is crucial to ensure that all aspects of the text work together seamlessly in order to provide a clear and unified message that reflects modern values of equality and fairness.

In this experiment, each AI model was tasked with rewriting selected excerpts from historical English legal reports. These excerpts, sourced from CHELAR, were chosen for their use of gender-specific language that reflects historical societal norms and legal conventions. The texts cover three distinct historical periods, allowing an assessment of how well AI models handle different linguistic styles and the evolution of legal language. The chosen excerpts are as follows (Table 6.11).

6.5.1 Analysis

The grey highlights in Table 6.11 indicate the gendered terms in each text, providing a basis for examining how effectively each AI model substitutes these terms with gender-neutral alternatives, while also showcasing distinct examples of gendered language that reflect the societal and legal conventions of their respective historical periods. Text A was extracted from a legal report dated from 1535 to 1599. It employs explicit gender markers, including terms such as "man", "husband" and "wife", alongside possessive adjectives like "his" and "her". The language used in this text assumes the male gender as normative, thus embodying a legal framework that predominantly recognised men as the primary agents in matters related to property and family. Such terminology reflects a period where the male role was not only central but assumed to be inherently dominant within the legal and familial hierarchy. This male-centric language encapsulates the historical expectation that men held authoritative

Table 6.11 Extracts of law reports sourced from the CHELAR featuring gender-biased language

Text A	It was resolved that if a man makes a feoffment to the use of himself for life, and afterwards to the use of his wife for her life, for the jointure of his wife, that such estate in remainder is within the intent of the said Act of 27 H. 8. (…) all the examples expressed in the Act are of a joint estate made to the husband and wife, and none of them to the wife only.
Text B	The case therefore must be determined as it stands upon the will, and consequently to enter into an enquiry what regard he had to his niece; how far he considered the Lord Guildford either in point of affection, or in gratitude for good offices received, or by reason of affinity by marriage, or the like, is not material, nor necessary to know; and it may be it is not possible now to know what induced him to limit his estate in the manner as by his will is expressed: but he having done it, we must agree with the Lord Dyer, that men's deeds and wills, by which they settle their estates, are the laws that private men are allowed to make, and they are not to be altered even by the King in his courts of law, or conscience; we must take it as we find it.
Text C	Thomas Fitz-Simons, his son and administrator, met with the same refusal from the administratrix, and from the same conviction acquiesced under it till his death in 1748; as did after him the respondent Christopher Fitz-Simons, who having administered to Raymond the original under-tenant, and possessed the lands under the lease from Espinasse, met with as peremptory a refusal from the administratrix to renew, as his father and brother had done. But notwithstanding these repeated refusals, both father and sons continued paying her their rent, and never mentioned either the bond or indorsement, nor set up the least pretence of right to the original lease by way of trust or otherwise.

roles, with women's identities often defined in relational terms, such as that of a wife. In Text B, sourced from the period 1650–1699, the gender bias is conveyed through the consistent use of masculine pronouns ("he" and "him") and possessive adjectives ("his") as well as terms like "men" and "King". This linguistic choice highlights how male actors were the central figures within legal and familial domains at that time. By exclusively employing masculine terms, the text reflects a period when societal structures often positioned men as decision-makers and key stakeholders, both legally and domestically. The normative use of masculine pronouns in this context implies that men were the presumed agents of legal action, while women remained in more peripheral roles. The reinforcement of male agency through language reveals a structural bias in historical legal documentation, which likely shaped the social and legal expectations surrounding gender roles. Text C, extracted from the 1750–1799 interval, further illustrates gender-specific language, employing terms such as "administrator", "administratrix", "father", "son(s)" and "brother". In this text, it is clear that the legal and familial roles are distinctly gendered. Such language reflects a legal framework where the distribution of roles and responsibilities was overtly delineated by gender, with male individuals occupying roles associated with authority and inheritance. Female roles, on the other hand, were often confined to secondary positions within the family hierarchy. The use of "administratrix" not only assigns gender but also implies a limited scope of authority for female actors within legal and property-related contexts. This explicit gender differentiation in legal titles and familial roles exemplifies the gendered nature of legal language, potentially influencing how these historical roles are perceived and applied in contemporary legal practice. Maintaining such terms within legal precedent can have substantial interpretative consequences, as it preserves a hierarchical view of gender roles that may clash with modern expectations of gender equality and neutrality within the legal system.

To assess the capabilities of the chatbots, a specific approach was adopted. Each AI model received the same instruction to rewrite the texts in a gender-neutral manner. The prompt was designed to encourage the replacement of gendered terms while ensuring that the original meaning and structure remained intact. The following prompt is written in the search field of each chatbot:

Prompt: Make the following text gender-neutral: "*[text]*".

The outputs were then analysed based on their effectiveness in neutralising gendered language, the consistency of applying neutrality throughout the text and any unintended changes in sentence structure or syntax. The results are presented in Table 6.12 and subsequent tables, which display the AI-generated revisions alongside the original texts. These tables highlight instances where gender-specific terms were successfully neutralised and where the AI introduced unsolicited modifications. Such modifications might include rephrased sentences, altered punctuation or slight changes in word choice. While these adjustments could enhance readability, they may also introduce subtle shifts in interpretative tone.

Table 6.12 provides a comparison of Text A and the outputs generated by the AI models ChatGPT, Copilot and Gemini. In this table, gender-biased language is highlighted in grey while gender-neutral expressions are marked in bold. Any additional changes made to the original text are underlined for clarity.

In Table 6.12, the output of each chatbot reflects a distinct approach to gender-neutral language, with varying levels of fidelity to the original

Table 6.12 Text A and its modifications carried out by the chatbots to make it gender-neutral

Text A	ChatGPT	Copilot	Gemini
It was resolved that if a man makes a feoffment to the use of himself for life, and afterwards to the use of his wife for her life, for the jointure of his wife, that such estate in remainder is within the intent of the said Act of 27 H. 8. (…) all the examples expressed in the Act are of a joint estate made to the husband and wife, and none of them to the wife only.	It was resolved that if a **person** makes a feoffment to **their** own use for life, and afterwards to the use of **their spouse** for **their** life, for the jointure of **their spouse**, that such estate in remainder is within the intent of the said Act of 27 H. 8. Additionally, all the examples expressed in the Act refer to a joint estate made to **both spouses**, and none are made to **one spouse** only.	It was resolved that if a **person** makes a feoffment to the use of **themselves** for life, and afterwards to the use of **their spouse** for **their** life, for the jointure of **their spouse**, that such estate in remainder is within the intent of the said Act of 27 H. 8. (…) all the examples expressed in the Act are of a joint estate made to the **spouses**, and none of them to the **spouse** only.	It was decided that if a **person** makes a feoffment for **their** own lifetime, and then for the lifetime of **their spouse** as a jointure, such a remainder interest falls under the purview of the Act of 27 H. 8. (...) All the examples provided in the Act involve joint estates created for both a husband and wife, and none are specifically for the wife alone.

text. Across all outputs, certain consistent substitutions are evident: "man" is universally replaced with "person", "his wife" with "their spouse" and "her" with "their". Furthermore, "husband and wife" is adjusted to "(both) spouses" by both ChatGPT and Copilot, demonstrating an effort to maintain inclusive language in line with modern standards.

Nevertheless, unrequested alterations in wording and structure occur in the outputs from ChatGPT and Gemini, each of which diverges from the source text in remarkable ways. ChatGPT, for example, introduces stylistic adjustments by rephrasing "to the use of himself" as "to their own use", a substitution that, while gender-neutral, shifts the original phrasing. Furthermore, ChatGPT inserts a full stop after "within the intent of the said Act of 27 H. 8", followed by the connector "additionally" at the beginning of the next sentence. This punctuation and structural change slightly modify the flow and tone of the original legal language, perhaps aiming for clarity but at the expense of strict fidelity to the source.

Gemini introduces even more extensive rephrasing, reformatting almost every sentence. For instance, "a feoffment to the use of himself for life" is rephrased as "a feoffment for their own lifetime" and "such estate in remainder is within the intent of the said Act" becomes "such a remainder interest falls under the purview of the Act". These changes are not limited to gender-neutral adjustments but include alterations in terminology and phrasing that impact the precision of legal language. The substitution of "falls under the purview of" for "is within the intent of" introduces a subtle change in nuance, as "purview" implies scope or jurisdiction whereas "intent" suggests purpose or design. Such modifications, while stylistically smoother, may dilute the precise legal meaning and intent of the original phrasing.

Gemini does not employ gender-neutral language as consistently as ChatGPT and Copilot. It continues to use terms such as "husband and wife" rather than substituting them with "spouses" and the term "wife" remains unchanged as well. This selective use of traditional gendered language suggests an inconsistent commitment to gender neutrality, which may diminish clarity in situations where inclusive language is essential.

Table 6.13 shows the results obtained for Text B

In Table 6.13, the chatbot outputs show similar patterns of language adjustment, particularly concerning gender neutrality and simplification

Table 6.13 Text B and its modifications carried out by the chatbots to make it gender-neutral

Text B	ChatGPT	Copilot	Gemini
The case therefore must be determined as it stands upon the will, and consequently to enter into an enquiry what regard he had to his niece; how far he considered the Lord Guildford either in point of affection, or in gratitude for good offices received, or by reason of affinity by marriage, or the like, is not material, nor necessary to know; and it may be it is not possible now to know what induced him to limit his estate in the manner as by his will is expressed: but he having done it, we must agree with the Lord Dyer, that men's deeds and wills, by which they settle their estates, are the laws that private men are allowed to make, and they are not to be altered even by the King in his courts of law, or conscience; we must take it as we find it.	The case must therefore be determined as it stands upon the will, and consequently, an inquiry into what regard **they** had for **their** niece—how far **they** considered Lord Guildford in terms of affection, gratitude for good offices received, or reason of affinity by marriage, or the like—is not material nor necessary to know. It may even be impossible to determine what induced **them** to limit **their** estate in the manner expressed in **their** will. However, since **this** has been done, we must agree with Lord Dyer that **individuals**' deeds and wills, by which they settle their estates, are the laws that private **individuals** are allowed to make, and these are not to be altered even by the King in **their** courts of law or conscience; we must take it as we find it.	The case therefore must be determined as it stands upon the will, and consequently to enter into an enquiry what regard **the individual** had to **their** niece; how far **they** considered Lord Guildford either in point of affection, or in gratitude for good offices received, or by reason of affinity by marriage, or the like, is not material, nor necessary to know; and it may be it is not possible now to know what induced **them** to limit **their** estate in the manner as by **their** will is expressed: but having done it, we must agree with Lord Dyer, that **people**'s deeds and wills, by which they settle their estates, are the laws that private **individuals** are allowed to make, and they are not to be altered even by the King in his courts of law, or conscience; we must take it as we find it.	The case must therefore be decided based on the will as it stands. Consequently, it's unnecessary to investigate the **person**'s relationship with **their** niece or **their** feelings towards Lord Guildford, whether due to affection, gratitude, familial ties, or other reasons. It may not be possible to determine what motivated **them** to limit **their** estate in this manner. However, since **they** have made this decision, we must agree with Lord Dyer that **individuals** are allowed to create their own laws regarding their property through their deeds and wills. Even the King cannot alter these arrangements in courts of law or conscience. We must accept the situation as it is presented.

of expressions. Each AI model makes modifications to the original legal text, though they vary in extent and adherence to the source material.

As observed in the previous text, all three chatbots address gender-biased language in comparable ways. Specifically, "his" and "him" are changed to "their" and "them" and "men" becomes either "individuals" or "people". These modifications advance the text towards inclusive language standards without significantly altering its legal intent. However, in addition to the requested gender-neutral substitutions, there are also numerous unsolicited alterations, including rephrasing, changes in word order and the introduction of additional punctuation.

ChatGPT, for instance, introduces rephrasing and minor structural adjustments that affect the flow of the text. It modifies "therefore must" to "must therefore" and rephrases "in the manner as by his will is expressed" as "in the manner expressed in their will". These changes, while subtle, shift the original phrasing to a slightly more conversational style. ChatGPT also simplifies phrases such as "either in point of" to "in terms of" and "it may be it is not possible now to know" to "it may even be impossible to determine". Moreover, it rephrases "but he having done it" to "however, since this has been done", a change that smooths out the original phrasing but introduces a more modern, less formal tone that may not align with the style of the legal text.

Copilot generally adheres more closely to the source structure but it also makes minor rephrasing choices, such as "people's deeds and wills" instead of "men's deeds and wills" and adjusts phrases like "private men" to "private individuals". These changes retain the legal specificity but adopt a more inclusive tone. Copilot maintains most of the original sentence structures, preserving the formal cadence of the legal language better than the other models.

Gemini, in contrast, makes significant and extensive rephrasing, resulting in an output that diverges notably from the original. This is evident in examples such as "but he having done it" being transformed into "however, since they have made this decision". The phrase "men's deeds and wills, by which they settle their estates, are the laws that private men are allowed to make, and they are not to be altered" is heavily simplified to "individuals are allowed to create their own laws regarding their property through their deeds and wills". Such extensive rephrasing and simplification result in a version that is stylistically more accessible but deviates from the formal and precise legal tone of the source text. By incorporating conversational elements and condensing complex phrases, Gemini generates an output that, while intelligible, sacrifices some legal precision and specificity issues of the original text. The text produced by Gemini is almost entirely underlined, indicating a degree of rewording that renders it markedly distinct from the original and likely less acceptable in a rigid legal context where fidelity to the original language is paramount.

An additional oversight across all chatbot outputs is the retention of "King", which could have been replaced with gender-neutral terms like "Sovereign" or "Monarch" to further modernise the text. This omission suggests that, while gender-specific pronouns and terms were addressed, other aspects of gender neutrality were inconsistently applied.

Table 6.14 explores the changes to Text C.

In Table 6.14, we observe a series of systematic adjustments across the outputs of these chatbots aimed at replacing gendered terms with gender-neutral language. The chatbots consistently replace phrases such as "his

Table 6.14 Text C and its modifications carried out by the chatbots to make it gender-neutral

Text C	ChatGPT	Copilot	Gemini
Thomas Fitz-Simons, his son and administrator, met with the same refusal from the administratrix, and from the same conviction acquiesced under it till his death in 1748; as did after him the respondent Christopher Fitz-Simons, who having administered to Raymond the original under-tenant, and possessed the lands under the lease from Espinasse, met with as peremptory a refusal from the administratrix to renew, as his father and brother had done. But notwithstanding these repeated refusals, both father and sons continued paying her their rent, and never mentioned either the bond or indorsement, nor set up the least pretence of right to the original lease by way of trust or otherwise.	Thomas Fitz-Simons, **their child** and administrator, met with the same refusal from the administratrix and, out of the same conviction, acquiesced under it until **their** death in 1748. Following this, the respondent Christopher Fitz-Simons, who administered to Raymond, the original under-tenant, and possessed the lands under the lease from Espinasse, encountered an equally peremptory refusal from the administratrix to renew, as had **their** father and **sibling**. However, despite these repeated refusals, both **parent** and **children** continued paying rent to her, never mentioning either the bond or endorsement, nor asserting any claim to the original lease by way of trust or otherwise.	Thomas Fitz-Simons, **their child** and administrator, met with the same refusal from the administrator, and from the same conviction acquiesced under it till **their** death in 1748; as did after **them** the respondent Christopher Fitz-Simons, who having administered to Raymond the original under-tenant, and possessed the lands under the lease from Espinasse, met with as peremptory a refusal from the administrator to renew, as **their parent** and **sibling** had done. But notwithstanding these repeated refusals, both **parent** and **children** continued paying **the rent**, and never mentioned either the bond or indorsement, nor set up the least pretence of right to the original lease by way of trust or otherwise.	Thomas Fitz-Simons, **their child** and administrator, encountered the same refusal from the administratrix and, similarly, acquiesced in it until **their** death in 1748. Following **them**, the respondent Christopher Fitz-Simons, who had administered to Raymond the original under-tenant_______and possessed the lands under the lease from Espinasse, also faced a definitive refusal from the administratrix to renew the lease, just as **their parent** and **sibling** had. Despite these repeated denials, both the **parent** and **children** continued to pay rent to the administratrix and never mentioned the bond or endorsement, nor asserted any claim to the original lease through trust or other means.

son" with "their child", "brother" with "sibling" and "father and sons" with "parent and children". Similarly, "his" and "him" are replaced by "their" and "them" throughout the text. These changes align with the goal of promoting inclusivity by eliminating male-centric language.

Beyond gender-neutral adjustments, ChatGPT and Gemini make further stylistic modifications that enhance readability but alter the tone and structure of the original text. ChatGPT, for instance, adds punctuation and rephrases specific legal terms, making the text less formal and more approachable. Examples include modifying "met with as peremptory a refusal" to "encountered an equally peremptory refusal" and changing "set up the least pretence of right" to "asserting any claim". These adjustments create a more straightforward, conversational tone, potentially making the text more accessible to a general audience, though at the cost of some legal precision.

Gemini goes a step further in restructuring the text for readability. It splits the content into three paragraphs, enhancing clarity and flow, and introduces similar modifications. Phrases like "from the same conviction acquiesced under it till" and "met with as peremptory a refusal" are rephrased as "similarly, acquiesced in it until" and "also faced a definitive refusal", respectively. Furthermore, Gemini simplifies the expression "but notwithstanding these repeated refusals" with "despite these repeated denials". These changes make the text easier to follow but diverge substantially from the original, potentially losing some of its formal tone and nuanced language.

One remarkable limitation across all chatbot outputs concerns the terms "administrator" and "administratrix". While the original text uses "administratrix" to specify a female administrator, the chatbots handle this term inconsistently. Gemini retains "administratrix" whereas Copilot replaces it with "administrator". While the masculine term "administrator" may initially evoke a return to gender-biased language where the masculine form is seen as the norm, it is worth noting that this term has become the standard and neutral designation in contemporary usage. The European Parliament, for instance, considers it appropriate for both genders (Papadimoulis 2018: 12). Despite these discrepancies, this oversight highlights a significant deficiency in the methodologies employed by AI models in their efforts to uphold gender neutrality within legal terminology.

6.5.2 Considerations

The analysis of chatbot outputs in addressing gender-biased language highlights both the capabilities and limitations of current AI-driven tools in achieving gender neutrality. Each of the three chatbots, namely Copilot, ChatGPT and Gemini, demonstrates distinct approaches, with varying levels of success in maintaining the integrity and intent of the original legal texts.

Copilot stands out as the most effective tool, largely due to its careful handling of gendered terms without significantly altering syntax or sentence structure. For instance, it replaces phrases like "his son" with "their child" while preserving the flow and meaning of the original text. Nevertheless, minor oversights remain; terms like "King" could have been replaced with more inclusive options, such as "Monarch" or "Sovereign", to align with contemporary standards of gender-neutral language. Despite these few areas for improvement, the output of Copilot is praiseworthy in balancing gender neutrality with textual fidelity, making it the most reliable of the three in this analysis.

In contrast, the output generated by Gemini presents significant issues. The extensive rephrasing in its output departs notably from the source material, suggesting either a misunderstanding of the prompt or a disregard for its specifications. Many phrases were simplified or restructured, resulting in a text that no longer accurately represents the original legal language, which is particularly problematic in legal contexts where precise wording is essential. This highlights a key challenge when using AI for language reform in specialised fields, that is, any substantial deviation from the original wording can obscure the legal intent, potentially compromising the meaning of the text. The performance of Gemini, therefore, underscores the importance of caution when relying on AI for any linguistic tasks in law.

ChatGPT, meanwhile, occupies a middle ground. It addresses gendered terms effectively but introduces some unsolicited changes, such as punctuation adjustments and rephrasing that were not part of the original prompt. While these alterations can sometimes improve readability, they risk compromising the precision and tone required in legal texts.

The tendency of ChatGPT to reword phrases, though not as extreme as in the case of Gemini, shows that AI can sometimes prioritise stylistic adjustments over strict fidelity to the source material. Thus, ChatGPT emerges as a competent tool for basic gender-neutral rewriting but it still requires oversight to ensure that the resulting text remains faithful to its legal context.

The inconsistencies across these tools reveal that AI is not yet fully capable of producing gender-neutral texts without human supervision. Each tool applied gender-neutral terms in different ways but none delivered fully satisfactory results without some degree of human intervention. This limitation points to the ongoing need for human expertise in guiding AI-driven processes to ensure the precise and contextually appropriate use of language. In contexts as complex as legal discourse, where meaning can hinge on specific terminology, human oversight remains essential.

Another consideration involves the prompts provided to the chatbots. While these prompts were designed to be straightforward, it is arguable that more explicit instructions could have helped clarify that no changes to structure or meaning were desired. The tendency of the chatbot to simplify or rephrase suggests a potential gap between user expectations and the operational protocols of these AI systems. This observation highlights a broader need for clearer communication in prompts, especially when working with AI in specialised fields like law.

It is also worth acknowledging that field-specific AI solutions, such as Law ChatGPT, may have been more skilled at preserving legal phrasing while addressing gender bias. Specialised AI tools are likely to have a better grasp of legal language conventions and could produce outputs that more accurately reflect the intended meaning of the text. However, this analysis intentionally focused on generic chatbots to assess how well they could handle gender-neutral language reform without domain-specific training. Gender-neutral language is a consideration that spans multiple fields and affects both professionals and laypeople, making it essential for general-purpose AI to handle such tasks competently.

6.6 Concluding Remarks

This chapter set out to explore and critically evaluate the capabilities of general-purpose chatbots in performing tasks within the legal domain, specifically assessing their proficiency in navigating and analysing the intricate language of law reports. Three key aspects, in particular, were examined in order to achieve this aim, namely the identification and replacement of *legalese* traits, the accuracy and reliability of translations and back-translations and the detection and replacement of gender-biased language.

With regard to the first aspect, that is, the identification and replacement of *legalese* traits, ChatGPT was evaluated as a representative chatbot. Unfortunately, its results were only partially coherent. Plain English terms replaced *legalese* elements sporadically, but not consistently. Moreover, when prompted to rewrite an extract from a law report, the chatbot produced a summary rather than a self-contained rephrasing in legal style. This suggests limitations in the ability of the chatbot to emulate precise legal language while avoiding excessive simplification.

As regards the second aspect, concerning the accuracy and reliability of translations and back-translations, this chapter identified several notable shortcomings in the machine-generated outputs from both chatbots and machine translation platforms. Issues ranged from lexical and syntactical errors to the use of non-standard terms and uncommon word combinations or collocations. In some instances, AI-generated "hallucinations", erroneous or nonsensical outputs, appeared, highlighting an area of unreliability. Conversely, the back-translations performed by both chatbots and MT systems showed consistent language solutions. Mistranslations were largely limited to individual terms, and nonsensical phrases were avoided, suggesting a relative stability in back-translation processes. It might be posited that back-translations were more accurate as intelligent machines may have "learnt" the initial source text.

The third and last area of analysis concerned the capability for AI solutions to detect gender-biased language and replace it with gender-neutral expressions. For this purpose, several chatbots were tested. The findings revealed several inconsistencies as not only did some chatbots fail to identify and replace gender-biased language correctly, but they also altered the input text unexpectedly. Specifically, output texts were often rephrased or simplified in structure and content, with punctuation adjusted independently. Such modifications indicate that certain chatbots struggled to follow the precise task instructions, instead performing unrequested alterations to the input text.

The analyses carried out in this chapter confirm scholars' concerns regarding the possibility for AI tools to produce inaccurate or incorrect outputs, including "hallucinations" or nonsensical content. Users are thus advised to accept AI-generated outputs only after careful evaluation and scrutiny. This means that it is essential for them to verify the information against reliable sources (Medianik 2018). Consequently, human intervention and supervision are crucial when consulting AI systems. Furthermore, users should possess a solid understanding of the subject matter in order to interpret and, if necessary, adjust AI-generated content appropriately.

It could be argued that legal AI-driven tools, designed specifically for the legal sector, should have been included in this analysis as they may offer more refined and reliable outputs. Nevertheless, this chapter set out to access and assess generic, field-unrelated chatbots. Chatbots such as ChatGPT, indeed, are regularly consulted by both professionals and laypeople (Thomson Reuters 2023a, b). Therefore, this chapter sought to explore the extent to which such generally trusted AI solutions are capable of catering for legal and linguistic needs of both professionals and laypeople.

Bibliography

Abbott, Ryan. 2020. *The Reasonable Robot: Artificial Intelligence and the Law.* Cambridge: Cambridge University Press.

Alarie, Benjamin, Anthony Niblett, and Albert H. Yoon. 2018. How Artificial Intelligence Will Affect the Practice of Law. *University of Toronto Law Journal* 68:106–124.

Alqodsi, Enas Mohammed, and Dmitry Gura. 2023. High Tech and Legal Challenges: Artificial intelligence-Caused Damage Regulation. *Cogent Social Sciences* 9:2. https://doi.org/10.1080/23311886.2023.2270751.

American Bar Association. 2020. *Model Rules of Professional Conduct.* https://www.americanbar.org/groups/professional_responsibility/publications/model_rules_of_professional_conduct/

Ashley, Kevin D. 2017. *Artificial Intelligence and Legal Analytics: New Tools for Law Practice in the Digital Age.* Cambridge: Cambridge University Press.

Autto, H., H. Haapio, and J. Nuottila. 2024. Contracts Rethought and Redesigned: A New Era with AI. *International Journal of Commerce and Contracting* 8 (1–2): 7–34. https://doi.org/10.1177/20555636241261278.

Bhatia, Vijay K. 2010. *Textbook on Legal Language and Legal Writing.* New Delhi: Universal law publishing Co. Pvt. Ltd.

Brooks, Chay, Cristian Gherhes, and Tim Vorley. 2020. Artificial Intelligence in the Legal Sector: Pressures and Challenges of Transformation. *Cambridge Journal of Regions, Economy and Society* 13 (1): 135–152. https://doi.org/10.1093/cjres/rsz026.

Buchanan, Bruce G. 2006. A (Very) Brief History of Artificial Intelligence. *AI Magazine* 26 (4): 53–60.

Buchanan, Bruce G., and Edward H. Shortliffe. 1984. *Rule-Based Expert Systems: The MYCIN Experiments of the Stanford Heuristic Programming Project.* Reading, MA: Addison-Wesley.

Calabresi, Augustus. 2021. Machine Lawyering and Artificial Attorneys: Conflicts in Legal Ethics with Complex Computer Algorithms. *Georgetown Journal of Legal Ethics* 34:789–806.

Calo, Ryan. 2015. Robotics and the Lessons of Cyberlaw. *California Law Review* 103:513–563.

Cavanillas, José M., Edward Curry, and Wolfgang Wahlster. 2016. *New Horizons for a Data-Driven Economy.* Cham: Springer.

Constantin, Felicia, Anamaria-Mirabela Pop, and Monica-Ariana Sim. 2024. Human Intelligence and Artificial Intelligence in Professional Translations – Redesigning the Translator Profession. Proceedings in Business and Economics. In *Strategic Innovative Marketing and Tourism.* Current Trends and Future Outlook—10th ICSIMAT, Ionian Islands, Greece, 2023. Springer Proceedings in Business and Economics, eds. Androniki Kavoura, Teresa Borges-Tiago, and Flavio Tiago. Cham: Springer, pp. 239–247.

Crawford, Kate, and Ryan Calo. 2016. There Is a Blind Spot in AI Research. *Nature* 538:311–313.

Curle, David. 2017. Alternative 20Legal 20Service Providers: Changing Buyer Perception. Online: https://www.lawjournalnewsletters.com/sites/lawjournalnewsletters/2017/06/01/alternative-legal-services-providers-changing-buyer-perceptions-2/?slreturn=20240029094735

Domingue, John, Nelia Lasierra, Anna Fensel, Tim van Kasteren, Martin Strohbach, and Andreas Thalhammer. 2016. Big Data Analysis. In *New Horizons for a Data-Driven Economy*, ed. José M. Cavanillas, Edward Curry, and Wolfgang Wahlster, 63–86. Cham: Springer.

Doomen, Jasper. 2023. The Artificial Intelligence Entity as a Legal Person. *Information & Communications Technology Law* 32 (3): 277–287.

Emsley, Robin. 2023. ChatGPT: These Are Not Hallucinations - They're Fabrications and Falsifications. *Schizophrenia* 9 (52): 1–2. See also https://vimeo.com/844688249/56fcfd10d6.

Escribe, Marie, and Ruslan Mitkov. 2023. Applying Incremental Learning to Post-editing Systems: Towards Online Adaptation for Automatic Post-editing Models. In *Corpora and Translation Education, Advances and Challenges*, ed. Jun Pan and Sara Laviosa, 35–62. Springer Nature Singapore: Singapore.

European Union Agency for the Operational Management of Large-Scale IT Systems in the Area of Freedom, Security and Justice (eu-LISA), The European Union Agency for Criminal Justice Cooperation (Eurojust). 2022. *Artificial Intelligence Supporting Cross-Border Cooperation in Criminal justice. Joint Report Prepared by eu-LISA and EUROJUST*. https://www.eulisa.europa.eu/Publications/Reports/AI%20in%20Justice%20-%20Report.pdf

Garner, Bryan A. 2004. *Black's Law Dictionary*. 8th ed. St Paul, MN: Thomson/West.

Giampieri, Patrizia. 2024. *Corpus-based Translation of Private Legal Documents*. Amsterdam: John Benjamins.

Gigi, Gisa Mariam, Nikhitha Rajesh, Sania A. T. Mohan, and Biju A. Thekkanath. 2023. AI Contract: Future and Scope in Legal System. *International Journal of Advance and Applied Research* 10 (6): 237–240.

Guerreiro, Nuno M., Elena Voita, and André F.T. Martins. 2023. Looking for a Needle in a Haystack: A Comprehensive Study of Hallucinations in Neural Machine Translation. https://doi.org/10.48550/arXiv.2208.05309

Hadfield, Gillian K. 2016. *Rules for a Flat World: Why Humans Invented Law and How to Reinvent It for a Complex Global Economy*. Oxford: Oxford University Press.

Hassani, Hossein, Sirimal Silva, Unger Emmanuel, Stephane Maedeh TajMazinani, and Stephen Mac Feely. 2020. Artificial Intelligence (AI) or Intelligence Augmentation (IA): What Is the Future? *AI* 1 (2): 143–155. https://doi.org/10.3390/ai1020008.

Kroski, Elyssa. 2020. *Law Librarianship in the Age of AI*. Chicago: American Library Association.

Laney, Dough. 2001. *3D data Management: Controlling Data Volume, Velocity, and Variety*. Technical report, META Group.

Leslie, David, Christopher Burr, Mhairi Aitken, Josh Cowls, Mike Katell, and Morgan Briggs. 2021. *Artificial Intelligence, Human Rights, Democracy, and the Rule of Law: A Primer. The Council of Europe*. https://doi.org/10.5281/zenodo.4639743

Lyko, Klaus, Marcus Nitzschke, Ngonga Ngomo, and Axel-Cyrille. 2016. Big Data Acquisition. In *New Horizons for a Data-Driven Economy*, ed. José M. Cavanillas, Edward Curry, and Wolfgang Wahlster, 39–61. Cham: Springer.

McCarthy, John. 1959. Programs with Common Sense. In *Symposium on The Mechanization of Thought Processes*, National Physical Laboratory, Teddington, Middlesex, 24th–27th November 1958. pp. 3–10. London: Her Majesty's Stationery Office. https://www-formal.stanford.edu/jmc/mcc59/mcc59.html

McCarthy, John, Martin Minsky, Claude E. Shannon, and Nathanielì Rochester. 1955. A Proposal for the Dartmouth Summer Research Project on Artificial Intelligence, August 31, 1955. *AI Magazine 27* (4): 12. https://doi.org/10.1609/aimag.v27i4.1904.

Medianik, Katherine. 2018. Artificially Intelligent Lawyers: Updating the Model Rules of Professional Conduct in Accordance with the New Technological Era. *Cardozo Law Review* 39:1497–1530.

Monostori, Lazlo. 2019. Artificial Intelligence. In *CIRP Encyclopedia of Production Engineering*, ed. Luc Laperrière and Gunther Reinhart, 47–50. Berlin: Springer.

Mullen, Keith. 2018. Artificial Intelligence: Shiny Object? Speeding Train?, American Bar Association. *RPTE eReport Fall Issue*. https://www.americanbar.org/groups/real_property_trust_estate/publications/ereport/rpte-ereport-fall-2018/artificial-intelligence/

Oseid, Julie A., Amy Vorenberg, and Melissa Love Koenig. 2019. OK, Google, Will Artificial Intelligence Replace Human Lawyering? *Marquette Law Review* 102:1270–1303. https://ssrn.com/abstract=3449500.

Papadimoulis, Dimitrios. 2018. *Gender-neutral Language in the European Parliament*. https://www.europarl.europa.eu/cmsdata/151780/GNL_Guidelines_EN.pdf.

Prieto Ramos, Fernando. 2024. Revisiting Translator Competence in the Age of Artificial Intelligence: The Case of Legal and Institutional Translation. *The Interpreter and Translator Trainer* 18 (2): 148–173.

Quinci, Carla. 2024. The Impact of Machine Translation on the Development of Info-Mining and Thematic Competences in Legal Translation Trainees: A

Focus on Time and External Resources. *The Interpreter and Translator Trainer* 18 (2): 290–312.

Raghavan, Vijai V., Venkat N. Gudivada, Govindaraju Venu, and C. R. Rao. 2016. *Cognitive Computing: Theory and Applications*. Amsterdam: Elsevier.

Regulation (EU) 2024/1689 of the European Parliament and of the Council, of 13 June 2024, Laying Down Harmonised Rules on Artificial Intelligence and Amending Regulations (EC) No 300/2008, (EU) No 167/2013, (EU) No 168/2013, (EU) 2018/858, (EU) 2018/1139 and (EU) 2019/2144 and Directives 2014/90/EU, (EU) 2016/797 and (EU) 2020/1828 (Artificial Intelligence Act). Available online: https://eur-lex.europa.eu/eli/reg/2024/1689/oj/eng (accessed on 2 September 2025).

Remus, Dana, and Frank Levy. 2017. Can Robots Be Lawyers? Computers, Lawyers, and the Practice of Law. *Georgetown Journal of Legal Ethics* 30:501–549.

Russell, Stuart J., and Peter Norvig. 2010. *Artificial Intelligence: A Modern Approach*. 3rd ed. London: Pearson.

Sheeba, Nirmalanathan. 2023. Artificial Intelligence's Effects on the Legal Sector: Transforming Legal Practice. *International Journal for Legal Research and Analysis* 2 (7): 4–18.

Susskind, Richard. 2023. *Tomorrow's Lawyers. An Introduction to Your Future*. 3rd ed. Oxford: Oxford University Press.

Susskind, Richard, and Daniel Susskind. 2022. *The Future of the Professions: How Technology will transform the work of human experts*. Oxford: Oxford University Press.

Thomson Reuters. 2023a. *ChatGPT and Generative AI Within Law Firms*. https://www.thomsonreuters.com/en-us/posts/wp-content/uploads/sites/20/2023/04/2023–Chat-GPT-Generative-AI-in-Law-Firms.pdf

Thomson Reuters. 2023b. *Report: Stepping into the Future: How Generative AI Will Help Lawyers Improve Legal Service Delivery*. https://legal.thomson-reuters.com/content/dam/ewp-m/documents/legal/en/pdf/reports/lawyers-harnessing-power-of-ai.pdf

Tiersma, Peter. 1999. *Legal Language*. Chicago: University of Chicago Press.

Turing, Alan M. 1950. Computing Machinery and Intelligence. *Mind a Quarterly Review of Psychology and Philosophy* 236:4334–4360.

Van Melle, William. 1978. MYCIN: A Knowledge-based Consultation Program for Infectious Disease Diagnosis. *International Journal of Man-Machine Studies* 10 (3): 313–322. https://doi.org/10.1016/S0020-7373(78)80049-2.

Visconti, Guido. 2021. *Climate, Planetary and Evolutionary Sciences: A Machine-generated Literature Overview*. Cham: Springer.

Weaver, John F. 2013. *Robots Are People Too*. Westport: Praeger Publishing.

Williams, Christopher. 2023. *The Impact of Plain Language on Legal English in the United Kingdom*. London/New York: Routledge.

Wu, Jiayang, Wensheng Gan, Zefeng Chen, Shicheng Wan, and Hong Lin. 2023. *AI-Generated Content (AIGC): A Survey*. https://doi.org/10.48550/arXiv.2304.06632

Yamane, Nicole. 2020. Artificial Intelligence in the Legal Field and the Indispensable Human Element Legal Ethics Demands. *The Georgetown Journal of Legal Ethics* 33:877–890.

Zhang, Ziheng, Wang, Ping, and Liu, Ji-long. 2022. *CRISPR. A Machine-Generated Literature Overview*. Berlin: Springer Nature.

AI and MT Resources

ChatGPT: https://chatgpt.com/
ChatSonic: https://writesonic.com/chat
Copilot: https://copilot.microsoft.com/
DeepL: https://www.deepl.com/en/translator/
Gemini: https://gemini.google.com/
Google Translate: https://translate.google.com/

7

Conclusions

In direct response to the first research question, specifically, whether diachronic analyses of legal language can be effectively and reliably conducted through corpus-based methodological approaches, the empirical findings unequivocally confirm that such analyses are not only methodologically feasible but demonstrably effective in revealing patterns of linguistic change over time. However, this validation requires critical qualification. Whilst employing robust, transparent and methodologically replicable corpus-linguistic techniques, the study has successfully demonstrated that distinctive linguistic features characteristic of *legalese*, including syntactically complex adverbial phrases, semantically vague expressions, lexically archaic terminology and ideologically problematic gender-biased language, can be systematically identified, quantified and tracked across both historical and contemporary legal corpora.

Nevertheless, the apparent success of these methodological approaches should not obscure their inherent limitations. The diachronic methodology adopted herein, whilst ostensibly adaptable and transferable across diverse legal genres and jurisdictions, remains constrained by the representativeness of available corpora, the potential for sampling bias and the challenge of maintaining chronological consistency across different legal

V. Leonardi, P. Giampieri, *Legal English through the Ages*,
https://doi.org/10.1007/978-3-032-02172-4_7

systems and temporal periods. Furthermore, the reliance on automated corpus analysis tools may inadvertently privilege quantifiable linguistic features whilst potentially overlooking subtle but significant qualitative shifts in legal discourse that resist computational detection. The methodology, therefore, whilst offering a valuable and replicable model for similar investigations, should be regarded as one component of a broader, more comprehensive analytical toolkit rather than a standalone solution to understanding legal linguistic evolution.

Regarding the second research question, which concerned the identification and analysis of observable trends in the historical evolution of legal language, the empirical results indicate a statistically significant yet contextually complex shift towards linguistic simplification. More specifically, the documented decrease in archaic terminology, semantically vague language constructions and institutionally embedded gender-biased linguistic forms appears to reflect the tangible influence of broader societal movements and targeted institutional reform efforts, most notably the plain language movement and associated legal reform initiatives, that have explicitly aimed at rendering legal texts more comprehensible to lay audiences.

A particularly significant finding of this study relates to the systematic reduction of gender-specific language in legal discourse and the corresponding adoption of gender-neutral terminology. Diachronic corpus analysis reveals the historical dominance of male-referential terms, such as *heirs male*, *executrix* or the generic *he*, which have now largely been replaced by inclusive alternatives such as *heirs*, *personal representative* or the singular *they*. These lexical changes are not merely stylistic updates but represent a broader ideological and institutional shift towards inclusivity and representational fairness in legal drafting. The decreasing frequency of explicitly gendered expressions, exemplified by *men* overwhelmingly outnumbering *women* in earlier texts, and the subsequent rise of inclusive phrases like *men and women* or referential constructions, *if a person* rather than *if a man*, underscore a deliberate move to eliminate linguistic bias. This trend reflects not only changes in social expectations but also legal and governmental initiatives, such as the UK's 2007 policy mandating gender-neutral language in legislation. Furthermore, the disappearance of gendered legal designations such as *heirs male* and *heirs female* from modern corpora highlights how legal language has adapted to contemporary values of equality and non-discrimination. The shift towards inclusive terminology thus demonstrates that gender is no longer treated as a marginal or symbolic linguistic issue but as a structural and ethical concern intrinsic to legal clarity, fairness and modernisation.

However, this apparent trend towards simplification demands critical scrutiny and contextual qualification. The observed rate of linguistic change remains markedly uneven and inconsistent across different legal genres, with statutory texts and legislative documents demonstrating considerably greater degrees of linguistic modernisation and stylistic reform than judicial opinions, law reports and case law materials, which persistently retain conservative stylistic features and traditional linguistic conventions. This disparity suggests that institutional resistance to change varies significantly across different components of the legal system, potentially reflecting varying professional cultures, institutional priorities and audience expectations.

Moreover, the notion of "simplification" itself requires problematisation. What appears as linguistic simplification may, in certain contexts, represent a shift towards different forms of complexity or technical specificity rather than genuine enhancement of comprehensibility for non-specialist audiences. The tension between maintaining legal precision and achieving accessibility remains an unresolved challenge that merits continued scholarly attention and practical experimentation.

In addressing the third research question, which examined the potential applications and limitations of artificial intelligence tools for legal linguistic analysis, the findings reveal a complex and nuanced picture that defies simplistic assessments. Whilst AI systems demonstrate promising capabilities in certain analytical domains, their current performance remains frustratingly inconsistent and contextually limited. The AI technologies analysed in this study demonstrated measurable competence in detecting and categorising specific lexical features characteristic of legalese, yet consistently struggled with context-sensitive terminology, syntactically complex constructions and the interpretation of abstract legal concepts that require a sophisticated understanding of jurisprudential principles.

These limitations are not merely technical but reflect fundamental epistemological challenges inherent in automated legal language processing. Legal discourse operates within complex interpretive frameworks that rely heavily on contextual understanding, cultural knowledge and professional expertise that current AI systems cannot fully replicate. Furthermore, the reliance on historical training data may perpetuate existing biases and limitations whilst failing to adapt to evolving legal concepts and emerging areas of law.

Consequently, whilst AI may indeed serve as a valuable complementary instrument in certain aspects of legal drafting, document analysis and routine linguistic processing tasks, it cannot and should not be regarded as a substitute for expert legal and linguistic judgement. The integration of AI tools into legal practice requires careful consideration of their limitations, potential biases and the ethical implications of automated decision-making in legal contexts.

Whilst this study provides substantive and methodologically rigorous insights into the evolution of legal English, it simultaneously identifies numerous areas that warrant extensive future scholarly exploration and methodological innovation. Future research endeavours would benefit significantly from expanding the analytical scope beyond the law reports examined in this study to encompass a broader range of legal genres, including statutes, contracts, legal briefs, administrative regulations and emerging forms of digital legal communication. Each of these genres exhibits distinctive linguistic patterns, professional conventions and communicative purposes that contribute to the overall complexity of legal discourse. Such genre-based expansion would facilitate a more comprehensive and nuanced understanding of how legal language varies, adapts and evolves across different legal sub-domains, potentially revealing genre-specific patterns of change that may not be apparent from analysis of individual text types. Additionally, this broader analytical scope would enable researchers to examine the relationship between formal legal requirements and actual linguistic practice across different professional contexts.

Equally critical is the extension of corpus-based studies to encompass a more diverse range of English-speaking jurisdictions, including but not limited to the United States, Canada, Australia, New Zealand, South

Africa and other Commonwealth nations where English serves as a legal language. Comparative research of this nature could reveal divergent patterns of linguistic development shaped by differing legal systems, institutional practices, colonial histories and contemporary cultural norms. Such comparative analysis would also illuminate the extent to which legal English represents a unified global phenomenon versus a collection of related but distinct national or regional varieties.

A particularly pressing area requiring deeper investigation concerns the syntactic and structural dimensions of legal language, which have received insufficient attention in existing scholarship. Whilst the present study necessarily concentrated on lexical markers and vocabulary-based features, numerous other linguistic elements, including sentence length, degrees of subordination, syntactic embedding patterns, passive voice constructions and punctuation conventions, significantly influence legal comprehensibility and warrant systematic empirical examination. Of particular importance is the role of modality in legal discourse. Modal verbs such as shall, must, may, for instance, serve crucial functions in expressing legal obligation, permission, prohibition and recommendation. The evolution of these modal elements over time may reflect broader institutional efforts to standardise legal language, clarify legal requirements or adapt to changing jurisprudential philosophies. The frequency, distribution and contextual usage of such modal expressions across different legal genres and jurisdictions would constitute a particularly fruitful avenue for future diachronic inquiry.

Another methodologically challenging yet theoretically significant area meriting extensive future research concerns the specialised appropriation of common vocabulary within legal contexts. Legal English frequently co-opts everyday lexical items, such as *consideration*, *execution*, *party*, *material* and *construction*, and redefines them with highly specific, technical meanings that differ substantially from their general usage in non-legal contexts. These dual-purpose terms create significant potential for confusion among lay readers and demand sophisticated semantic analysis that extends well beyond surface-level lexical identification and categorisation. As this study focused primarily on overtly recognisable markers of *legalese*, the systematic investigation of such semantically complex terms remains an important but substantially underexplored dimension of legal linguistic research. Future studies might productively employ advanced corpus-linguistic techniques, including collocational analysis and semantic field mapping, to trace how ordinary vocabulary acquires specialised legal meanings and how these meanings evolve over time.

Closely related to the challenge of terminological complexity is the fundamental issue of vagueness and indeterminacy in legal language, which represents a defining characteristic of legal discourse that serves important functional purposes whilst simultaneously creating interpretive challenges. Whilst the present study addressed semantically vague lexical items at a general level, it did not systematically examine doctrinally indeterminate expressions, such as *reasonable*, *due diligence*, *best efforts*, *material breach* and *good faith*, which are inherently context-dependent and continuously shaped by evolving judicial interpretation and developing legal doctrine. Understanding the precise role and historical evolution of such terms requires sophisticated interdisciplinary approaches that necessarily incorporate legal theory, jurisprudential analysis and doctrinal scholarship, methodological dimensions that extend beyond the traditional reach of corpus linguistics alone but are essential for achieving a comprehensive appreciation of legal abstraction and interpretive flexibility. Future research might productively combine corpus-linguistic analysis with detailed case law examination and jurisprudential analysis to trace how courts interpret and apply vague legal concepts over time.

The rapid and continuing development of artificial intelligence technologies presents both unprecedented analytical opportunities and significant methodological challenges for the expanding field of legal linguistics. Contemporary AI systems, whilst demonstrating considerable promise in their application to specific tasks such as automated legal drafting, document simplification, contract review and routine legal research, remain fundamentally constrained by limited contextual understanding, particularly in relation to the culturally specific, idiomatic and abstract dimensions of legal discourse that require deep professional knowledge and cultural competence. The capacity of current AI systems to address novel or rapidly evolving legal issues is inherently limited by their dependence on historical training data and pattern recognition algorithms, which may be ill-equipped to handle unprecedented legal questions or emerging areas of law. Moreover, legal practitioners, scholars and policymakers must remain vigilant regarding ethical concerns, data privacy issues, algorithmic bias and compliance with developing regulatory frameworks such as the European Union's AI Act and similar legislative initiatives in other jurisdictions.

Given the dynamic and rapidly evolving nature of AI development, any scholarly assessment of AI's role in legal linguistics must be regarded as inherently provisional and subject to continuous revision. Consequently, there exists a pressing and ongoing need for sustained empirical research that not only rigorously evaluates the current capabilities and limitations of existing AI models but also actively supports the development of domain-specific tools trained on carefully curated legal corpora and designed to address the nuanced requirements of legal reasoning and professional legal communication.

In conclusion, it is hoped that this study has contributed meaningfully and substantively to the scholarly understanding of the complex historical evolution of legal language and the expanding methodological possibilities afforded by contemporary corpus linguistics and emerging AI technologies. By systematically identifying key linguistic shifts, highlighting significant genre-based disparities and suggesting productive new directions for empirical and theoretical inquiry, this research aspires to serve as a methodologically rigorous foundation for continued interdisciplinary exploration at the intersection of linguistics, law and digital humanities.

As legal systems worldwide increasingly seek to improve transparency, accessibility and public comprehension whilst maintaining necessary precision and professional standards, the future trajectory of legal language research will necessarily depend on developing and implementing integrated approaches that combine empirical rigour, linguistic sensitivity and responsible technological innovation. Through such collaborative and methodologically diverse efforts, the challenging but essential goal of fostering clearer, more inclusive and more effective legal communication may be progressively and meaningfully realised, ultimately serving both legal professionals and the broader public interest in accessible justice and transparent governance.

Index

V. Leonardi, P. Giampieri, *Legal English through the Ages*,
https://doi.org/10.1007/978-3-032-02172-4_7

FSC
www.fsc.org
MIX
Papier | Fördert gute Waldnutzung
FSC® C083411

Kolibri 360 GmbH
Ferdinand-Jühlke-Straße 7
99095 Erfurt, Deutschland
produktsicherheit@kolibri360.de